Scenic Driving

CALIFORNIA

Help Us Keep This Guide Up to Date

Every effort has been made by the author and editors to make this guide as accurate and useful as possible. However, many things can change after a guide is published—establishments close, phone numbers change, hiking trails are rerouted, facilities come under new management, etc.

We would love to hear from you concerning your experiences with this guide and how you feel it could be improved and kept up to date. While we may not be able to respond to all comments and suggestions, we'll take them to heart and we'll also make certain to share them with the author. Please send your comments and suggestions to the following address:

The Globe Pequot Press
Reader Response/Editorial Department
P.O. Box 480
Guilford, CT 06437

Or you may e-mail us at:

editorial@GlobePequot.com

Thanks for your input, and happy travels!

A FALCON GUIDE

Scenic Driving

CALIFORNIA

Second Edition

STEWART M. GREEN

FALCON®

GUILFORD, CONNECTICUT
HELENA, MONTANA

AN IMPRINT OF THE GLOBE PEQUOT PRESS

A FALCON GUIDE ®

All photos by Stewart M. Green
Maps created by Trailhead Graphics © The Globe Pequot Press

ISSN 1551-3610
ISBN 0-7627-3481-7

Manufactured in the United States of America
Second Edition/First Printing

To buy books in quantity for corporate use
or incentives, call **(800) 962–0973, ext. 4551,**
or e-mail **premiums@GlobePequot.com**

Contents

Locator Map vi
Acknowledgments vii
Introduction ix
    How to Use This Book xii
Map Legend xiv

THE SCENIC DRIVES

1   Redwood Highway Scenic Drive: Eureka to Crescent City 1

2   Smith River Scenic Byway: US 101 to Collier Tunnel 9

3   Sonoma-Mendocino Coast Scenic Drive: Marin City to US 101 17

4   Sonoma-Napa Valleys Scenic Drive: Santa Rosa to Hopland 27

5   Big Sur Coast Scenic Drive: Carmel to Morro Bay 37

6   San Andreas Fault Scenic Drive: I–5 to Hollister 47

7   Klamath River Scenic Drive: I–5 to Willow Creek 53

8   Lava Beds National Monument Scenic Drive 61

9   Cedar Pass-Fandango Pass Scenic Drive 69

10   Lassen Volcanic National Park Scenic Drive 77

11   Yuba Pass Scenic Drive: Nevada City to CA 89 87

12   Lake Tahoe Scenic Drive: South Lake Tahoe to Truckee 93

13   Carson Pass Scenic Byway: Jackson to Woodfords 101

14   Sonora Pass Scenic Drive: Sonora to US 395 107

15   Tioga Pass Scenic Drive: Big Oak Flat Road to Lee Vining 115

16   Yosemite National Park Scenic Drive: Oakhurst to Mariposa 123

17   Sequoia and Kings Canyon Scenic Drive: Minkler to Lemon Cove . . 133

18   Angeles Crest Scenic Byway: La Canada to Mountain Top Junction . 143

19   Rim of the World Scenic Byway: San Bernardino to Redlands 151

20   Palms to Pines Scenic Drive: Banning to Palm Desert 157

21   Mexican Border Scenic Drive: El Cajon to Boulevard 163

22   Joshua Tree National Park Scenic Drive 169

23   Anza-Borrego Desert Scenic Drive 177

24   Mojave Desert Scenic Drive 185

For More Information 191
Index 199
About the Author 208

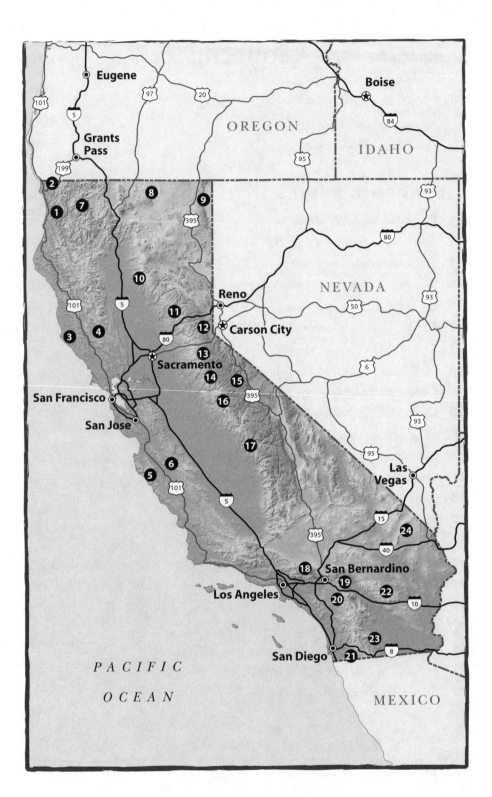

Acknowledgments

Scenic Driving California was, beyond a doubt, a most excellent adventure. My goal was to find, drive, photograph, research, and write about California's most beautiful and scenic highways. The only downside was having to limit the book to only twenty-four drives. I began with a list of forty-five possibilities and slowly pared them down to the drives I liked best. The rest will have to wait for a future volume. Not everyone will necessarily agree with my selections, having their own favorite drives, but these are the most representative of California's scenic drives, the best of the best. Some are part of the U.S. Forest Service's Scenic Byway program, while others incorporate some of the BLM's Back Country Byway drives and the official California state scenic drives; but not all of the excellent designated drives in these programs are described in this book. I urge you to buy *Scenic Driving Back Country Byways,* which I wrote for The Globe Pequot Press, to get more details on the rest of these BLM drives.

I give my sincere thanks to Falcon Publishing and The Globe Pequot Press for the fabulous opportunity to write this book back in the early 1990s and then to do this great second edition. A special thanks to Randall Green, my first editor in Helena, Montana, for his helpful comments, suggestions, and editorial expertise that made this a better book. Also, many thanks to Liz Taylor and Cary Hull at The Globe Pequot Press for editorial direction for this new edition. Editors make us writers better; I appreciate their efforts.

I am grateful to the many federal and state employees in California who generously dispensed information, answered questions, and reviewed portions of the manuscript for accuracy. These include Jim Warner at Kings Canyon National Park, Ginger Burley at Yosemite National Park, Arthur C. Webster III at Joshua Tree National Park, Elizabeth Knight at Lassen Volcanic National Park, Chris Roundtree with Lava Beds National Monument, Mark C. Jorgenssen at Anza-Borrego Desert State Park, and Donn Headley of Angeles National Forest. *Gracias* to my brother Mark Green in Sonoma, California, for aiding and abetting this project.

Lastly, a hearty and loving thanks to my two sons, Ian and Brett Green, who traveled all these California drives with me as humorous young lads. They shared starlight hikes among redwoods, polished slab climbs at Tuolumne Meadows, Sierra campfires that warded off May cold, summer heat in the Mojave Desert, walks along deserted beaches, as well as traffic jams in Pasadena, a Sunday drive around Fresno in search of a new tire, a midnight campground car burglary outside Lake Tahoe, and the rest of the nonsense found during ten hectic weeks on the road. I appreciate those fleeting special times we shared.

Introduction

California stretches along the edge of North America, perched on the watery rim of the vast Pacific Ocean. California, in a sense, is an island surrounded by both water and desert, an insular land shaped by the earth's most basic forces and populated by an astonishing diversity of plants, animals, and people. Its primeval landscape, suffused with golden light, dictates, defines, and measures us against its ancient rhythms.

California—the promised land, the land at the end of the rainbow. That's what early American settlers thought after crossing the bleak continent, wading its snows and enduring its heat, and finally reaching this fertile country with its plentiful rain, pleasant climate, and abundant resources. As long as the promised "lands beyond sundown" lay open to exploration and exploitation, Americans walked across the hard miles to this new country and the new hope it offered. It's still like that more than 160 years after the peak of the famed California Trail. People still find the most populous of the states an irresistible golden magnet. Californians, as one wag put it, are people who were born somewhere else and then came to their senses.

California is a land of startling variety. Its landscape offers every geographic shape and form and every climate. Precipitous peaks, chiseled by glaciers, lift snow-capped summits into the matchless turquoise sky. Abrupt desert mountains, baked in a crucible of brilliant sunlight, form obtuse angles with creosote-studded bajadas. Vegetable fields, fruit orchards, and vineyards weave a green tapestry across broad valleys. Snow, hundreds of inches deep, blankets California's highest ranges; sere desert basins lie almost untouched by rain; and dense fog shrouds the redwood-lined coast.

COAST, VALLEY, PEAK, AND DESERT

The state, with 158,693 square miles, is roughly divided into four main geographic provinces—the Coast Ranges, the Central Valley, the Sierra Nevada and Cascade Mountains, and the Basin and Range Desert regions. Climate and topography lend each area a unique flora and fauna.

The Coast Ranges can be further divided into separate ranges. The Klamath Mountains spread across rough, forested country up to 8,000 feet high in north-eastern California. The Coast Ranges themselves stretch from near Crescent City to San Luis Obispo, a maze of mountains that includes the famed redwood forests, the Napa wine country, and the Santa Cruz, Diablo, and Santa Lucia ranges above the Big Sur Coast. These ranges all lie along the heralded San Andreas Rift, an active fault zone that stretches some 650 miles from the Mexican border to Cape Mendocino. The Transverse Ranges, some of the only east-west trending mountain ranges in the United States, lie north of the Los Angeles Basin, while the Peninsular Ranges march southward from the basin to the border with Baja California.

The Central Valley is drained by the Sacramento and San Joaquin Rivers and forms a broad, level plain for 500 miles from Bakersfield to Redding. This sea was once rich in wildlife and wetlands but is now America's garden, growing almost every type of crop. Vast fields and orchards, watered by melting snow in the mountains, create a patchwork quilt broken only by arrow-straight roads, silver silos, and country towns.

The Sierra Nevada and Cascade Mountains form a twisting spine down eastern California. The Cascades, beginning with Lassen Peak and extending to Oregon and Washington, are punctuated by symmetrical, volcanic peaks. Mount Shasta with its snowy summit lifting to 14,162 feet is itself a sleeping giant. This dormant volcano could awaken any day and spread fiery destruction across its flanks. The Sierra Nevada, "snowy range" in Spanish, rises in a 400-mile-long towering wall of lofty peaks excavated by millions of years of glaciation. The range's high point is 14,494-foot Mount Whitney, which is the nation's highest point outside Alaska. Nearby lies Death Valley, North America's lowest point at 282 feet below sea level. The Sierra also houses some of California's stunning natural wonders—granite-walled Yosemite Valley, the massive sequoia trees at Sequoia National Park, the precipitous gorge at Kings Canyon National Park, and shimmering Lake Tahoe.

The Basin and Range province isolates California from the rest of the nation. Its northern section is characterized by thick volcanic plateaus formed when lava, measured in cubic miles, spread across the land's surface. Two of North America's great deserts—the Sonoran Desert and the Mojave Desert—meet and mingle in southern California. Rough mountain ranges separated by wide basins scatter across this arid region of scanty rainfall and fierce temperature ranges.

California is an amazing place for the naturalist. Its topographic diversity shelters a startling variety of plants and animals in almost every type of ecosystem found on earth, from offshore canyons and tide pools to mixed conifer forests and delicate alpine tundra. The state harbors some 5,200 plant species, with over 30 percent endemic to California, meaning they live here and here alone. The state is called the California Floristic Province by ecologists. It is the home of the bristlecone pine, the world's oldest living thing; the sequoia, the world's largest living thing; and the coast redwood, the world's tallest living thing. Sixteen oak species live here, with eleven exclusive to California. Pine trees are represented by twenty-one distinct species, with eight endemic to the state.

The state's wildlife is equally diverse. But wholesale habitat destruction caused by its ever-growing population and the accompanying development threatens California's wildlife and wildlands. California's known vertebrate species total 748. Almost 40 percent of its freshwater fish, 30 percent of its amphibians, and 10 percent of its mammals are endemic. Animals include the ubiquitous black bear, fleet-footed pronghorn antelope, bighorn sheep, several rattlesnake species, California gray whale, sea otter, desert tortoise, and mountain lion. The grizzly bear, featured on the state flag, and the jaguar are both extinct here. More than 550 bird species have been identified in California. Vast flocks of migratory birds pass through on the Pacific Flyway; the majestic, endangered California condor now survives only because of a successful captive breeding program.

California presents a spectacular assortment of natural wonders, scenic attractions, historic points of interest, and recreational opportunities. Its numerous national parklands include Yosemite, Sequoia, Kings Canyon, Lassen Volcanic, Death Valley, Joshua Tree, and Redwood National Parks; Muir Woods National Monument; Point Reyes National Seashore; and Golden Gate National Recreation Area. Nineteen national forests scatter across the state, attracting recreationists to 2,500 lakes, more than 13,000 miles of trails, and 1,800 miles of Wild and Scenic Rivers. The Pacific Crest National Recreation Trail, beginning on the Mexican border, wends its way north to Oregon across numerous mountain ranges. The bucolic Sonoma and Napa Valleys invite travelers to sample wines from one of the world's premier grape-growing regions. The state's 1,264-mile-long Pacific coastline offers sweeping sand beaches and rocky, windswept headlands. The Mojave National Preserve, administered by the Bureau of Land Management and National Park Service, is a stunning 1.4-million-acre desert marvel.

CALIFORNIA DRIVES

Scenic Driving California explores and discovers the best of California. The twenty-four drives, following more than 2,000 miles of highways and back roads, showcase the wonder and mystery of California to both traveler and resident alike. The drives sample the state's beauty spots, scenic wonders, and hidden jewels. They thread across the state, introducing highway travelers to the diversity that is California. Along the drives, highway recreationists find secluded glens, soaring redwoods, plunging waterfalls, ghost towns, abandoned gold mines, lava flows, damp caves, active volcanic areas, windswept shores battered by Pacific breakers, shimmering alpine lakes, wagon ruts from pioneer trails, and elegant stands of Joshua trees. The scenic drives also stray far from the urban path into the still-wild heart of California.

These twenty-four drives are only the beginning of California's scenic drives. These are admittedly some of the Golden State's best and most beautiful highways, but others lie beyond, inviting travelers to discover their wonders with new appreciation and understanding. It is simply impossible to detail all the scenic drives found in California. Travelers will also want to explore Ebbetts Pass over the Sierras, the fabulous back roads over the Coast Ranges both north and south of San Francisco, the Trinity Heritage Scenic Byway west of Redding, the Sierra Vista Scenic Byway in Sequoia National Forest, the Sunrise Scenic Byway east of San Diego, the Bureau of Land Management's Back Country Byways lacing the Mojave Desert, the various state highways crossing Death Valley National Park, and U.S. Highway 395 along the Sierra Nevada's abrupt eastern escarpment.

BEING PREPARED

Be prepared for emergencies and inclement weather while traveling California's scenic drives. Many of the roads twist and curve across steep mountainsides. Maintain a safe speed, use pullouts to allow other traffic to pass, stay in your own lane, and watch for blind corners. Weather can quickly change and drastically alter driving conditions. Drive carefully on rain-soaked roads, and, in winter, use proper snow tires and carry chains, extra clothes, and a shovel. Dense fog along the coastal drives often creates visibility problems. Slow down and keep alert. Watch for heavy traffic in urban areas and allow ample time to travel through cities. Most of the drives feature frequent viewpoints and scenic pull-offs for sightseeing. It's a good idea to top off the gas tank before embarking on any of these trips. Be prepared for hot weather in the state's desert areas. Be sure your car is in proper working order and carry plenty of water.

Travelers and campers are, unfortunately, potential crime victims. Stow all valuables out of sight in a parked car. Better yet, take them with you when leaving a vehicle. Campers should be wary of auto break-ins at popular overnight destinations. Keep all valuables, including money, cameras, and video equipment with you in your tent at night. Bears are a serious problem at many campgrounds. Keep all food stowed and covered in your car. Bears recognize ice chests as food sources and will break windows to get at them.

The scenic drives cross both public and private land. Respect private property rights by not trespassing. Remember federal laws protect both archeological and historic sites, including Native American ruins and artifacts, petrified bone and fossils, and historic structures. Camp only in designated sites to minimize impact, put out all campfires, and carry your trash out.

HOW TO USE THIS BOOK

Scenic Driving California describes and interprets twenty-four of the best scenic highways and back roads throughout the state. Each drive is complemented with a detailed route map, photographs of attractions and scenery, and trip planning information.

Each drive description, under the heading **The Drive,** follows the route from start to finish—explaining points of interest, appreciating the natural history, retelling the area history, and interpreting the drive for a greater understanding. The narrative text provides detailed travel information and presents the drive and its attractions in one direction. If you travel the route in the opposite direction, simply start at the end of the drive description.

Each map shows the drive's route, highway numbers and road names, campgrounds, points of interest, towns and cities along the way, recreation areas, national and state parks, national forests, and connecting roads.

Each trip planning section includes summaries of specific information for each drive. These self-explanatory sections allow quick access to relevant drive and trip details to help you make the most of your time on the byway.

General description provides a brief summary of the length and scenic features of the drive.

Special attractions are prominent points of interest, features, and activities found along the drive route.

Location gives the area of California where the drive is located.

Drive route number and name denotes the specific highway and road numbers and names that the drive travels.

Travel season notes the best times of the year to make the drive and whether the route is closed by snow in winter. Remember that opening and closing times of roads are always approximate and depend on regional weather conditions. Always check local conditions before setting out on your drive.

Camping includes listings of most NPS national park and monument, state park and recreation area, USDA national forest, BLM, regional, county, and city public campgrounds along the drive. Private campgrounds are generally not listed. Contact information for private campgrounds is easily obtained on the Internet. Consult the Web sites of specific governmental agencies for up-to-date information on making camping reservations.

Services lists communities along the drive where you can obtain visitor services, including lodging, dining, groceries, telephone, medical services, and gasoline.

Nearby attractions are major attractions, points of interest, and activities found within 50 miles of the drive. This list is by no means comprehensive but is intended to point you toward the best attractions.

The **For More Information** section at the end of the book lists names, telephone numbers, addresses, and Web sites of helpful organizations, including national parks and monuments, state parks, national forests, BLM public lands, chambers of commerce, and visitor bureaus. Before embarking on your scenic driving adventure, contact them for additional information and maps.

Map Legend

Featured Route	▬▬▬▬▬
Interstate Highway	═══(25)═══
U.S. Highway	═══(27)═══
State Highway	───(58)───
County, Local, or Forest Road	───[558]───
Trail	--------
Point of Interest	▫
Campground	▲
Picnic Area	⊼
Pass	) (
Tunnel	≈
Mountain, Peak, or Butte	▲
River, Creek, or Drainage	～～～
Reservoir or Lake	⬭
State Line	CALIFORNIA
National Park, National Forest, Large State Park, or other Federal Area	▨
Wilderness Area	▨

Redwood Highway Scenic Drive

EUREKA TO CRESCENT CITY

GENERAL DESCRIPTION: This 78-mile section of U.S. Highway 101 parallels the rugged Pacific coast, passing redwood groves and a rugged wave-carved shoreline of beaches, cliffs, and sea stacks.

SPECIAL ATTRACTIONS: Redwood National Park, Del Norte Coast Redwoods State Park, Prairie Creek Redwoods State Park, Humboldt Lagoons State Park, Patrick's Point State Park, Humboldt Bay National Wildlife Refuge, Eureka, Fort Humboldt State Historic Park, Crescent City, hiking, backpacking, fishing, world's tallest tree, redwood forests.

LOCATION: Northwestern California, from Eureka to Crescent City, 20 miles south of the Oregon border.

DRIVE ROUTE NUMBER AND NAME: US 101 (Redwood Highway).

TRAVEL SEASON: Year-round. Fog often envelops the road in summer, while heavy winter rains make hazardous driving conditions.

CAMPING: Hundreds of campsites, including primitive ones on the beach, in state parks, nearby Six Rivers National Forest, and private RV campgrounds.

SERVICES: All services in Eureka, Arcata, McKinleyville, Trinidad, and Crescent City. Limited services in Orick and Klamath.

NEARBY ATTRACTIONS: Smith River Scenic Byway, Jedediah Smith Redwoods State Park, Six Rivers National Forest, Oregon coast, Klamath River scenic drive, King Range National Conservation Area, Humboldt Redwoods State Park, Avenue of the Giants, Grizzly Creek Redwoods State Park.

THE DRIVE

The Redwood Empire stretches almost 500 miles from south of Monterey to a small pocket in southwestern Oregon along California's coastal ranges. This immense span of land, wreathed in summer fog and bounded by winter storms, is home to *Sequoia sempervirens,* the coast redwood. The Redwood Highway, US 101, traverses 78 miles of the empire's best redwood country between Eureka and Crescent City in northwestern California. This long strip of land is northern California's frontier with the ocean and boasts an almost unsurpassed natural beauty with craggy headlands jutting boldly into frothy surf, majestic stands of pristine redwood trees, broad bays and estuaries that teem with wildlife, and glistening sweeps of sand that form

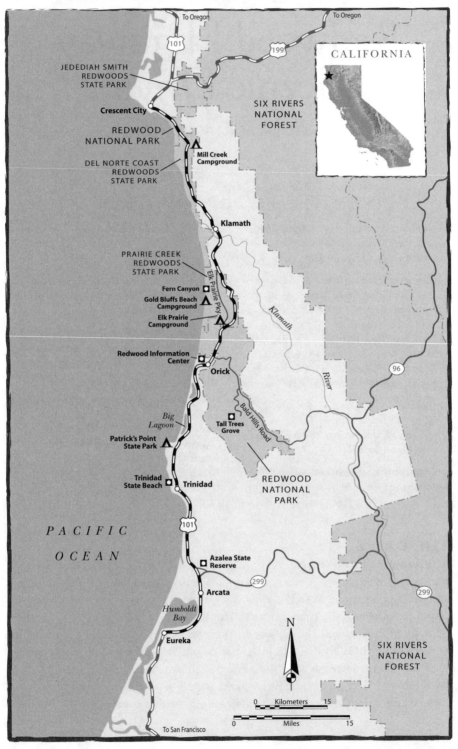

the tenuous boundary between land and sea. The land along the drive is truly unique, one of California's greatest and most memorable scenic attractions.

California's north coast is a land of heavy rain. As much as 100 inches falls on parts of the Redwood Coast, making lush forests and thick meadowlands. Most of the rain falls in winter when Pacific storms lash against the coastal mountains. Temperatures are also cool. January's average high in both Eureka and Crescent City is fifty-three degrees. Summer hardly warms up, with average July temperatures in Eureka only a paltry sixty degrees; temperatures in Crescent City climb to a sixty-nine degree average. Eureka is the usual winner of the coolest city year-round in the continental United States, with little variation between summer and winter. Expect thick fog in summer along the coast and in the redwood forests. Sometimes it burns off by midday, but the mist usually hangs around all day. Biologists estimate as much as 12 percent of the moisture redwoods need is derived from the summer fogs. A good raincoat and hat are needed for both hikers and beachcombers.

EUREKA

The drive begins in Eureka, the largest city on California's northern coast. Eureka is a charming, historic town that started as a prosperous seaport for the Trinity mining boom to the east. San Francisco land speculators and merchants saw beckoning opportunity on the north coast in 1850, and several different companies raced northward to grab land and potential profits. Irishman James Ryan's group claimed the east shore of Humboldt Bay, a long inland bay named for famed naturalist Baron Alexander von Humboldt, and established a new town dubbed Eureka. Eureka is a Greek word meaning "I have found it!" Within three years Eureka housed a population of 3,000. After the mining boom busted, the port became a major logging center. The harvested wood was, of course, redwood. By 1855 nine mills operated around Humboldt Bay.

The city today has a population of 26,128 and offers many restored houses, including the elegant Carson Mansion, an Old Town area, and numerous sights and services. Eureka also has several fine museums such as the Humboldt Bay Maritime Museum and the Clarke Memorial Museum with its excellent collection of Native American basketry. Fort Humboldt State Historic Park preserves the site of an 1850s military garrison that established order between settlers and Indians. Capt. Ulysses S. Grant, later a Civil War hero and president, was stationed here before being drummed out of the service for drunkenness in 1854. On leaving Eureka, Grant prophesied to his friend Post Surgeon Jonathon Clark, "My day will come, they will hear from me yet." Eureka's Old Town is worth a stroll. This "skid row" collection of brothels, sailor's taverns, card houses, and flophouses has been renovated into a trendy area with art galleries, cafes, and shops. "Skid row" itself is a North Coast logging expression. Logs were laid crossways on steep slopes or marshes and logs pulled by oxen teams were skidded along the improvised road to railheads and mills.

HUMBOLDT BAY TO PATRICK'S POINT

The scenic drive, following four-lane US 101, leaves Eureka and swings around broad Humboldt Bay. The bay is California's second largest and is enclosed on the west by long sand spits with a narrow, treacherous channel that has grounded many ships. The bay was first discovered by Russian-American Fur Company traders in 1806. The bay's east part, called Arcata Bay, is part of Humboldt Bay National Wildlife Refuge. This fertile wetland of tidal flats and marsh is a stopover for birds on the Pacific Flyway. The bay supports more than 250 bird species and 75 fish species. Arcata lies 8 miles north of Eureka on the Arcata Bottoms floodplain. The town, second largest in Humboldt County, is home to Humboldt State University and the Humboldt Crabs baseball team. Arcata offers a pleasant downtown plaza, the 600-acre Arcata Community Forest, and the nearby 213-acre Lanphere-Christensen Dunes Preserve on the Samoa Peninsula. Here, dune plant communities from both the south and north coasts overlap in a unique transition zone.

From Arcata the highway runs north across low farmland and through McKinleyville, a small town renamed in 1901 for assassinated President William McKinley. The area's industry includes bulb and tree farms, cheese, dairies, and truck farming. The thirty-acre **Azalea State Reserve** lies east of the road on the Mad River. The site is spectacular in May when the aromatic pink western azaleas bloom. Beyond McKinleyville, the highway hugs the coast, passing Clam Beach County Park and Little River State Beach. The state beach offers picnicking, surf fishing, and clamming; the county park has a campground.

Trinidad sits a few miles north at Trinidad Head, a large promontory that juts into the ocean. This headland was discovered and christened Trinidad by Spanish explorer Don Bruno Hecata on June 11, 1775. A large pine cross erected on the site marked the territory as a Spanish possession. The wooden cross was replaced by a stone one in 1913. Trinidad, like Eureka, grew out of the mining boom in the nearby mountains, serving as a supply and whaling port and later as a shipping center for lumber bound for world markets. Trinidad State Beach, just north of town, offers good beachcombing for driftwood and moonstones.

Patrick's Point State Park is another headland north of Trinidad. The 640-acre park is covered with grassy meadows sprinkled with spring wildflowers and a fringe of forest that includes Sitka spruce, Port Orford cedar, red alder, and hemlock. Sand beaches and abrupt cliffs and promontories chiseled by the relentless surf compose the park's landscape. The area's rich game, vegetation, and sea life attracted the Yurok, who lived here seasonally. They ate sea lions as well as plentiful mussels, leaving huge shell middens at their campsites. The park offers Sumeg, a reconstructed Yurok village, along with a native plant garden. Three park campgrounds—Agate Beach, Abalone, and Penn Creek—provide 124 sites with water, restrooms, and showers. Several good hiking trails lace the promontory. Two-mile Rim Trail, following an old Yurok path from Agate Beach to Palmer's Point, is one of the best. The park is also one of the best whale-watching spots on the Redwood Coast. The gray whales follow a 12,000-mile, eight-month migration from Arctic feeding grounds to winter calving lagoons off Baja California. From November to January and from March through May are the best times for whale watching. Binoculars are helpful in spotting the whales.

Past Patrick's Point the highway curves around several huge inland lagoons—Big, Stone, and Freshwater Lagoons. These comprise **Humboldt Lagoons State Park,** a large area of both salt and freshwater marshes and dense woods that shelter numerous migrating birds on the Pacific Flyway such as ducks, herons, egrets, and pelicans. Long sand spits front the ocean on the west, and densely forested mountains rise steeply over the wetlands. The park offers boating; fishing for trout, salmon, and steelhead; and primitive camping.

REDWOOD NATIONAL PARK

At the north end of Freshwater Lagoon, the highway bends inland along Redwood Creek. Here among the sand dunes sits the Redwood Information Center. It is the southern gateway to Redwood National Park, a unique 112,613-acre national and state parkland jointly managed by the National Park Service and California State Parks. The park scatters along the coast from here to Crescent City like a string of pearls. Eastward stretches the Redwood Creek section with its tall trees, and northward lie Prairie Creek Redwoods State Park, Del Norte Coast Redwoods State Park, and Jedediah Smith Redwoods State Park. Logging over the last century decimated 85 percent of California's coastal old-growth redwoods, leaving huge stumps where massive giants once stood. Redwood National Park, incorporating the three state parks, preserves some of the best forest left, including the world's tallest living thing. The park was declared a World Heritage Site for its unique forests in 1982. Redwood Information Center is a good place to stop for information on camping and hiking, and to view exhibits detailing the park's unusual natural history, coastline, and history.

Past the center, the road enters Orick. This small town nestles in a broad pastoral valley flanked by redwood-studded mountains. Dairy farms and small ranches are scattered along the highway. The Yuroks inhabited the area seasonally, and the town's name is derived from their word "Ore'q" meaning "mouth of the river." The town offers all services to travelers including gas, lodging, restaurants, and RV parks.

The Bald Hills Road takes off east from the highway just north of Orick. This narrow road, with grades as steep as 15 percent, twists into the Bald Hills above Redwood Creek. Just up the road is the 1-mile Lady Bird Johnson Grove self-guided nature trail. Ten miles up the road, the 3-mile round-trip **Tall Trees Trail,** which is accessible from the road by shuttle bus, drops steeply down to Redwood Creek and the world's tallest tree. This spirelike redwood towers 367.8 feet above its massive base. It was discovered by National Geographic naturalist Paul Zahl in 1964. The tree, along with many other 300-footers, grows on a moist gravel bench above a Redwood Creek meander. The discovery of the tree on privately owned timberland helped ensure the establishment of the national park in 1968. Prior to that, environmental organizations, including the Save-the-Redwoods League and Sierra Club, had urged the protection of California's remaining big trees. But much of the land that was purchased for the park was already clear-cut and in dire need of rehabilitation.

PRAIRIE CREEK REDWOODS STATE PARK

The drive runs north up Prairie Creek from Orick and quickly reaches Prairie Creek Redwoods State Park, a spectacular 14,000-acre sanctuary of pristine redwood forests. Eight miles of US 101 wend through the park, past silent groves that reach skyward. A four-lane, 12-mile-long bypass skirts the east boundary of the park for those in a hurry. The park features several dirt side roads that make fabulous excursions. Cal Barrel Road runs 3 miles through mature redwood forest. The Coastal Drive turns west at the north end of the park and runs down through redwoods to an unimpeded view of Gold Bluff Beach and the Pacific Ocean, before turning north to US 101 on the south side of the Klamath River. The Davison Road is a favorite; it begins 3 miles south of the park boundary and uncoils 4 miles through second-growth forest to Gold Bluff Beach. It then runs north below the bluff alongside the crashing surf for another 4 miles to the secluded trailhead for Fern Canyon.

Fern Canyon is simply one of the most beautiful spots imaginable. A short trail leaves the parking lot, crisscrosses Home Creek, and enters Fern Canyon, a 50-foot-deep gorge etched into soft sandstone. Above the pebbled canyon floor, five-finger ferns and other species blanket the walls with a verdant, hanging garden. Quiet reigns in this green kingdom, broken only by occasional bird songs, wind rippling the lofty treetops, and the distant roar of waves breaking on the strand. Redwoods, Sitka spruce, and Douglas fir loom over the canyon, blocking sunlight on rare clear days. An excellent primitive twenty-five-site campground sits on the dunes a couple of miles south of Fern Canyon.

The park's other campground, Elk Prairie, offers seventy-five sites and sits among giant redwoods just off US 101 6 miles north of Orick. Nearby is the park's "prairie," a large open meadow. Elk Prairie and Gold Bluff Beach are home to the park's two herds of endangered Roosevelt elk. These elk are members of the deer family and are larger than their Rocky Mountain cousins. An adult Roosevelt bull weighs 1,000 pounds and boasts a spectacular rack of antlers 3 feet high. Remember that, despite their docile appearance, these are wild animals and are particularly aggressive during the fall rut. A long pull-off lane on the drive allows visitors to safely park off the highway and view the grazing elk. Other animals found in the redwood forest include black bear, rabbit, squirrel, mountain lion, bobcat, coyote, and fox. More than 250 species of birds have been identified in the park's wide variety of habitats. Notable birds are the spotted owl and marbled murrelet, both dependent on old-growth forests.

Fog shrouds tall redwood trees in Del Norte Coast Redwoods State Park along U.S. Highway 101, the Redwood Highway.

More than 75 miles of hiking trails thread the park, making it a walker's paradise. Stop along the drive in either Prairie Creek or Del Norte Coast State Parks and hike into the redwood forest. It's an unforgettable experience. Standing there among the silent trees is to stand in the forest primeval. The redwoods soar overhead, caring nothing for their great antiquity and offering a serene aloofness to our own scattered lives. The oldest of the trees have witnessed as many as fifty human generations that have come and gone. No wonder author John Steinbeck called redwoods "ambassadors from another time." These impressive trees tower over 350 feet, weigh more than 2 million pounds, live as long as 2,000 years, and supply enough wood to build several houses. Yet these gentle forest titans grow from seeds hardly larger than a pinhead; the seeds come from a cone that is smaller than most western evergreens produce, less than an inch long.

The coast redwood once spread over much of the Northern Hemisphere, growing in diverse locales including Alaska, Siberia, Greenland, Europe, and North Dakota. Subsequent changes in climate and topography reduced those great redwood forests to their present small range on California's foggy coast. Their closest relatives are the giant sequoia atop the crest of the Sierra Nevada and the rare dawn redwood found only in a secluded Chinese valley and a transplanted stand in Jedediah Smith Redwoods State Park.

KLAMATH AND DEL NORTE COAST REDWOODS

The highway drops down from Prairie Creek and crosses the mouth of the 263-mile-long Klamath River, the state's second-largest river. The Klamath is famed for its huge runs of Chinook salmon and steelhead that migrate upriver in autumn to spawn and die. The town of Klamath, built on the river's north shore, was erased on the terrifying night of December 22, 1964, when the river rose to unprecedented levels after weeks of heavy rain and snow saturated the coastal ranges. Klamath is now a popular stop for fishermen and offers all services; be sure to sample its famous smoked salmon jerky. Nearby sits the Trees of Mystery, a hokey tourist attraction made famous by Ripley's *Believe It Or Not!* Farther north lies Requa, a small town that was once a thriving mining and lumber camp and earlier a Yurok village. A county road runs west from the scenic drive through Requa to Klamath Overlook with a great view of the mighty river emptying into the ocean. The Coastal Trail travels north along the coast from here to Crescent City.

The highway continues north from Klamath and after a few more miles reemerges on the coast at False Klamath Cove. It then enters 6,400-acre **Del Norte Coast Redwoods State Park,** another division of Redwood National Park, with 50 percent old-growth redwood forest and 8 miles of wild shoreline. This road section is lined with towering redwoods, butting against the asphalt like wooden pillars. An excellent hike travels 3 miles along Damnation Creek Trail, an old Yurok trail, from the highway to the seashore, losing 1,000 feet along the way. Splendid old redwoods loom over the path, their spirelike tops hidden by swirling mist. Lush undergrowth of sword ferns and rhododendrons carpet the forest floor. The park's 145-site campground, in second-growth redwood forest logged in the 1920s, sits east of the drive on Mill Creek.

At the north end of the state park, US 101 curves northwest and enters **Crescent City,** another old seaport founded in 1853. Jedediah Smith Redwoods State Park, another gorgeous part of Redwood National Park, lies just east of town on U.S. Highway 199. The Smith River scenic drive continues up US 199 to the Oregon border. US 101 runs north 19 miles from Crescent City past Lake Earl State Park and Easter lily fields to Pelican State Beach and the Oregon border.

Smith River Scenic Byway

US 101 TO COLLIER TUNNEL

GENERAL DESCRIPTION: This 33-mile scenic byway traverses the spectacular Smith River Canyon as it winds eastward from Crescent City on the Pacific coast to the Oregon border.

SPECIAL ATTRACTIONS: Jedediah Smith Redwoods State Park, Redwood National Park, Six Rivers National Forest, redwood forests, hiking, rafting.

LOCATION: Extreme northwestern Calfornia, from just north of Crescent City to Grants Pass, Oregon.

DRIVE ROUTE NUMBER: U.S. Highway 199.

TRAVEL SEASON: Year-round. Heavy rain and possible snow in the higher road elevations can make hazardous driving conditions.

CAMPING: Three Six Rivers National Forest campgrounds and 108 campsites in Jedediah Smith State Park.

SERVICES: All services at Crescent City; limited services at Gasquet.

NEARBY ATTRACTIONS: Redwood National Park, Pacific coast, Siskiyou Wilderness Area, Oregon Caves National Monument, Del Norte Coast Redwoods State Park, Battery Point Lighthouse Museum and Del Norte County Historical Society Museum (Crescent City), Prairie Creek Redwoods State Park, Klamath River scenic drive.

THE DRIVE

There's magic in rivers. Sit beside a river and it unlocks some of the land's deepest secrets. Listen to its flow, watch its waters glisten in the sunlight, hear the stories it tells of far-off winter snows, cascading waterfalls, tumbling rapids, and water-worn cobbles. The Smith River, tinted emerald by its riverbed rocks, unravels a tale in its tumbling currents of ancient, untrammeled wildness, of tall trees standing quietly like sentinels along its banks in cathedral groves, of the furtive comings and goings of Indians and the mountain man for which it was named. The Smith River drive, a designated U.S. Forest Service Scenic Byway, follows US 199 as it weaves along the river for 33 miles through what is simply some of the best and most beautiful country in all of California. This is the kind of place that takes hold of you and won't let go. It imprints itself on your memory and becomes a resting place in hectic times.

The three-forked Smith River arises high atop the Siskiyou Mountains and boasts the distinction of being California's last undammed river system with 315 miles of wild and scenic waterway. The coastal mountains dissected by the river basin are not particularly rocky and high, none reach over 7,000 feet, but they form a rugged tangle of forested ridges that march from the Siskiyou crest almost to the river's floodplain on the Pacific coast. The drive follows the Middle Fork of the Smith River and traverses the Smith River National Recreation Area. The 305,337-acre area is managed by U.S. Forest Service to protect the region's unique scenery, pristine rivers and creeks, wildlife, fisheries, rich ecological diversity, and historical sites.

Summer weather is generally ideal along the Smith River, although fog and cool temperatures are often found along the coast. Expect highs between seventy and eighty-five degrees, with rising temperatures as you drive inland. Summer rain is generally infrequent and short-lived. Winters are cool and rainy, with daily high temperatures in the forties and fifties. It can be colder with occasional snow in the higher elevations at the Collier Tunnel. Be prepared for heavy rain from October through April. The average annual rainfall at Gasquet is 94 inches, and the coastal area here receives as much as 120 inches.

CRESCENT CITY

The drive begins just north of Crescent City where U.S. Highway 101 intersects US 199. Turn east on US 199. Crescent City, famed for its Easter lily farms, was laid out in 1852 along a crescent-shaped harbor. The town offers a rough, weatherworn look with its cool, foggy days and sea breezes. A tsunami or tidal wave in 1964, spawned by a great Alaskan earthquake, almost leveled the town. The Battery Point Lighthouse Museum is an interesting stop on the city's waterfront. All services, including gas, food, lodging, and restaurants, are found in Crescent City.

JEDEDIAH SMITH REDWOODS STATE PARK

The byway, after exiting US 101, quickly climbs into rounded hills and twists into a deep, silent forest of towering redwoods in Jedediah Smith Redwoods State Park. The 10,000-acre park is California's northernmost redwood parkland. It is named for pioneer trailblazer, mountain man, and fur trader Jedediah Smith. Smith was the first white man to travel overland from the Mississippi River to the Pacific coast, discovering South Pass in Wyoming along the way. This low Rocky Mountain divide later opened the western gates to a flood of emigrants who journeyed across the California and Oregon trails in the 1840s and 1850s. In 1828 Smith was expelled from California, then Mexican territory, and set northward with a small party and more than 300 horses and mules to the Hudson Bay outposts in Oregon. The party often made less than a mile a day through the rugged coastal mountains. Indians harassed them constantly, thinking the horses were a new type of elk. Eventually, Smith's party reached the beach and rested for several days on the site of today's Crescent City before pushing on to Oregon where Umpquas massacred all but Smith and three men. Smith died three years later at the hands of Comanches on the Santa Fe Trail at the age of thirty-three.

The first 4 miles of the drive are breathtaking. Tall coast redwoods, *Sequoia sempervirens,* rear up along the narrow, winding road, and a dense undergrowth of ferns, rhododendrons, and azaleas carpets the forest floor. The park was established in 1929 and contains forty-six memorial redwood groves. The park's largest tree in Stout Memorial Grove soars 340 feet high with a 22-foot-thick trunk. The coast redwood, except for a 14-mile incursion into Oregon, is exclusively a California tree. The redwoods are the world's tallest living things, thriving in a moist, cool, 500-mile-long fog belt from just south of Monterey Peninsula to southern Oregon. They prefer this strip of lowland mountains between the stinging sea breezes and the warmer inland ranges that mimics the mild weather of their heyday millions of years ago in the Tertiary epoch when they spread over much of western North America, China, Europe, and even the Arctic. The redwood is not a drought-tolerant species; it needs the fog moisture during California's dry summer months. Fog along the northern coast contributes as much as 12 inches of the region's annual precipitation.

The redwoods here at Jedediah Smith Redwoods State Park flourish along damp riverside terraces above the Smith River, growing in almost pure stands with only shade-tolerant shrubs and trees carpeting their feet. A good stop along the drive is the mile-long Simpson Reed Discovery Trail in the roadside Simpson Reed Grove. The path leaves a parking area and winds among the forest giants, passing fallen trunks, dense fern thickets, sprawling vine maples, western hemlocks, huckleberries, and cloverlike redwood sorrel.

The byway continues through the redwoods and after 4 miles crosses the Smith River, its placid waters skimming over gravel bars. A side road, California Highway 197, turns north here and follows the river north to US 101. A side trip well worth taking is the meandering Howland Hill Road, a redwood-lined lane that follows Mill Creek southwest to Howland Summit and Crescent City. The road begins in Hiouchi. The state park's main facilities nestle along the river almost a mile east of the highway bridge. The park offers 108 campsites with restrooms and nearby showers, along with a slew of outdoor opportunities, including hiking on the park's seventeen trails, swimming, and fishing. The park also harbors a stand of rare dawn redwoods, a tree thought to be extinct until discovered in a remote Chinese valley in 1948. A Humboldt State University professor brought these trees from China as seedlings.

UP THE SMITH RIVER

The byway heads east up the Smith River's Middle Fork from the state park's eastern boundary. A Redwood National Park information center sits just beyond the turnoff for the park campground. A short distance beyond, as the road and river bend northeast, Forest Road 427 heads up the river's South Fork. This sparkling

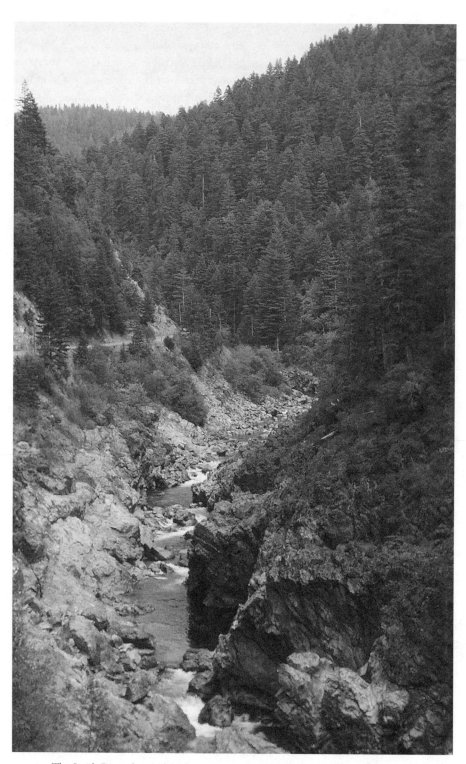

The Smith River plunges through a rocky canyon below the Smith River Scenic Byway.

stream is in a deep, wooded canyon. Just past Hiouchi, the byway enters Smith River National Recreation Area and Six Rivers National Forest. The river is considered the crown jewel in the nation's Wild and Scenic River System. After entering the national forest, the byway climbs away from the open valley and enters the Smith River's slashing canyon. The winding highway clings shelflike to steep mountain slopes, while the river cuts through a narrow, rock-lined gorge below. After a few miles, the canyon broadens below 2,620-foot Gasquet Mountain and enters the country town of Gasquet at the confluence of the Smith River's North and Middle Forks. Gasquet offers most visitor services, and a roadside ranger station provides information on the area's hiking trails, wilderness areas, campgrounds, and fisheries. Panther Flat, the largest forest campground along the river with thirty-nine sites, lies just beyond Gasquet.

Past Gasquet, both the climate and vegetation begin changing. The weather warms and dries as the highway ascends the canyon floor and the surrounding plant communities correspondingly change. The lush vegetation of the fog belt is left behind, but an equally diverse population of plants clot the steep-sided mountains. Impressive old-growth stands of Douglas fir mingle with Port Orford cedar (a representative of the Pacific Northwest rainforest) on moist slopes, while incense cedar, madrone, tan oak, pines, poison oak, and white fir form a dense mixed woodland. The Smith River area boasts of seven separate plant communities. The land's remote and rugged character makes excellent habitat for more than 300 wildlife species, including endangered bald eagles and peregrine falcons that nest in the area. Mountain lion, black bear, bobcat, mink, gray fox, raccoon, skunk, and blacktail deer roam the forest. River life includes otter, mergansers, ducks, osprey, kingfishers, a variety of snakes, and, of course, the steelhead and salmon for which the river is justly famed. Steelhead are oceangoing rainbow trout. They grow in the twenty-pound range in the Smith River and run from December into March. Salmon run September to December. A fishing license is required, and the limit is two fish.

The Smith River country also offers superb hiking trails. The 14-mile **South Kelsey Historical Trail,** a National Recreation Trail, is one of the best. The path follows an 1851 army supply route from Crescent City to the site of old Fort Jones. The first 7 miles march along the river's South Fork before climbing onto timbered ridges in the Siskiyou Wilderness Area and the lofty summit of 5,775-foot Baldy Peak. Spectacular views abound. Other good hikes include the 1-mile Myrtle Creek Trail, the 3.75-mile Craig's Creek Trail, and the 2.5-mile Doe Flat Trail. Ask at the Gasquet ranger station for maps and information. The river also gives great rafting adventures. The 12-mile section above Gasquet is a good run, while the placid waters through Jedediah Smith Redwoods State Park are ideal canoeing waters. The South Fork provides thrilling kayaking on tough rapids hemmed in by rocky cliffs.

Past Panther Flat, the canyon again narrows down. Numerous pull-offs allow river access for fishing and swimming. The drive passes nineteen-site Grassy Flat Campground, and a few miles farther lies thirteen-site Patrick Creek Campground. The highway slims down and twists up the rocky river canyon. Steep side canyons with moss-covered trees and cliffs, dense undergrowth, and occasional cascading waterfalls line the walls above the river. The Smith River spills over boulder-choked rapids and gathers in deep, aquamarine-colored pools in the mountain shadows below the drive.

The canyon and road widen at Washington Flat and bend northward past 4,778-foot Wounded Knee Mountain and 3,702-foot Monkey Ridge. The highway, now three lanes, soon leaves the Smith River, which arcs southeast to its headwaters on 5,708-foot Rocky Knob atop the Siskiyou range crest. The road follows Griffin Creek upward to the scenic byway's end at Collier Tunnel and 2,200-foot-high Collier Roadside Rest Area among high, rounded ridges. The rest area makes a good turnaround spot. Retrace the byway back down to Crescent City or continue on through the tunnel, drop down Kettle Creek to Oregon, and follow US 199 to Grants Pass.

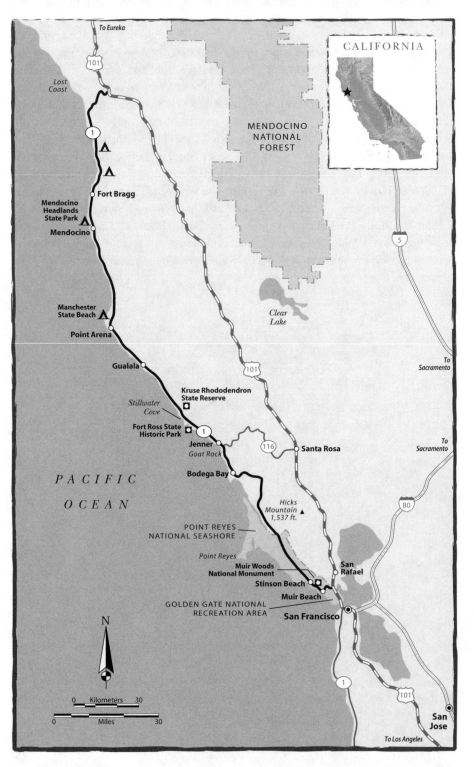

To Eureka

101

Lost
Coast

1

Fort Bragg

Mendocino
Headlands
State Park

Mendocino

MENDOCINO
NATIONAL
FOREST

CALIFORNIA

5

Manchester
State Beach

Point Arena

Clear
Lake

Gualala

Kruse Rhododendron
State Reserve

To
Sacramento

101

Stillwater
Cove

Fort Ross State
Historic Park

1

Jenner

Goat Rock

Bodega Bay

116

Santa Rosa

To
Sacramento

PACIFIC

OCEAN

Hicks
Mountain
1,537 ft.

80

POINT REYES
NATIONAL SEASHORE

Point Reyes

Muir Woods
National Monument

Stinson Beach

Muir Beach

GOLDEN GATE NATIONAL
RECREATION AREA

San Francisco

San
Rafael

N

1

0   Kilometers   30

0   Miles   30

101

San
Jose

To Los Angeles

Sonoma-Mendocino Coast Scenic Drive

MARIN CITY TO US 101

GENERAL DESCRIPTION: This 209-mile-long drive borders the Pacific coast north of San Francisco. The highway passes historic sites, redwood forests, abrupt headlands, sandy beaches, windswept coves, and numerous recreation areas.

SPECIAL ATTRACTIONS: Muir Woods National Monument, Point Reyes National Seashore, Golden Gate National Recreation Area, San Andreas Rift Zone, Sonoma Coast State Beaches, Fort Ross State Historic Park, Kruse Rhododendron State Reserve, Point Arena Lighthouse, Van Damme State Park, Mendocino Headlands State Park, Mendocino, Fort Bragg, hiking, redwoods, beaches.

LOCATION: West-central California. The drive runs north on California Highway 1 from U.S. Highway 101 in Marin City just north of San Francisco to US 101 north of Willits.

DRIVE ROUTE NUMBER AND NAME: California Highway 1 (Shoreline Highway).

TRAVEL SEASON: Year-round. Summer mornings are often foggy. Winters are wet, windy, and cool. Watch for slick pavement.

CAMPING: Numerous campgrounds are along the route.

SERVICES: All services at Marin City, Bodega Bay, Jenner, Gualala, Manchester, Mendocino, and Fort Bragg.

NEARBY ATTRACTIONS: San Francisco, Golden Gate Bridge, Sonoma, Napa Valley, Clear Lake, Standish-Hickey State Recreation Area, Smithe Redwoods State Reserve, Richardson Grove State Park, Avenue of the Giants, Jackson State Forest, Santa Rosa, Guerneville, Russian River, Armstrong Redwoods State Reserve, China Camp State Park, Mount Tamalpais State Park.

THE DRIVE

This 209-mile-long scenic drive follows CA 1 up California's spectacular Pacific coast from the Marin Peninsula north of the Golden Gate Bridge to US 101 south of Eureka. The highway traverses steep, wave-carved headlands, quiet sandy coves, grassy terraces punctuated by grazing cattle, towering redwood trees in moist canyons, long sweeping beaches, and dense woodlands of oak and pine. The shoreline, called the Sonoma-Mendocino Coast for its two counties, is a wildly beautiful meeting of sea and land. Much of the area is protected by numerous state beaches and parks, Muir Woods National Monument, Golden Gate National Recreation Area, and Point Reyes National Seashore.

The Sonoma-Mendocino Coast lies in California's fog belt. Thick fog, particularly in summer, hangs over the shoreline and backs up against the coastal mountains. The fog is the result of moist air blowing over cold offshore currents. Fog forms when the air condenses into tiny water droplets. Inland, even just a few miles, the fog dissipates as the sun warms the air. Point Reyes is considered one of California's foggiest and windiest spots. Some coastal areas, notably the Point Arena headland, are "banana belts" that are warm and virtually fog free because of protective mountains and ocean currents. Expect cool temperatures, with summer highs ranging from sixty to seventy degrees, and breezy afternoons. September and most of October bring glorious, balmy days. September days average sixty-five degrees with temperatures occasionally climbing into the eighties. Clear skies dominate, with fog occurring on only one out of every eight days. Winters are cool and rainy. Most of the coast's annual precipitation comes from wet Pacific storms. December and January both average 7 inches of rainfall along the Mendocino coast. Temperatures are moderate, falling between forty and sixty degrees. Expect heavy rain, slick roads, and stiff winds during stormy weather. A raincoat over a sweater usually provides plenty of protection for winter hikers, beachcombers, and whale-watchers. Wet weather continues into spring, but greenery adorns the grasslands and forests.

MUIR WOODS NATIONAL MONUMENT

The drive begins in Marin City just north of San Francisco and the Golden Gate Bridge. Exit off US 101 and head west on CA 1, the Shoreline Highway. After a couple of miles, the highway leaves the town behind and passes along a rounded ridge lined with eucalyptus and oak trees. The road quickly narrows and begins winding across the hillsides—a character it assumes for the next 200 miles. Vehicles over 35 feet in length are prohibited. The traveler will not encounter another traffic light until Fort Bragg, more than 160 miles up the coast. Just over 3 miles from the drive's start, the highway intersects the Panoramic Highway, which climbs north into 6,300-acre Mount Tamalpais State Park and the Muir Woods Road. The park, one of the Bay area's most beloved natural areas, offers pastoral beauty with 200 miles of hiking trails, camping, and picnicking. The view from atop 2,571-foot Mount Tamalpais encompasses the entire Bay region.

The Muir Woods Road spirals down to Muir Woods National Monument, a small 560-acre national parkland that preserves the last virgin stand of coast redwoods in the San Francisco Bay area. The forest was spared from logging when Congressman William Kent bought it in 1905; he later donated the land to the federal government. After Pres. Theodore Roosevelt established the national monument in 1908, Kent urged the new park be named for famed California naturalist and writer John Muir. Muir later told Kent, "This is the best tree-lover's monument that could possibly be found in all the forests of the world." The tall trees nestle in Redwood Canyon, lifting their towering crowns high above the damp forest floor.

Ferns, including the sword fern, lady fern, California polypody, and bracken fern, moss, and redwood sorrel blankets the forest undergrowth, while red alders line trickling Redwood Creek. Six miles of trails explore the park. Most popular is a short loop that follows the creek up to the Cathedral Grove. The tallest tree here measures 252 feet high. A visitor center, snack bar, and gift shop are at the trail's start. The monument is very popular, making parking in its small lots a perennial problem.

MUIR BEACH AND STINSON BEACH

Return to CA 1 by following the Muir Woods Road west down Redwood Creek for 3 miles. Muir Beach lies in a curved, south-facing cove south of the road intersection. The drive twists toward the northwest like an asphalt ribbon above tawny bluffs, rugged sea stacks, and crashing surf before dipping into shallow canyons and emerging onto bold headlands with expansive views. **Muir Beach Overlook** offers one of the best views on clear days. The Farallon Islands, one of the largest seabird nesting areas in American waters, jut like haystacks above the ocean horizon to the southwest. Closer at hand is the Point Bonita Lighthouse and the entrance to the fabled Golden Gate, named by explorer John C. Fremont in 1846. The coastal region from the Golden Gate to Point Reyes is managed by the National Park Service as 75,398-acre Golden Gate National Recreation Area. The park, one of the largest urban national parks in the world, includes 28 miles of coastline as well as Alcatraz, Marin Headlands, and the Presidio of San Francisco.

The highway straightens out when it reaches **Stinson Beach,** an old resort town. The large beach stretches alongside the road, attracting swimmers and sunbathers. Nearby Bolinas Lagoon is protected from ocean waves by a thin sand spit. At low tide, it is a tidal mudflat inhabited by numerous birds and waterfowl. A great blue heron and snowy egret rookery lies in a shallow canyon at the Audubon Canyon Ranch just east of the lagoon. From March to July, visitors can hike into the canyon and view the birds' nests high atop the Schwartz Grove redwoods. The Panoramic Highway, one of California's most scenic back roads, begins in Stinson Beach and climbs east into Mount Tamalpais State Park.

The highway joins the San Andreas Rift Zone at Stinson Beach and follows it north up Olema Valley and Tomales Bay. The famed fault separates the North American crustal plate from the Pacific plate and stretches some 650 miles from northern Mexico to Cape Mendocino, where it plunges into the ocean. The two plates have been slowly creeping past each other for the last thirty million years at an annual rate of about 2 inches. Underlying rocks, contorted and broken by faulting, are easily eroded, forming the broad valley the drive traverses. The coast range east of here is composed of sandstone and chert. The granite rocks on the low hills to the west were moved 350 miles from the south by the fault. During the great 1906 San Francisco earthquake, horizontal movement along the fault here was 20 feet. The San Andreas Rift Zone contains numerous large and small faults. As the two plates grind against each other, pressure builds to a breaking point and the faults jump and release the pressure.

POINT REYES NATIONAL SEASHORE

The turn to Point Reyes National Seashore sits just north of Olema. Down a narrow lane are the park headquarters and an excellent visitor center. Spectacular 71,068-acre Point Reyes National Seashore, administered by the National Park Service, preserves a magnificent slice of California coastline. The region is geographically part of the coastal ranges with brushy, chaparral-coated hillsides, grasslands that waver under ocean breezes, pine- and fir-choked ridges and vales. A wild 20-mile-long beach is pounded by Pacific breakers and scoured by gales. The triangular peninsula, a scrap of Sierra granite hauled north by the fault, was named El Punta de Los Reyes by Spanish explorer Don Sebastian Vizcaino on January 6, 1603. That day was Epiphany, the twelfth day of Christmas and the Feast of the Three Kings. Sir Francis Drake beached his ship, *The Golden Hinde,* a few years earlier in 1579 to make needed ship repairs for his round-the-world voyage. After five weeks Drake dubbed the land New Albion, claimed it for England by placing "a plate of brasse, fast nailed to a great and firme post," and sailed west into the sunset.

Point Reyes is a great place to explore. A couple of roads pierce the Peninsula's interior and allow trail access to numerous points of interest. Two trails begin near the Bear Valley Visitor Center—the 0.6-mile Earthquake Trail along the San Andreas Fault and the 0.7-mile Woodpecker Nature Trail. Nearby is Kule Loklo, a replica of a Coast Miwok village. The Miwoks were a hunting and gathering tribe that harvested this rich land for centuries before the Spanish and English arrived. Popular trails include the Sky Trail and the Coast Trail. The Sky Trail leads to the summit of 1,407-foot Mount Wittenberg, the park's high point. Diverse ecosystems inhabited by varied plant communities and animals await the walker along the Coast Trail. The park, lying on the Pacific Flyway, boasts 361 bird species, including eight hawk species, herons, egrets, numerous ducks, and woodpeckers. Exotic deer, such as the fallow and axis deer, have flourished here since the 1940s. A tule elk refuge sits on Tomales Point. Sea lions colonize the rocky shore of Point Reyes itself. A nearby overlook gives a good view of the large seals. Point Reyes is also an excellent and popular whale-watching spot. More than 100 California gray whales a day are usually sighted during the peak migration in January. Four walk-in campgrounds scatter across the park.

ALONG THE SONOMA COAST

From Point Reyes, the drive runs north along the east shore of Tomales Bay, a long sea arm that separates Point Reyes peninsula from the mainland. The San Andreas Fault plunges underwater and runs along the bay's floor. The rounded hills of Bolinas Ridge, broken by grass and trees, stair-step eastward from the drive. The high-

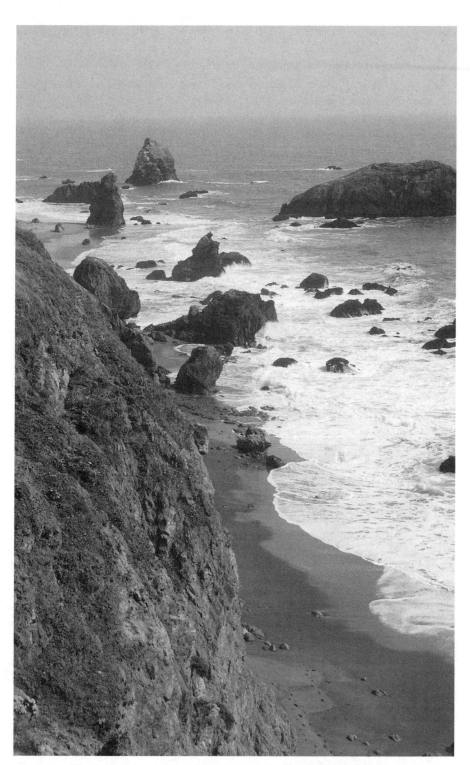

The Pacific Ocean washes against rocky sea stacks along the Mendocino Coast.

way bends inland near the bay's north end, crosses rolling hills, and enters Sonoma County and the Sonoma Coast.

The countryside slowly changes after leaving Point Reyes. Gone are the dense forests and tall coastal peaks. In their place is a bucolic landscape, with low grassy hills seamed by creeks and rivers. After entering Sonoma County, the drive turns abruptly west and drops back down to the shore at Bodega Bay, a charming seaside town that served as the backdrop for Alfred Hitchcock's classic 1962 film *The Birds*. The harbor here is enclosed by a sand spit. Bodega Head was named in 1775 for Don Juan Francisco de la Bodega y Cuadra, a lieutenant aboard the Spanish ship *Sonora*.

The next 10 miles from Bodega Bay to Jenner and the Russian River is lovely country. The highway rolls over grass-covered terraces backed by tawny hillsides. Coves and sandy beaches, broken by cliffs and bluffs, line the shoreline below the drive. A succession of state-owned beaches, dubbed the **Sonoma Coast State Beaches,** scatter along the highway. Bulky Bodega Head is a piece of granite dragged north on the San Andreas Fault. It offers good hiking trails. Salmon Creek, Portuguese, Gleasons, Duncan's Landing, Wright's, Shell, and Goat Rock State Beaches lie just off the drive. Numerous pullouts allow beach access. Wright's Beach has a twenty-seven-site campground and Bodega Dunes offers ninety-eight sites with showers and restrooms. **Goat Rock State Beach** is a dramatic meeting of land and ocean, with a side road that runs along a ridge to the craggy rock. In winter, towering whitecaps crash against the cliffs. It's illegal to climb on the rock; treacherous waves and currents have drowned many people here. Safe rock climbing is found on nearby Sunset Rock, a small crag perched on a grassy table below the entrance road to Goat Road. None of the state beaches along the highway are good for swimming. Dangerous undertows, riptides, sleeper waves, and cold water conspire against the swimmer. Most visitors indulge in surf fishing, picnicking, walking, and beachcombing in the rocky tide pools.

CA 1 joins California Highway 116 on the Russian River just east of Jenner. CA 116 makes a good inland excursion. The highway winds along the deep Russian River, its banks flanked with willows, eucalyptus, cypress, and mixed conifers. At Guerneville the route leaves the river and plunges through dark woods to Santa Rosa and US 101.

FORT ROSS STATE HISTORIC PARK

The drive travels north from Jenner and the Russian River, and, after crossing Russian Gulch, begins spiraling and edging across steep slopes almost 1,000 feet above the cobbled beach. This road section is one of the most dramatic on the northern coast. It lies adjacent to the offshore San Andreas Fault. Breathtaking views are found from airy pullouts. This is open grazing country; watch for cattle sharing the road. Eventually, the highway drops onto an undulating terrace, crosses the San Andreas Rift Zone, and reaches Fort Ross State Historic Park, which was the site of imperial Russia's farthest American outpost.

Fort Ross was initially settled by ninety-five Russians and forty Aleuts of the Russian-American Fur Trading Company in 1812. The group built a 14-foot-high timber stockade that featured forty cannons and corner lookouts. Warehouses, a jail, barracks, and the commandant's house were created inside the compound, while a village surrounded it. The place was named "Rossiya" or Little Russia, and later corrupted to Fort Ross. The Russians set to work trapping sea otters and quickly brought the species to the verge of extinction. The colonists then turned to farming, but the damp climate and rodents decimated their efforts. In 1841 the Russians decided to cut their losses and sold the fort and all its property to John Sutter for $30,000. Sutter hauled everything, including 1,700 cattle, 940 horses and mules, and an arsenal of weapons to Sacramento. Most of the fort is now reconstructed and open as a living history exhibit. The park boasts an excellent visitor center with numerous interpretative exhibits. Hiking trails meander around the park over grasslands, through cypress groves, and above the rocky shore. The park also offers a twenty-eight-site campground tucked in a sheltered beachside ravine.

STILLWATER COVE AND KRUSE RHODODENDRONS

The drive runs northwest along grassy terraces from Fort Ross. Sixteen miles north of Jenner it passes Stillwater Cove Regional Park, a pleasant overnight stop with twenty-three campsites. Salt Point State Park lies 4 miles farther up the coast. This scenic 4,000-acre park encompasses abrupt headlands that plunge into foaming surf; shallow valleys dense with cypress, pine, and redwood; sandy beaches rimmed with cliffs; and rocky tide pools nestled in quiet coves. The park not only offers 7 miles of coastline, but includes the rolling hills east of the highway. Numerous trails thread the park. The 1.5-mile Stump Beach Trail leads along bluffs above the ocean and gives great views to January whale-watchers. Visitors also enjoy excellent beachcombing, rockfishing, tide pool exploring, and abalone diving. The park's ninety-nine-site Woodside Campground has showers and restrooms.

Kruse Rhododendron State Reserve sits up the highway from Salt Point. This 317-acre nature preserve yields one of the Sonoma Coast's most beautiful natural wonders in April and May when its rhododendrons spread a canopy of pink blossoms throughout the second-growth forest. Nowhere else in California do rhododendrons grow in such profusion or as tall as the 30-foot giants here. The reserve, reached via Kruse Ranch Road, can be explored by trail. A small picnic area sits at the parking lot.

CA 1 continues north, running across a grassy shelf past Horseshoe and Rocky Points to Stewarts Point, a small town along the bold promontory above the sea. The last 11 miles of the Sonoma Coast passes the Sea Ranch, a controversial luxury, vacation-home subdivision that was once part of a 17,500-acre Mexican land grant called Rancho de Herman. A battle between developers and conservationists culminated in the establishment of the California Coastal Commission and continued public access to 10 miles of state-owned beach.

MENDOCINO COAST

Past Sea Ranch, the highway crosses the Gualala River and enters Mendocino County and Coast. For the next 90 miles, the serpentine drive winds across a brooding landscape, traversing steep ridges, crossing numerous creeks and rivers, and swinging around coves. The ocean, always in sight, dictates geography and climate. Strong winds constantly scour the sea-facing bluffs, rippling fields of grass and sculpting exposed trees. It's a land that seems in eternal motion—cloud shadows trail across wooded hills; unceasing waves batter rocky headlands; and gray fog hides the earth's sharp edges, making forms uncertain and hazy.

Gualala, a derivation of the Pomo Indian word *wala'li,* meaning "meeting of the waters," lies at the mouth of the Gualala River. Until the 1960s this small town was a bustling redwood lumber town. Nearby is **Gualala Point Regional Park** with trails, picnicking, and a campground. The river is popular with steelhead fishermen in winter. The drive continues up the coast through open meadows and Monterey cypress groves on broad marine terraces and reaches Point Arena after 16 miles.

Point Arena, first sighted by Captain George Vancouver in 1792, was a rollicking seaport in the late nineteenth century. The nearby Point Arena Lighthouse, a six-story, automated beacon, warns sailors of underwater dangers. Until the first lighthouse was built in 1870, many ships found a watery grave here, including ten on a stormy November night in 1865. Visitors can tour the old lighthouse, marching up its 147 steps to a spectacular coastal view. **Manchester State Beach** hugs the coast for 5 sandy miles from the point. The park offers camping, beachcombing, surf fishing, and good bird watching. Elk, another old lumber town, sits 14 miles up the road on Greenwood Creek. The town's last lumber mill closed in 1932, leaving a charming village of Victorian homes. Numerous sea stacks, their rocky pinnacles white with bird guano, stud nearby Greenwood Cove. Greenwood Creek State Beach is on the site of the old lumber mill and offers a mile-long stretch of beach.

Just north of Elk, the highway sweeps across the Navarro River and enters the heartland of the Mendocino Coast. The towns of Mendocino and Fort Bragg sit along this 40-mile-long coast, surrounded by some excellent state parks including Van Damme, Mendocino Headlands, Russian Gulch, and MacKerricher parks. Van Damme and Mendocino Headlands are the first parks encountered.

Van Damme, 3 miles south of the town of Mendocino, spreads its 1,831 acres for 5 miles along the Little River. The park is covered with second-growth redwood forest and is laced with trails. Fern Canyon Trail winds for 2.5 miles through lush undergrowth. The Pygmy Forest section boasts dwarfed Bolander and Bishop pine, Mendocino pygmy cypress, and manzanita trees as old as one hundred years that are only 2 feet tall and less than an inch thick. Acidic soils and poor drainage stunt the trees. The park has a popular seventy-four-site campground. **Mendocino Headlands State Park** lies just up the highway. This spectacular coastal slice is a monument to sea erosion with sea stacks and headlands carved by relentless waves. The park—offering hiking, whale watching, and excellent tide pools—forms a pristine greenbelt along Mendocino's west edge and preserves the town's unique shore from development.

MENDOCINO TO FORT BRAGG

Mendocino, perched atop dramatic bluffs, is a quaint, rustic town with a New England ambience. Many of the town's Victorian homes were built by homesick pioneers who settled here during its nineteenth-century lumber boom. The town was founded in 1852 by shipwrecked William Kasten and quickly became a logging center that shipped thousands of feet of redwood to San Francisco. After the last sawmill closed in 1937, Mendocino's fortunes slowly ebbed until the 1960s when it became an artists' colony. It's a trendy, stylish place today with boutiques, health-food restaurants, and galleries. A walk around the town's designated National Historic District reveals the charm of its gingerbread architecture and the wild beauty of its coastline. Be prepared on busy summer weekends for crowded streets and a lack of parking spots.

    Russian Gulch State Park and **Jug Handle State Reserve** are just north of Mendocino. Russian Gulch features thick forests, a wide bay, and a thirty-site campground. Jug Handle preserves a staircase of five wave-cut terraces. Each level is 100 feet higher and 100,000 years older than the one below and is populated by different plant communities.

    Fort Bragg, the coast's largest town between San Francisco and Eureka, is a working town, unlike its sister city to the south. Loggers, mill workers, and fishermen live here. The town was founded in 1855 as a military fort to keep Indians on the Mendocino Reservation. In 1867 the area was opened to settlers, and Fort Bragg became a lumber town. It still retains its working-class roots with the local Georgia-Pacific mill. The town also boasts the only traffic lights along the scenic drive. The California Western Railroad, affectionately called the "Skunk Train," is Fort Bragg's main tourist attraction. The track snakes 40 miles inland through redwood forests to Willits. The trains run daily in summer and include both half- and full-day runs. The seventeen-acre Mendocino Coast Botanical Garden is another interesting stop.

    MacKerricher State Park, the largest coastal state park on the drive, lies 3 miles north of Fort Bragg. The park is a superlative area, with sharp cliffs and headlands. It has one of northern California's longest beaches, windswept sand dunes, rocky islands, tide pools, fields of wildflowers, and a freshwater lagoon. A short trail leads out to Laguna Point, a good spot to sight gray whales December through April during their migration. Harbor seals are often seen here frolicking in the surf and sunning on rocks. The park features 143 sites in three secluded campgrounds with restrooms, showers, and beach access.

THE LOST COAST

The last 26 miles of CA 1 along the coast travel a remote, lonely land. The road twists across marine terraces and drops down through shallow canyons. Roadside pullouts offer marvelous views and trails that lead to hidden beaches and coves. Westport is a small town with sparse services and was once the largest seaport between San Francisco and Eureka. In the 1880s the town was the center of a massive freight operation that supplied inland cities. The completion of the railroad to Fort Bragg, however, spelled the beginning of the end for Westport. The highway straightens out north of Westport for a few miles. **Westport-Union Landing State Beach** lies along this road section. The park is a marvelous place to get away from crowds. A campground with one hundred primitive sites scatters along the top of a lofty bluff and offers ocean views.

The drive continues up the coast. Ten miles from Westport the highway turns inland and leaves the Mendocino Coast behind. The shoreline north of here, called the Lost Coast, is a ragged vastness of wild mountains, stormy beaches, and few people and roads. The last 17 miles of CA 1 follow a winding, old logging road. Obey the numerous caution signs and drive slowly. The road corkscrews up steep canyons past lush woodlands before emerging atop lofty ridges. Several pullouts yield excellent viewpoints. Eventually, the road begins spiraling down across ridge lines before spanning the South Fork of the Eel River and entering Leggett. US 101, the drive's end, lies just outside Leggett. A northward turn leads to Eureka and the Redwood Country. A south turn heads to Ukiah, Santa Rosa, and San Francisco.

Sonoma–Napa Valleys Scenic Drive

SANTA ROSA TO HOPLAND

GENERAL DESCRIPTION: A 132-mile-long drive that makes an open loop through the pastoral wine country of the Sonoma and Napa Valleys.

SPECIAL ATTRACTIONS: Santa Rosa, Jack London State Historic Park, Sonoma Valley, Sonoma, Sonoma State Historic Park, Napa, Napa Valley, wineries, Bale Grist Mill State Historic Park, Calistoga, Old Faithful Geyser, Mount St. Helena, Robert Louis Stevenson State Park, Clear Lake, hiking.

LOCATION: West-central California, from Santa Rosa just north of San Francisco to Hopland.

DRIVE ROUTE NUMBERS AND NAMES: California Highways 12 (Sonoma Highway), 29 (St. Helena Highway), and 175; U.S. Highway 101 (Redwood Highway).

TRAVEL SEASON: Year-round.

CAMPING: Several public campgrounds, including three state park campgrounds, lie along the drive. Reservations for state park sites are necessary in summer.

SERVICES: All services at Santa Rosa, Sonoma, Napa, Yountville, St. Helena, Calistoga, Kelseyville, Lakeport, and Hopland.

NEARBY ATTRACTIONS: Sonoma Coast State Beaches, Russian River, San Francisco, Golden Gate Bridge, Muir Woods National Monument, Point Reyes National Seashore, Golden Gate National Recreation Area, Fort Ross State Historic Park, San Pablo National Wildlife Refuge, Marine World Africa USA, Armstrong Redwoods State Reserve, Petaluma Adobe State Historic Park.

THE DRIVE

This 132-mile scenic drive makes an open loop between Santa Rosa and Hopland, both on US 101. The drive, following three California highways, traverses California's wine country in the Sonoma and Napa Valleys; crosses high, rolling mountains tangled with dense woods; and passes Clear Lake, the largest natural lake entirely within the state. Numerous historic sites line the highways, including the ranch and home of famed author Jack London, the Mexican colonial town of Sonoma, and the ghost-town site of Silverado made famous by writer Robert Louis Stevenson.

The wine country offers pleasant weather year-round, with wet winters and dry summers. Expect cool temperatures between forty and sixty degrees and regular rain during winter. Seventeen inches of Sonoma's total annual rainfall of 27 inches

CALIFORNIA

MENDOCINO
NATIONAL
FOREST

20

29

Clear
Lake

To Ukiah

Lakeport
Lakeport
Peak

Hopland

175

Big
Valley

Clear Lake
State Park

Kelseyville

Mount
Konocti
4,299 ft.

Clearlake

20

Lower Lake

29

MAYACAMAS MOUNTAINS

Mount Hannah
1,212 ft.

Loch
Lomond

29

Cobb

Boggs
Mountain

175

Cloverdale

Cobb
Mountain

Collayomi
Valley

Middletown

ALEXANDER

Pine Mountain
1,011 ft.

VALLEY

29

128

Mount St. Helena
4,339 ft.

Robert Louis Stevenson
State Park

Healdsburg

Sugarloaf Mountain
910 ft.

101

Calistoga

Bothe-Napa Valley
State Park

Bale Grist Mill
State Historic Park

St. Helena

Lake Hennessey
Recreation Area

128

Annadel
State Park

Sugarloaf Ridge
State Park

NAPA

Haystack
Mountain

Santa Rosa

Oakmont

Kenwood

VALLEY

Yountville

Jack London
State Historic
Park

Mount
Veeder

29

Bodega
Bay

Sonoma
Mountain
2,299 ft.

Valley of the Moon

12

Sonoma

Napa

1

Petaluma

Sonoma Valley

121

29

N

PACIFIC

OCEAN

101

37

80

0   Kilometers   10

0   Miles   10

POINT REYES
NATIONAL
SEASHORE

To San Francisco

San Francisco
Bay

Vallejo

falls between December and February. Spring continues with rain but yields warmer days and wildflower-strewn hillsides. Temperatures become hot by June. Daily highs often creep into the nineties, and skies are generally clear and dry. Fog often shrouds the lower valleys on summer mornings. Autumn days, with the summer tourists gone and the vineyards ablaze with color, are warm and clear.

SANTA ROSA AND SONOMA VALLEY

The drive begins by following CA 12 (Sonoma Highway) east from Santa Rosa and US 101. Santa Rosa, with a population of 147,000, is Sonoma County's largest city and economic hub. One of the city's best attractions is the **Luther Burbank Home and Gardens.** Luther Burbank, a renowned, self-taught horticulturist, worked here for fifty years improving and developing cultivated plants like Shasta daisies and Santa Rosa plums in the area's rich soils and mild climate. Burbank died in 1926 and is buried near his house, which is open daily to visitors. Other Santa Rosa points of interest include the Sonoma County Museum and the Robert L. Ripley Memorial Museum, which houses worldwide memorabilia from local son Robert "Believe It or Not!" Ripley.

The highway quickly runs through Santa Rosa's eastern suburbs and swings southeast into the Sonoma Valley, a broad valley flanked by the Sonoma Mountains on the west and the Mayacamas Mountains on the east. This 17-mile-long valley, nicknamed the Valley of the Moon by local author Jack London in a popular novel, is home to more than thirty wineries. Sonoma is supposedly a local Native American word meaning "many moons."

Annadel State Park sits south of the highway immediately after entering the valley. This 5,000-acre park spreads over rolling hills broken by trickling streams and coated with oak woodlands and grassy meadows. Thirty-five miles of trails lace the hills, leading to lush canyons with redwoods, Douglas firs, and ferns. A popular hike leads 3 miles to Lake Ilsanjo, a good lake to fish for black bass. The lake's name is derived from its former owners—Ilsa and Joe. Spring Lake Regional Park, just northwest of Annadel, offers a thirty-one site campground next to the seventy-two-acre lake.

Hood Mountain Regional Park and Sugarloaf Ridge State Park drape over the Mayacamas Mountains across the valley from Annadel. Both parks boast a variety of plant communities spread across steep mountainsides and slicing canyons. Sugarloaf Ridge, a rugged 2,500-acre park, reaches a high point of 2,729 feet atop Bald Mountain. Over 25 miles of trail snake across the park, passing big leaf maples, madrones, coast redwoods, several oak species, and, in springtime, some 187 flower species that include owl's clover, iris, lupine, Indian paintbrush, and periwinkle. The views from both Bald and Hood Mountains are marvelous. Fifty campsites, with tables, food lockers, and water, scatter through an evergreen forest at Sugarloaf. Hikers should carry water and watch for poison oak and rattlesnakes.

The drive follows the verdant Valley of the Moon for 18 miles from Santa Rosa to Sonoma, twisting down the valley past sun-drenched vineyards and several small towns such as Kenwood, Glen Ellen, El Verano, and Boyes Hot Springs. Numerous back roads explore the countryside, many making excellent and safe bike tours. Eight wineries, including Kenwood Vineyards, lie in residential Kenwood. Kenwood hosts the World Championship Pillow Fight every Fourth of July. Just down the road sits the old resort community of Glen Ellen and **Jack London State Historic Park.** The 800-acre park, west of the scenic drive, creeps up the northeast flank of Sonoma Mountain.

Jack London was born in San Francisco in 1876 and became one of the best known and most successful writers of his time with books like *White Fang* and *The Call of the Wild*. In 1905 London and his second wife, Charmian, bought acreage in Sonoma Valley and established the Beauty Ranch. By 1911, at age thirty-five, he had acquired more than 1,100 acres and work began on his four-story Wolf House mansion. The house, however, mysteriously burned down in 1913 only days before the Londons were to move in, leaving fragmented stone walls. London died in 1916 and was buried under a lava boulder on a grassy hill beside two pioneer children. Charmian London built the nearby House of Happy Walls, which today houses a collection of London's papers, rejection slips, library, travel souvenirs, and memorabilia. Several easy trails stroll around the state park, exploring the same paths London rode.

The old resort towns of El Verano and Boyes Hot Springs are just north of Sonoma. Boyes Hot Springs, the geographical center of the valley, is famed for its thermal mineral springs. An Englishman named Captain Henry E. Boyes developed the springs after learning of their medicinal powers.

SONOMA

Sonoma, one of California's oldest and most historic towns, lies on the undulating hills between the Mayacamas Mountains and the watery delta of Sonoma Creek above San Pablo Bay. Originally established as California's northernmost mission in 1823 to counter the Russian presence at nearby Fort Ross, the town was laid out by Comandante Alferez Mariano Vallejo around a spacious central plaza, the largest in California, and named Pueblo de Sonoma. Low-slung adobe "haciendas" or houses and "palacios" or palaces were erected, and Vallejo built a prosperous fiefdom. On June 14, 1846, Sonoma fell into the hands of a group of armed American settlers and trappers angered by the Mexican law that prohibited them from owning property. The group was led by explorer Captain John C. Fremont. They took over Sonoma without a shot, declared California an independent republic, and raised the Bear Flag over the town plaza. The flag, the basis for today's California flag, featured a red stripe, a star in memory of the Lone Star Republic in Texas, and a crudely drawn bear. Shortly afterward, Sonoma and California came under the American flag as part of the spoils of the Mexican-American War. Vallejo remained in Sonoma as a leading citizen and land baron, became a delegate to California's

California Highway 175 twists across the Mayacamas Mountains north of the Napa Valley.

first constitutional convention in 1849, and was elected a state senator and mayor of Sonoma.

Sonoma features many frontier buildings, including the Mission San Francisco de Solano, the Vallejo home, and the Sonoma Barracks that are preserved in **Sonoma State Historic Park.** Sonoma, besides being the cradle of modern California, is also the birthplace of the state's viticulture. The mission padres planted grapevines in the early 1800s and made rustic wines. In 1856 Count Agoston Haraszthy, a Hungarian emigrant, planted the first major American vineyard with European grapes and founded Buena Vista Winery. It is east of Sonoma on a eucalyptus-lined lane. It offers tastings and tours of the original stone wine cellar as well as of caves built by Chinese workers in 1862. In town itself is Sebastiani Vineyard, a large winery with a comprehensive tour and complimentary samples. Besides wine, travelers can also sample Sonoma's famous cheeses at the Vella Cheese Company, with its superb Monterey cheeses, and the Sonoma Cheese Factory, home of the famed Sonoma Jack cheeses. Sonoma offers all visitor services and the visitor bureau on the Plaza doles out free information on the region.

The drive turns south in Sonoma and continues for a few miles to Schellville, where the highway bends abruptly eastward. The road runs past ranches, grazing cattle and horses, vineyards, and undulating hills coated with tawny grass at the southern end of the Mayacamas Mountains. After 11 miles, CA 12 intersects CA 29 just south of Napa. The city of Napa sits astride the Napa River at the southern end of the 30-mile-long Napa Valley, California's most famous wine region.

Sonoma–Napa Valleys Scenic Drive　　　　　　　　　　　　　**31**

NAPA VALLEY

The Napa Valley is considered with the Sonoma Valley as one of the world's great wine regions. It offers porous, well-drained soils and a dry Mediterranean climate conducive to growing excellent grapes. While early American settlers grew grapes from cuttings from Sonoma's mission vineyards, Charles Krug is considered the valley's first true vintner after introducing Riesling grapes in 1861. The valley's acclaimed vintages today are dry wines, and grapes include Pinot Noir, Riesling, Chardonnay, Cabernet Sauvignon, Chenin Blanc, and others. More than 200 wineries with some 32,000 acres of vineyards carpet the valley floor. Napa wine connoisseurs still agree with writer Robert Louis Stevenson's 1880 assessment of California wines as "bottled poetry."

The Napa Valley, because of its superb climate, fine lodging and dining, pastoral beauty, and excellent wines, is deservedly popular with visitors. Weekends, particularly in autumn when the grapes are crushed, are hectic with bumper to bumper traffic. Better to travel on weekdays and avoid the rush. Most valley wineries offer tours, and some require reservations and charge tasting fees. Beginning tasters are well-advised to take the informative tours at the larger wineries like Robert Mondavi before exploring the small vineyards. Current winery lists with addresses and phone numbers are found at local chambers of commerce. It's best to call ahead to smaller wineries for hours and tours. A good sampling of the valley's wines and wineries often includes stopping at a large, medium, and small winery, preferably in different parts of the valley, as each has its own distinctive wines. Select a designated, nondrinking driver in advance when touring the wine country, and remember to drink sensibly.

NAPA TO CALISTOGA

The drive turns north on CA 29 and quickly enters the city of Napa, the southern anchor and business center for the prosperous valley. The word "napa," like so many California place names, is a Native American word meaning grizzly bear or derived from "napo," meaning house. The name was given to Vallejo's large land grant here and later applied to the county. Napa, now a large sprawling city, began in 1848 as a river port on the San Pablo Bay and later became a busy tannery town.

The drive runs north on CA 29 for 25 miles to Calistoga, passing through the heart of the Napa wine country and the picturesque towns of Yountville and St. Helena. Yountville, 9 miles north of Napa via a four-lane highway, is a quaint, upscale village with numerous historic stone buildings. In 1836 North Carolina trapper George Yount built the valley's first house and planted the first vineyard here on a Mexican land grant. The town is also home to the Veterans Home of California and chic shops and restaurants. Nearby is Domaine Chandon, maker of fine sparkling wines, and S. Anderson Vineyard. St. Helena, like neighboring Yountville, is a town of expensive shops and restaurants. The **Robert Louis Stevenson Museum** is housed in a wing of the Silverado Museum. The collection is a must-see for the Stevenson aficionado and includes more than 8,000 items from his life and literature. The exhibits detail Stevenson's first childhood letters, first editions of his treasured books, manuscripts and letters, drawings, and photographs. Nearby is the Napa Valley Wine Library with more than 3,000 books on wine and wine making.

Most of the Napa Valley's better-known vintages are produced on the 8-mile section between Yountville and St. Helena. Robert Mondavi Winery, one of the largest, sits west of the highway at Oakville. Other wineries on this highway stretch include Beaulieu, Girard, Rutherford Hill, Sutter Home, Spring Mountain, and Heitz Wine Cellar. At St. Helena lie Christian Brothers, Beringer, and Krug wineries. Beringer Vineyards, open since 1876, offers its famed aging caves dug by Chinese workers, the ornate Rhine House mansion, and an excellent thirty-minute tour followed by a tasting. Charles Krug Winery is the valley's oldest and boasts four distinctive tours that explore all facets of Napa Valley wine making. The popular Cabernet Sauvignon Seminar covers this fine grape and its hearty wines. North of St. Helena are Frog's Leap, Deer Park Winery, and Burgess Cellars.

Two of the valley's premier champagne makers—Hanns Kornell Champagne Cellars and Schramsberg—sit north of St. Helena. Schramsberg, the first hillside winery in Napa Valley, ages its exquisite sparkling wines in 125-year-old caves hollowed out of volcanic ash deposits. Robert Louis Stevenson spent an afternoon in 1880 with founder Jacob Schram tasting wines in the cellar. He later wrote, "To Mr. Schram this was a solemn office . . . and he followed every sip and read my face with proud anxiety. I tasted all. I tasted every variety and shade of Schramberger . . . ." Today the vineyard offers sales but no tasting.

Two state parks also lie in the northern Napa Valley. The **Bale Grist Mill State Historic Park,** a few miles north of St. Helena, preserves a flour mill built by English doctor Edward T. Bale in 1846. **Bothe–Napa Valley State Park** straddles the mountain ridges just south of Calistoga. The 1,700-acre park spreads along Ritchie Creek and offers numerous hiking trails, a picnic area, a fifty-site campground with showers, and a swimming pool.

CALISTOGA

Calistoga crowns the northern end of the Napa Valley, nestled in the narrow valley between lofty peaks. Mormon entrepreneur Samuel Brannan platted the town in 1859 as a luxurious spa to attract well-heeled San Franciscans. Numerous hot springs were the main attraction. The local Indians called the area "Colaynomo" or Oven Place, but Brannan, after opening his grand hotel, called it Calistoga. Legend says that when he announced his new Saratoga of California, he muddled his speech saying it was the Calistoga of Sarifornia. The town remains a popular tourist haven. Visitors still bathe in the hot springs, take hot mud baths, and explore the upper valley's wineries, including the elite Cuvaison, Stonegate Winery, and Chateau Montelena. More wineries lie northwest of Calistoga on California Highway 128 in the Alexander Valley. The Sharpsteen Museum and Sam Brannan

Cottage make a good stop in Calistoga and include a detailed diorama of the town in 1865.

Volcanism coupled with the San Andreas Rift system explains the underground hot springs at Calistoga as well as the geology of the Napa and Sonoma Valleys and the surrounding mountain ranges. The northwest-to-southeast-trending valleys were formed by faults associated with the famed San Andreas Fault to the west. The valley floors filled with gravel and silt washed from the highlands, forming rich, porous soils that are ideal for grape growing. The soils here also impart unique taste characteristics to valley wines. Deposits of volcanic ash and rust-colored volcanic rocks blanket the area mountains. Most of the volcanoes that erupted sit north of Napa Valley around Clear Lake. Hot rock does, however, lie just underground at Calistoga, creating the bubbling hot springs and the unique 60- to 100-foot-high Old Faithful Geyser, which erupts about every thirty minutes. In a petrified forest, encased and preserved by volcanic ash just west of Calistoga, the largest log stretches 126 feet long and 8 feet in diameter.

MOUNT ST. HELENA

CA 29 turns north in Calistoga, swings through vineyards at the mountain base, and begins swiftly climbing northward above Jericho Canyon. The drive continues into the mountains, its narrow lanes spiraling up through dense oak thickets and past glades of wind-rippled grass. After 5 miles, it reaches a saddle east of 4,339-foot Mount St. Helena and **Robert Louis Stevenson State Park.**

The 3,200-acre park, mostly wilderness, drapes over the chaparral, oak, and pine-covered slopes of Mount St. Helena. The peak is one of the highest in the Coast Ranges and towers over the surrounding countryside. An unsubstantiated local myth says the peak was named for a Russian princess. In truth, it and the Napa Valley town were named in 1855 for the St. Helena Division of the Sons of Temperance. The park is, of course, named for the famed Scottish author Robert Louis Stevenson, who honeymooned with his new wife, Fanny Osbourne, at the abandoned town site of Silverado on Mount St. Helena's flanks in May of 1880. He later wrote the classic *Silverado Squatters,* a slim volume that detailed his experiences in the Napa country. Stevenson wrote of the park's dominant peak, "The mountain . . . feeds in the springtime many splashing brooks. From its summit you must have an excellent lesson in geography. Three counties, Napa, Lake, and Sonoma, march across its cliffy shoulders . . . Its sides are fringed with forest, and the soil, where it is bare, glows warm with cinnabar."

A rough parking area is atop Mount St. Helena's eastern shoulder at a high saddle. Here sit the ruins of the Toll House on the old Calistoga-Lakeport stage road that CA 29 now follows. A trail begins here and winds west a mile to a granite, book-shaped marker that commemorates old Silverado and the Stevensons' honeymoon site. The trail scrambles west to a fire road and leads 5 miles to the mountain's summit, some 4,000 feet above the Napa Valley. The view from atop is astounding on a clear day. The blue Pacific Ocean glimmers to the west; Mount Diablo lifts its grassy flanks to the southeast; and to the north Mount Shasta and Lassen Peak poke above the horizon, their snowcapped summits glimmering like distant alabaster towers.

MIDDLETOWN TO CLEAR LAKE

From the ridgeline, the drive drops steeply northward and follows St. Helena Creek to Middletown, a small town lying midway between Calistoga and Lower Lake. The drive turns northwest here on California Highway 175 and heads up the broad Collayomi Valley. The quiet highway runs through grassland and forest on the valley floor, passing small ranches with grazing cattle. After about 5 miles, the road begins climbing through a forest of gray pine, oak, and manzanita. Two miles later, the road crests at 2,600-foot Whispering Pines, a secluded, cool residential community set among towering sugar pines. The highway twists northwestward, passing a succession of small communities, Boggs Mountain State Forest, and brushy, tree-choked canyons. As the road drops, it follows the broad valley of Cole Creek, with shade from oak trees dappling the asphalt. After 18 miles, CA 175 rejoins CA 29 and runs west around Mount Konocti to Kelseyville.

Mount Konocti, a conical 4,299-foot peak, dominates the Clear Lake area. The peak and surrounding area is part of the Clear Lake volcanic field, a dormant region of recent volcanoes and lava flows. Konocti is built of volcanic cinders and lava. It stopped erupting some 250,000 years ago, although some activity on its northeast base occurred only 10,000 years ago. Numerous earthquakes and a large underground pocket of molten magma that create fumaroles and hot springs indicate the area is still geologically active. Clear Lake, covering 43,000 acres, is the largest natural lake totally within California and is the state's second-largest freshwater lake. It formed when landslides blocked its western drainage to the Russian River, and lava flows blocked its eastern drainage. The Clear Lake area is a fine rockhounding region, offering "Lake County diamonds" or excellent quartz crystals. A good spot to find the crystals is on Perini Road southwest of Lower Lake. Other collectible rocks include calcite, chert, jasper, and obsidian.

The area around Kelseyville is renowned for its delicious pears. Benjamin Kelsey founded the town in 1847, when he bought land from General Vallejo. Local Pomos, however, killed Kelsey in 1849 for harsh treatment of his laborers. The Pomos ceded their lands here in 1851 for "Ten head of beef cattle, three sacks of bread and sundry clothing." Today, orderly pear and walnut orchards march across the rolling hills around the small, quiet town of Kelseyville. **Clear Lake State Park** lies on the lakeshore just north of town. The park offers 2 miles of shoreline; waterskiing; swimming; fishing for crappie, catfish, perch, bass, and bluegill; and 112 campsites in four campgrounds.

BIG VALLEY TO HOPLAND

The drive traverses Big Valley west of Kelseyville, passing orchards and vineyards and reaches the southern outskirts of Lakeport after 8 miles. Turn south on CA 175 here. CA 29 continues north into Lakeport. The scenery along the next 18 miles is simply stunning. The drive corkscrews up precipitous slopes and deep canyons to the forested crest of the Mayacamas Mountains before dropping steeply down to Hopland and the Russian River. Dense forest and thick chaparral line the serpentine roadway; marvelous views of Clear Lake and the surrounding mountains unfold from each pullout. Little traffic is encountered on this lonely road section. The drive ends on US 101 at Hopland. The town's main industry used to be hops for brewing beer until the 1950s. Now vineyards and wineries flourish in the surrounding Sanel Valley. Fetzer Vineyards, the biggest winery here, offers a large in-town tasting room. The excellent Hopland Brewery, a microbrewing operation, opened in 1983 and includes a brewpub. Numerous crafts and antiques stores make Hopland a popular shopping stop. Travelers can return to the San Francisco Bay area by turning south on US 101. Squaw Rock, just south of town, is a popular summer swimming hole on the Russian River.

Big Sur Coast Scenic Drive

CARMEL TO MORRO BAY

GENERAL DESCRIPTION: A 122-mile-long highway that twists down the scenic central California coastline from Carmel to Morro Bay.

SPECIAL ATTRACTIONS: Carmel, Point Lobos State Reserve, Garrapata State Park, Big Sur Coast, Andrew Molera State Park, Pfeiffer Big Sur State Park, Julia Pfeiffer Burns State Park, Hearst-San Simeon State Historical Monument, William R. Hearst Memorial State Beach, San Simeon State Beach.

LOCATION: Western California between San Francisco and Los Angeles.

DRIVE ROUTE NUMBER AND NAME: California Highway 1 (Cabrillo Highway).

TRAVEL SEASON: Year-round. Watch for fog along the drive in summer. Heavy winter rains make the pavement slick and may create landslides that close the highway.

CAMPING: Hundreds of campsites, including walk-in tent sites and RV sites, are in national forest, state park, and private campgrounds along the drive. Reservations, particularly in summer, are strongly recommended.

SERVICES: All services in Monterey, Carmel, Morro Bay, and San Luis Obispo.

NEARBY ATTRACTIONS: Monterey, Pinnacles National Monument, Fremont Peak State Park, San Juan Bautista State Historic Park, Morro Bay Museum of Natural History, Pismo State Beach, San Luis Obispo County Historical Museum, Mission San Luis Obispo de Tolosa.

THE DRIVE

This 122-mile-long scenic drive follows CA 1 and twists along the spectacular Big Sur Coast between Carmel and Morro Bay on central California's Pacific shoreline. The highway, designated an All-American Road, is simply one of the world's most breathtaking drives, a must-do adventure for any California traveler. Here, the steep ridges of the remote Santa Lucia Range plunge down to a rocky, wave-battered coast, making an abrupt transition from wild peak to wild ocean. The roadway follows this transition zone, snaking along precipitous headlands, crossing grassy meadows above ragged coves, and traversing thirty-three bridges that span deep canyons and gorges. It's a superb landscape that serves as a fitting boundary between North America and the Pacific Ocean.

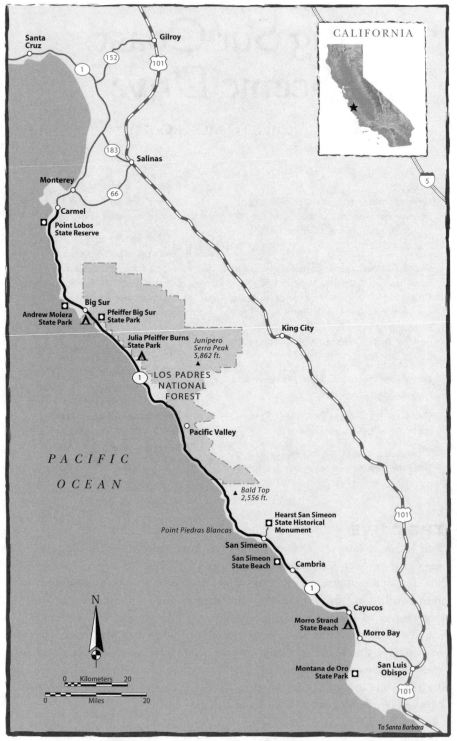

CALIFORNIA

Santa Cruz

Gilroy

152

101

183

Salinas

Monterey

66

Carmel

Point Lobos State Reserve

Andrew Molera State Park

Big Sur

Pfeiffer Big Sur State Park

Julia Pfeiffer Burns State Park

Junipero Serra Peak 5,862 ft.

King City

LOS PADRES NATIONAL FOREST

1

PACIFIC OCEAN

Pacific Valley

Bald Top 2,556 ft.

Hearst San Simeon State Historical Monument

Point Piedras Blancas

San Simeon

San Simeon State Beach

Cambria

1

101

Cayucos

Morro Strand State Beach

Morro Bay

Montana de Oro State Park

San Luis Obispo

101

N

0   Kilometers   20

0   Miles   20

To Santa Barbara

5

The climate along the Big Sur Coast is mild year-round. Around Monterey Bay on the drive's north end, the weather varies little between winter and summer. Only ten degrees difference separates the mean temperatures for August and January, making the climate here the most uniform in the United States. Summer brings thick fog banks that wrap the coast in gray shrouds. The fog usually burns off by midday, but temperatures are often cool. Bring a sweater for those days. Inland temperatures on the mountains and valleys above the coast can be hot with daily highs reaching into the nineties. Thunderstorms are infrequent, although light showers may accompany the fog. The upper part of the drive between Big Sur and Carmel is cooler and damper than the southern section. Autumn brings warm, clear days until winter storms sweep off the Pacific in December. Heavy rains lead to frequent landslides along the road. Forty-two landslides blocked the highway during the wet winter of 1982–83. One took over a year to clear away. The greenery in spring adorns the coastal meadows and forests, and the days are clear and breezy with occasional showers.

MONTEREY

Monterey is considered the birthplace of California. Juan Rodriguez Cabrillo, a Portuguese sailor exploring for Spain, discovered Monterey Bay in 1542. CA 1 is called the Cabrillo Highway in honor of California's first European explorer. In 1602 Sebastian Vizcaino celebrated mass under Monterey's own "Plymouth Rock," an old spreading oak tree. Almost two centuries later, explorer Gaspar de Portola and Father Junipero Serra established a presidio and mission on the bay's fertile south shore; and the town, called Monterey, grew into a lively port and the provincial capital of Alta California. Monterey later became a major fishing port and fish cannery, immortalized in John Steinbeck's classic 1945 novel *Cannery Row* as "a poem, a stink, a grating noise, a quality of light, a tune, a habit, a nostalgia, a dream." Today, the Sardine Capital of the World attracts tourists who stroll its charming streets.

Monterey retains its historic flavor with more eighteenth- and nineteenth-century buildings than any other California town. The self-guided "Path of History" winds 2.7 miles through the downtown past whitewashed adobe buildings with red tile roofs. Other popular attractions include Steinbeck's Cannery Row, Fisherman's Wharf, Monterey State Historic Park, and the spectacular Monterey Bay Aquarium. The aquarium explores 60-mile-long Monterey Bay's diverse habitats and its 10,000-foot-deep canyons, kelp beds, and tidal flats.

CARMEL TO POINT LOBOS

The drive begins in the arts town of Carmel, a picturesque hamlet nestled along Carmel Bay just south of Monterey on CA 1. It is one of California's least commercial towns, yet it is also one of the most popular. Visitors flock to play golf on its many championship courses, including prestigious Pebble Beach Golf Links, to shop its exclusive stores and galleries, and to admire the scenery at Point Lobos

State Reserve. Carmel also boasts a bohemian past of famed writers, artists, and photographers who rejoiced in the area's supreme natural beauty. The artists' colony included writers Jack London, Mary Austin, Lincoln Steffens, Upton Sinclair, and Robinson Jeffers, and photographers Ansel Adams and Edward Weston. Jeffers, the poet laureate of Big Sur Country, lived in Tor House on the Carmel Bay coast. This distinctive American poet embodied the region's strong spirit of place and invoked its wildness and freedom in his powerful poetry— ". . . each November great waves awake and are drawn/ Like smoking mountains bright from the west/ And come and cover the cliff with white violent cleanness."

The drive drops down from Carmel, crosses the Carmel River, and passes **Carmel River State Beach,** a generally uncrowded stretch of sand bordered by windswept cypress and eucalyptus trees. Good birding is found in the river's marsh delta. A mile past the state beach lies **Point Lobos State Reserve,** perhaps California's most beautiful coastal parkland. This 1,276-acre nature preserve of rocky headlands, wave-carved coves, narrow shell-strewn beaches, and sea stacks, juts into south Carmel Bay. Its 6-mile coast is a wonderful place of relentless surf and wind. Tide pools teeming with life—sea urchins, hermit crabs, starfish, anemones—are exposed on the rough shore at low tide. Numerous birds including seagulls, comorants, brown pelicans, and herons soar overhead. Colonies of barking sea lions populate the quiet coves, leading to the point's early Spanish name, *Punta de los Lobos Marinos,* or Point of the Sea Wolves. Sea otters are often seen frolicking in the surf or offshore kelp beds. The California Sea Otter Game Refuge begins south of Point Lobos and runs down to Big Sur. The reserve is also well-known for its diverse flora, with more than 300 plant species inhabiting its terrain. It's a good place to see the elegant Monterey cypress, a rare tree that grows only on Point Lobos and nearby Cypress Point. These gnarled, twisted trees, buffeted by fierce coastal winds, line the park's rocky cliffs and headlands. To preserve the park's beauty, only 450 visitors are allowed into the park at any one time. Plan to come early or wait in line along the highway on weekends. Park visitors will agree with Robert Louis Stevenson, who supposedly modeled Spyglass Hill in *Treasure Island* after Point Lobos, that the site is "the most beautiful meeting of land and sea on earth."

BIG SUR COAST

The drive runs through Carmel Highlands and enters Big Sur Country past Point Lobos. This is a spectacular stretch of coast where the Santa Lucia Range plunges into the blue Pacific Ocean. The Santa Lucias, also called the Big Sur Hills, spread southward from the Carmel River to the Cuyama River. Much of the range is administered by Los Padres National Forest, part of which is the remote 95,152-acre Ventana Wilderness Area. The high point is 5,862-foot Junipero Serra Peak.

The drive's next 30 miles cling to the seaward face of the Santa Lucias above the crash of the Pacific surf. The road is narrow with numerous pullouts. Use them to enjoy the scenery or allow traffic to safely pass. The first stop is 2,879-acre **Garra-pata State Park** along the coast just north of Soberanes Point. This day-use park-land, named by the Spanish for the lowly wood tick, boasts gleaming white beaches flanked by granite buttresses, arches, and grottos. Some good trails lace the bluffs above the water and the coves offer fishing for greenling and surf perch. A good trail climbs east from the highway 1.5 miles up Soberanes Creek to a verdant grove of redwoods nestled in the chaparral-covered hills.

The highway twists south from Garrapata past Kaiser and Rocky Points to the **Bixby Creek Bridge,** a dramatic concrete span that arches over Bixby Creek's deep gorge. The famed bridge, measuring 718 feet long and 260 feet high, consumed some 6,600 cubic yards of concrete poured into forms supported by 300,000 board feet of Douglas fir. The bridge, also called Rainbow Bridge, was completed in 1932. The highway itself was finished in 1937, hacked out of the remote coast by convict labor who battled violent weather and tough engineering problems for nine years. The road cost more than $10 million or $71,000 per mile.

The coast here at the end of the nineteenth of the century was one of California's least accessible regions. In the 1890s Dr. John Roberts, a Monterey physician, often made house calls along the coast by riding on horseback on a spiraling wagon track. He gradually mapped and plotted a road course that ran from Monterey to San Luis Obispo. Roberts and state senator James Rigdon estimated the cost of the road to be $50,000 and got legislation passed in 1919 to construct the road. In the late 1950s state engineers and land developers sought to modernize and straighten the road, turning it into an interstate-like highway. Big Sur's landowners realized the folly of the plan and fought to preserve the coast. The highway, withdrawn from the state freeway system, was dedicated in 1966 by Lady Bird Johnson as California's first official scenic drive.

The drive hugs the coast and then climbs away from a bridge to a lofty view-point above Hurricane Point. Good views of the ocean and the north coast are found here. Look to the south to see shipwrecks near Point Sur at low tide. The road drops southward, crosses the Little Sur River, and edges around Little River Hill to Point Sur. This rocky point was once nicknamed "the graveyard of the Pacific" for its numerous offshore shipwrecks including the S.S. *Los Angeles* in 1873. The automated Point Sur Lighthouse that now graces the site is operated by the Coast Guard. This thirty-four-acre spit of land is also a state historic park. Regular ranger-led tours visit the lighthouse. The point also makes a great spot for winter whale watching. Massive fifty-ton California gray whales, California's state mammal, make an annual 12,000-mile round-trip migration south to Baja California from Alaska in autumn to breeding and birthing grounds in Mexican waters before heading north with the spring. Bring a pair of binoculars to look for these gentle giants surfacing offshore.

The highway bends southeast after Point Sur and traverses a wide bench between the mountains and the sea. After a few miles, it passes 4,800-acre **Andrew**

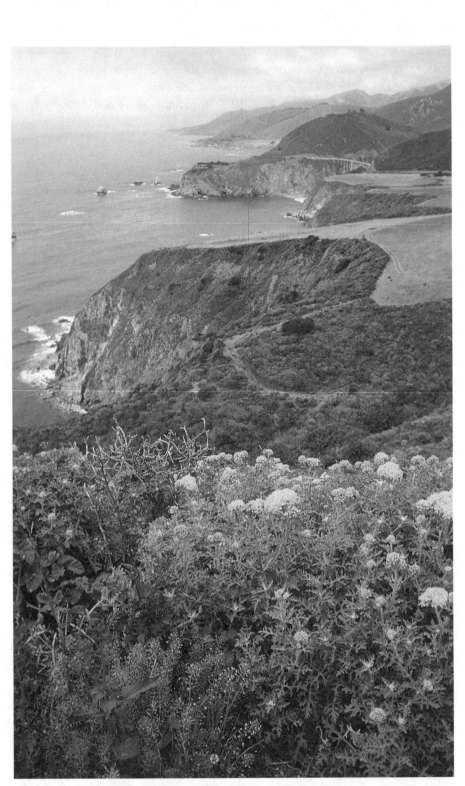

The drive runs along the Santa Lucias toward the Bixby Creek Bridge, which spans a precipitous gorge.

Molera State Park along the lower section of the Big Sur River. The usually uncrowded park offers several trails, a 2-mile-long beach, and a primitive twenty-four-site walk-in campground a quarter mile from the highway parking lot. This area, bounded on the north by the Little Sur River and the south by the Big Sur River, was part of an 8,949-acre Mexican land grant called Rancho El Sur in 1839. The early Spanish called the coast here *El Pais Grande del Sur* or "the Great Land of the South." Americans shortened it to Big Sur.

It's past Point Sur that Big Sur aficionados consider the "true" Big Sur to begin. A town called **Big Sur** stretches the 6-mile-length of the Big Sur River valley with scattered houses and a few stores along CA 1. This backwater, picturesque valley has long been an artists' colony, attracting those who felt that even Carmel was too civilized. Novelist Henry Miller lived here from 1947 to 1964. He wrote of Big Sur: "That same prehistoric look. The look of always. Nature smiling at herself in the mirror of eternity."

PFEIFFER BIG SUR STATE PARK

Past Molera State Park, the highway swings inland and follows the Big Sur River valley southeast through abrupt wooded mountains. Pfeiffer Big Sur State Park, one of California's most popular state parks, is soon encountered. This small 1,006-acre park abuts the Ventana Wilderness Area and is flanked by Pfeiffer Ridge and Cabezo Prieto. A thick woodland of oak, sycamore, big-leaf maples, willows, cottonwoods, and redwoods crowd the river valley, while trees that prefer drier climes, oak, chaparral, and the endemic Santa Lucia fir, scatter across the higher ridges. The spectacular coastal redwoods grow in isolated groves here. Their thick, fire-resistant trunks lift skyward, casting a canopy of sun-dappled shade over the moist, fern-covered forest floor. An excellent trail wanders through the redwoods to Pfeiffer Falls. Other trails climb into the nearby wilderness area. The park offers 214 wooded campsites.

A mile past the state park, Forest Road 19S05 drops down narrow Sycamore Canyon to scenic Pfeiffer Beach. This ragged coast is lined with rocky, wave-battered crags and narrow sand beaches. It was the first place settled on the Big Sur Coast when the Pfeiffers, for whom the beach and state park are named, home-steaded here in 1869. Another excellent side trip begins at Andrew Molera State Park and follows the old Coast Road for 11 miles to Bixby Bridge. This dirt road offers spectacular views of Big Sur Country as it corkscrews up and over lofty ridges and peaks, but it may be impassable when wet.

Past the Sycamore Canyon turn, the road rolls down to Nepenthe and its wide vista almost 1,000 feet above the azure Pacific Ocean. Filmmaker Orson Welles once owned a cabin here. Just south of Nepenthe sits the **Henry Miller Memorial Library,** an unassuming house among tall redwoods. This small library is open by appointment only; it preserves books, manuscripts, and paintings by one of Big Sur's most famous bohemian residents. Miller willed his personal collection to longtime friend Emil White, who in turn donated it to the Big Sur Land Trust for further preservation.

The Cabrillo Highway hugs the coast for the next 60 miles, occasionally venturing down near the pounding surf but usually edging along precipitous, chaparral-shrouded mountainsides high above the rocky strand. Except for the narrow band of asphalt-covered road, this remote, rugged land still remains as Spanish explorer Juan Cabrillo saw it in 1542, fifty scant years after Columbus's discovery of the New World. He noted in his journal, "All the coast passed this day is very bold; there is a great swell and the land is very high. There are mountains which seem to reach the heavens, and the sea beats on them."

Julia Pfeiffer Burns State Park, about 7 miles south of Nepenthe, is another great park on the coast. Excellent hiking trails thread across the steep hillsides, dropping down to 2 miles of rocky coastline, and walking up trickling creeks lined with redwoods near the southern end of their range. One hike passes Saddle Rock to the cliffs above Waterfall Cove where an 80-foot waterfall drops into the surf far below. The park has some walk-in and group camping, picnic facilities, and winter whale-watching programs.

The drive continues south, swings around Lopez Point, and enters the northern section of Los Padres National Forest. A couple of miles later, the road passes 33-site Kirk Creek Campground and tiny Mill Creek Picnic Area. A prison labor camp for 150 well-behaved San Quentin inmates sat at Kirk Creek. The inmates' sentences were reduced three days for every two worked, and escape attempts into the dry, unpopulated surrounding country were rare. The Nacimiento-Ferguson Road, the only road over the Santa Lucia Range, twists east over the range crest to US 101. A side road climbs to the summit of 5,755-foot Cone Peak and overlooks the vast Ventana Wilderness to the north. Inquire at a national forest office for road conditions.

PACIFIC VALLEY TO PIEDRAS BLANCAS

The small community of Pacific Valley sits on a wide marine terrace below the mountain escarpment. A national forest ranger station here dispenses information, maps, and wilderness permits. A short hike east from the station climbs to 75-foot-high Salmon Creek Falls. This area offers some good coastal access on public lands. Sand Dollar Picnic Area and forty-four-site Plaskett Creek Campground sit along this road section. Jade Cove south of Plaskett Point boasts excellent jade hunting along the cobbled beaches. The beaches and cove are unseen from the highway; look for signs and pullouts. A path drops down a stairway on a cliff to the cove. Two jade types are found here—rare nephrite jade and common green Monterey jade. Over a period of months in 1971, three divers excavated an 8-foot-long, 9,000-pound boulder of nephrite jade valued at $180,000. At Willow Creek is a picnic area above the rocky beach. Higher, on the highway, is Willow Creek Vista with scenic views of the coast receding to the southeast horizon.

Past Willow Creek the highway uncoils across precipitous ridges high above the ocean. Numerous pullouts allow scenic views. Drive carefully and slowly through this section; maximum speeds are less than 30 miles an hour. The road passes several rugged headlands—Ragged Point, Breaker Point, Point Sierra Nevada, and Point Piedras Blancas—that jut into the heaving water. Piedras Blancas, named for its white, guano-covered rocks, has a 145-foot-high lighthouse. The area is used for marine wildlife studies, including the thick kelp forest that covers the bay south of the lighthouse. The kelp is anchored to the ocean floor and grows to heights of 100 feet, serving as home to numerous sea creatures. A walk along the beach reveals tangles of kelp with remains of life clinging to the damp seaweed, including baby octopi, skeleton shrimp, sea spiders, sponges, and kelp crabs. The area also offers good spots to sit above the ocean and watch sea otters frolic in the kelp beds.

HEARST CASTLE

The landscape changes dramatically after Piedras Blancas as the road crosses grassy marine terraces above the low, rocky coastline. Chaparral-covered mountains rise beyond the coastal terrace. **William Randolph Hearst Memorial State Beach** lies near San Simeon. It offers good sunbathing, picnicking, and fishing.

High above San Simeon sits California's second-busiest tourist attraction—the Hearst San Simeon State Historical Monument. This extravagant castle, built by publishing magnate William Randolph Hearst beginning in 1919, has one hundred rooms including thirty-one bathrooms, two libraries, and a billiards parlor, and is adorned with art treasures from around the world. The first-floor vestibule decorated with 2,000-year-old mosaic tiles from Pompeii. The mansion cost more than $10 million, or as much as the total cost of CA 1. The estate, donated to California by the Hearst Corporation in memory of its maker, can be toured daily. It takes almost two days to see the entire place.

A few miles past the turn to the Hearst estate lies **San Simeon State Beach.** This great beach, accessed by several roadside parking areas, spreads along the shore beneath low, broken cliffs topped by windswept grass. The state park also offers two excellent campgrounds on the east side of the highway. San Simeon Creek Campground has 115 sites, and primitive Washburn Campground offers sixty-seven sites on the rolling grassland.

CAMBRIA TO SAN LUIS OBISPO

Cambria, 3 miles south of San Simeon Beach, is nestled in a broad valley carved by Santa Rosa Creek. Groves of Monterey pine mix with open grasslands on the bold, rolling hills surrounding the town. The pine is endemic to California and grows in a very restricted range around Monterey, Año Nuevo Point, two islands off Baja California, and around Cambria. It prefers sandy soils from marine sediments and moisture-laden summer fogs. Monterey pine, along with close relatives knob cone and Bishop pines, once grew across much of coastal California in a mild climate. All three pines grow today in relict stands. The Monterey pine, however, is widely used worldwide for reforestation and ornamental purposes.

The drive runs southeast from Cambria up broad Perry Creek valley and down Ellysly Creek and reaches the north end of scallop-shaped Estero Bay. The road heads east and then south through Cayucos, past Cayucos and Morro Strand State Beaches to the town of Morro Bay on the tiny inlet of Morro Bay. The town is dominated by 576-foot-high **Morro Rock,** named by early Spanish explorers for its bold headland. The rock is also called the "Gibraltar of the Pacific." It is the interior remains of an ancient volcano that once lifted its cone here. South of the rock are large middens or piles of broken seashells left by the early Chumash. Some artifacts found here are as old as 6,000 years. Morro Bay and Morro Rock are both wildlife preserves, inhabited by numerous birds, including falcons, great blue herons, egrets, and 250 other bird species living or wintering here. The bay, sitting along the Great Pacific Flyway, is an important rest stop for migrating birds. This area, including the fertile estuary, is considered one of the nation's top bird-watching spots. The town offers an excellent Museum of Natural History that explores the surrounding hills and ocean habitats. Although the scenic drive ends at Morro Bay, CA 1 bends inland at Morro Bay and runs as a four-lane highway another 12 miles to US 101 and the historic town of San Luis Obispo.

San Andreas Fault Scenic Drive

I–5 TO HOLLISTER

GENERAL DESCRIPTION: A 110-mile-long drive that begins on the western edge of the San Joaquin Valley, follows long grassy valleys formed by the San Andreas Rift Zone, and traverses the edge of the Gabilan Range to Hollister.

SPECIAL ATTRACTIONS: San Andreas Rift Zone, Pinnacles National Monument, San Benito River, Gabilan Range, hiking, rock climbing.

LOCATION: West-central California, from San Joaquin Valley to just south of San Jose.

DRIVE ROUTE NUMBER: California Highways 198 and 25.

TRAVEL SEASON: Year-round.

CAMPING: Only one campground lies along the drive—Pinnacles Campground, Inc. This private campground, with 125 shaded sites, is in Bear Valley on dead-end California highway 146 just off the drive before Pinnacles National Monument.

SERVICES: All services available in Coalinga and Hollister. Don't plan on finding any services along the drive.

NEARBY ATTRACTIONS: Fremont Peak State Park, San Juan Bautista State Historic Park, Monterey, Point Lobos State Reserve, Natural Bridges State Beach, Santa Cruz, Mission Nuestra Senora de la Soledad, Santa Lucia Range, Los Padres National Forest.

THE DRIVE

This 110-mile scenic drive follows CA 198 and CA 25 and traverses a series of long fault-line valleys formed by the San Andreas Rift Zone. The route passes along the east side of the Gabilan Range, which is one of the inner Coast Ranges between Coalinga in the San Joaquin Valley and Hollister east of Monterey Bay. The countryside is unpopulated and almost pristine, broken only by a few ranches or fences. Each season brings its own rhythm and distinct flavor. After spring rains, the rumpled land is verdant with green grass and sprinkled with colorful wildflowers. Summer heat desiccates the savannas and turns the straw-dry grass a tawny brown. This is a drive to savor, to slow down and admire the view, to stop and watch the wind ripple the grass, to watch a hawk soar overhead.

The weather here is typically Mediterranean with hot, dry summers and cool, rainy winters and springs. Winter and spring bring rain and cool temperatures sweeping in from the Pacific. Expect highs between fifty and seventy degrees. Sum-

mers are generally hot, with daily highs climbing to ninety or one hundred degrees. The dry heat punishes the land, pulling moisture from the grasses, trees, and streams. Occasional clouds or showers blot the storm of sunlight.

ACROSS THE DIABLO RANGE

The drive begins at the isolated intersection of I–5 and CA 198 on the west side of the agriculturally developed San Joaquin Valley. Gas, food, and lodging are all available at this road junction. The first 3 miles run west to the junction of CA 198 and California Highway 33 and then south 9 miles to Coalinga. The road rolls over undulating grass-covered hills called Anticline Ridge before dropping past irrigated fields to Pleasant Valley and Coalinga. This area is dotted with oil wells, part of the Coalinga Oil Field. Coalinga, at 162 feet high, is a small community nestled against grassy hills on the west side of Pleasant Valley. The town is home to oil and farm workers and offers all services to travelers.

Leaving Coalinga, the highway climbs into the hills of the Diablo Range and follows the winding trickle of Wartham Creek westward. The Diablo Range, a series of low mountains seamed with abrupt rain-carved canyons, runs northwest above the San Joaquin Valley to 3,849-foot Mount Diablo just east of San Francisco Bay. The road twists and turns along the creek, passing ranch homes, grazing cattle and horses, and steep sand-colored hills. Stately cottonwood trees scatter along the creek bed, and junipers dot the hillsides. As the road gains elevation, oaks blanket the hills with blotches of dark green. Farther up the drive, the road and canyon straighten; spindly gray pines appear on the hills. "Digger" or gray pines, a common conifer on California's hot lowland slopes, have thin, 10-inch-long, gray needles that droop raggedly from the branches. The needles deflect much of the drying sunlight and offer small evaporative surfaces. The gray pine generally thrives in association with blue oak, another drought-tolerant tree. Oaks are typical California trees. Of the state's thirteen species, eleven oaks are endemic to the California Floristic Province.

PRIEST VALLEY TO RABBIT VALLEY

Twenty-one miles from Coalinga, the drive climbs away from Wartham Creek, crosses a divide, and drops into 2,300-foot-high Priest Valley. This picturesque valley, flanked by Twin Peaks and Round Mountain on the northeast and Mustang Ridge on the southwest, is as pretty a place as anywhere in California. Spreading oaks stud the grassy hillsides. Gray pines, cottonwoods, willows, and dense meadows line Lewis Creek as it winds across the valley. The valley was named in the early 1850s when William Galman and Captain Walker found a priest and one hundred Native Americans encamped here while capturing wild horses. The valley is also the site of the last stand of the infamous bandit Joaquin Murrieta in 1853. After being brutally wronged by American miners, Murrieta vowed revenge and systematically murdered all the offenders. He and his gang then took up banditry. The state put a $5,000 reward on his death or capture and the hunt was on. Captain Harry

Love and twenty rangers took the challenge and tracked Murrieta to an arroyo here in July of 1853. He was ambushed at night and killed. His head was cut off and taken to San Jose as proof of his demise. The head, preserved in alcohol, was later exhibited all over California.

After a few more miles, the highway climbs out of the valley floor up steep hillsides to the top of Mustang Ridge, a long ridge along the San Andreas Fault that separates Priest Valley and Lewis Creek from Peachtree Valley to the west. There are spectacular vistas up Lewis Creek. The road switchbacks steeply with 7 percent grades down the western slope of Mustang Ridge, reaching the broad floor of Peachtree Valley 4 miles from the ridge crest. The highway intersects CA 25 in the valley. Turn north on CA 25. CA 198 continues west to U.S. Highway 101 just south of King City.

CA 25 runs northwest up the Peachtree Valley along the seep of San Lorenzo Creek. Dry savanna country, green in spring and tan in summer, covers the valley floor and the mountainsides. Occasional oaks lurk among the grasslands. Fields of wheat, watered by sprinklers, grow alongside the drive. For 20 miles, the highway traverses Peachtree Valley, turns up Lewis Creek into Bitterwater Valley, and then up Rabbit Valley. The bucolic landscape here, with humpbacked ridges sweeping away from the sunny valley floor in great tawny grasslands and dense live oak thickets, belies the angry nature of the underlying earth.

SAN ANDREAS FAULT

The land at first seems to hold no great, mysterious secrets. But underground hides California's most famous and most studied earth feature—the San Andreas Fault. California is splintered with faults, most running southeast to northwest through long, linear valleys like Peachtree, Bitterwater, and Rabbit Valleys. The San Andreas Fault or Rift Zone is the dividing line between the North American crustal plate and the Pacific plate and runs more than 600 miles from the Sea of Cortez in northern Mexico to the Mendocino Coast north of San Francisco. The Pacific plate is slipping northwest on an average of 2 inches a year. Often the plates lock together until they spring apart, moving with a sharp jolting earthquake. An 1857 quake on the Carrizo Plain south of here recorded an amazing 33-foot slippage. Hollister, at the drive's terminus, rocks almost every day with small, sometimes imperceptible earthquakes. A 1985 quake in Cienaga Valley, just south of Hollister off CA 25, broke and spilled a 20,000-gallon wine keg in the Almaden winery. The winery's main building is built atop the fault itself, which is slowly wrenching the building apart.

Past Rabbit Valley, the drive climbs over a slight divide and runs up another high, narrow valley flanked by Buck Ridge on the east and the rugged Gabilan Range on the west. The road passes wheat fields and Dry Lake, a parched lake bed. Keep an eye out for pronghorn antelope grazing along the grassy roadside. The highway bends west past the San Benito turnoff, crosses a ridge, drops into Bear Valley, and reaches the intersection with CA 146. An excellent side trip turns west on CA 146 and travels 5 miles to the visitor center at Pinnacles National Monument.

Scattered oaks and tawny grasslands cover rough hills above the San Andreas Fault in Rabbit Valley on California Highway 25.

PINNACLES NATIONAL MONUMENT

Pinnacles National Monument is truly one of California's least known and least appreciated national parks. The 24,206-acre monument, administered by the National Park Service, preserves a ragged jumble of eroded spires, buttes, buttresses, ramparts, arêtes, and cathedrals in the otherwise pastoral Gabilan Range. Huge boulders and fallen debris form a roof over sharp, narrow canyons where streams carve underground caverns. The rock here is volcanic rhyolite and breccia deposited around a huge, 8,000-foot-high volcano some twenty-two million years ago and 195 miles to the south near Lancaster. The volcano, built atop the San Andreas Rift Zone, then began creeping northwest along the fault to its present position. The other portion of the volcano, called the Neenach Formation, still lies alongside the fault far to the south. Erosion did the rest of the work, sculpting, molding, and scouring the rock into its eerie, fractured shapes. The park remains a lesson in geology that tells tales of the uplifting and tearing down of great mountains, the long procession of life, and the earth's constant change.

Chaparral covers 82 percent of the monument and is the dominant ecosystem. It flourishes on steep slopes with coarse soil and scanty water. The common scrubby plants of chaparral include chamise, buckthorn, holly-leaved cherry, and manzanita. The riparian plant communities along meager streams are the park's most species-rich areas, with tall shade trees, including sycamores, cottonwoods, willows, and oaks, and a lush undergrowth of moss, ferns, and flowers. Lichens, the rock colonizers, inhabit the monument's rocks, spreading slowly across their surface, taking thirty years to cover a square inch and slowly breaking down the solid rock to soil. Most of Pinnacles is a wilderness area that harbors diverse wildlife. Birds include the ubiquitous turkey vulture and raven, screech owls, prairie falcons that nest in rocky aeries, scrub jays, nuthatches, quail, acorn woodpeckers, hawks, and owls. Mammal species are raccoon, blacktail deer, mountain lion, bobcat, skunk, gray fox, pocket mice, and deer mice. Hikers need to keep a wary eye out for rattlesnakes, a common resident of the hills and scree slopes.

Pinnacles offers visitors a range of outdoor opportunities. A private 125-site campground sits just east of the monument boundary on CA 146 with tables shaded by towering oaks. Twenty-six miles of maintained trails lace the monument. The **Bear Gulch Visitor Center** exhibits the monument's geology, including a seismograph recording daily action on the nearby San Andreas Fault, natural history, and history. A few good hikes leave from near the visitor center. The Moses Spring/ Bear Gulch Caves Trail climbs up to several of the park's caves. The excellent 5.3-mile High Peaks Trail ascends steeply to the High Peaks, the rocky heart of Pinnacles. The Chalone Peak Trail reaches the monument's high point—3,304-foot North Chaldone Peak. The monument also offers excellent rock climbing on steep, pocketed rock and up slender spires. Springtime is the prime time to visit Pinnacles, when a blaze of wildflowers spreads carpets of color across the ridges and meadows.

ALONG SAN BENITO RIVER

The drive runs north from the Pinnacles turnoff up Bear Valley. After 5 miles, the highway leaves the broad fault valley, rolls across a few shallow canyons, and drops alongside the meandering San Benito River as it flows toward Monterey Bay. The river valley broadens as the road runs north. The forested Gabilan Range, beloved by author John Steinbeck, looms to the west. The range's northernmost mountain is 3,169-foot Fremont Peak, part of Fremont Peak State Park. Here, in 1846, Capt. John C. Fremont raised the American flag on California soil in defiance of the Mexican government. The park has a campground and a trail to the mountain summit. Marvelous views unfold of Monterey Bay, Salinas Valley, and San Benito River Valley. Fields of grapes, part of the Almaden wine district, line the drive.

The road turns away from the river at Paicines, skirts the east side of Swanson Bluff, and follows Tres Pinos Creek. A few miles farther, it passes through Tres Pinos and low rolling hills covered with grass. The drive then drops into broad Hollister Valley. Three miles later it enters Hollister, the center of a rich agricultural region. A few miles west of Hollister on California Highway 156 sits **Mission San Juan Bautista,** a state historic park that preserves the fifteenth Spanish mission in California; it was established in 1797. The surrounding town is a popular visitor attraction and still retains the ambience and flavor of a nineteenth-century California town. A little farther west lie Monterey and Santa Cruz on the shores of Monterey Bay.

Klamath River Scenic Drive

I–5 TO WILLOW CREEK

GENERAL DESCRIPTION: This drive twists alongside the Klamath and Trinity Rivers for 147 miles through deep canyons and over densely wooded ridges in northern California.

SPECIAL ATTRACTIONS: Klamath River, Trinity River, Pacific Crest Trail, Klamath National Forest, Six Rivers National Forest.

LOCATION: Northwestern California just south of the Oregon border.

DRIVE ROUTE NUMBER: California Highway 96.

TRAVEL SEASON: The highway is open year-round. Watch for wet pavement, heavy rain, and occasional snow in winter.

CAMPING: Several national forest campgrounds and private RV parks sit alongside the drive. A few others are just off the drive.

SERVICES: All services in Yreka and Willow Creek; limited services along the drive.

NEARBY ATTRACTIONS: Marble Mountain Wilderness Area, Red Buttes Wilderness Area, Rogue River National Forest, Yreka, Mount Shasta, Salmon-Trinity Alps Wilderness Area, Russian Wilderness Area, Redwood National Park, Prairie Creek Redwoods State Park, Smith River Scenic Byway, Pacific coast beaches, Eureka.

THE DRIVE

CA 96 twists for 147 miles through the deep gorges of the Klamath and Trinity Rivers in the remote Klamath Ranges of northwestern California. The Klamath River, running from southern Oregon's Upper Klamath Lake through the Cascade and Klamath Mountains to the Pacific Ocean, marks the southern and eastern boundary of the rumpled Siskiyou Mountains. The Scott Bar, Marble, and Salmon Mountains stretch south of the river. In California, the 265-mile-long Klamath River is second only to the Sacramento River in the amount of water it empties into the Pacific. This is a rugged land seamed with precipitous canyons and lorded over by densely forested peaks. The drive offers travelers a chance to roam far from California's well-used highways into a sparsely populated region with less than five people per square mile. The area teems with wildlife such as the legendary and elusive man-ape Sasquatch. Numerous pullouts line the road for scenic views and river access. Allow at least six hours to drive the narrow winding route.

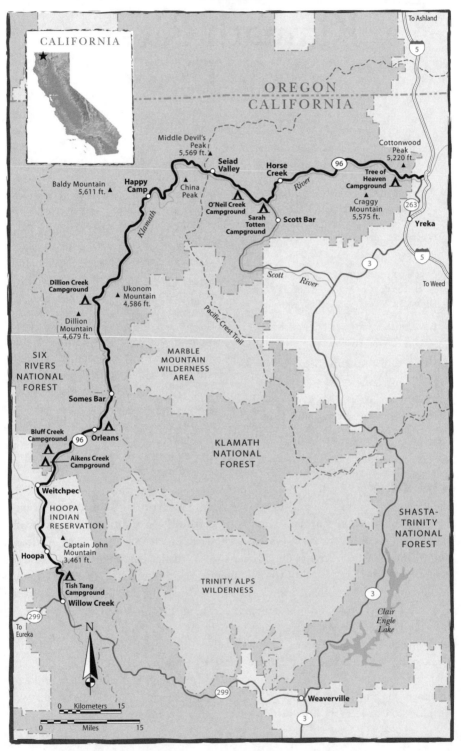

CALIFORNIA

To Ashland

5

OREGON
CALIFORNIA

Middle Devil's
Peak
5,569 ft.

Seiad
Valley

Horse
Creek

96

Cottonwood
Peak
5,220 ft.

Baldy Mountain
5,611 ft.

Happy
Camp

China
Peak

River

Tree of
Heaven
Campground

O'Neil Creek
Campground

Klamath

Sarah
Totten
Campground

Scott Bar

Craggy
Mountain
5,575 ft.

263

Yreka

5

Dillion Creek
Campground

Ukonom
Mountain
4,586 ft.

Scott

River

To Weed

Dillion
Mountain
4,679 ft.

3

Pacific Crest Trail

SIX
RIVERS
NATIONAL
FOREST

MARBLE
MOUNTAIN
WILDERNESS
AREA

Somes Bar

Bluff Creek
Campground

96

Orleans

KLAMATH
NATIONAL
FOREST

SHASTA-
TRINITY
NATIONAL
FOREST

Aikens Creek
Campground

Weitchpec

HOOPA
INDIAN
RESERVATION

Captain John
Mountain
3,461 ft.

Hoopa

Tish Tang
Campground

Willow Creek

TRINITY ALPS
WILDERNESS

3

Clair
Engle
Lake

299

To
Eureka

N

0   Kilometers   15

0   Miles   15

299

Weaverville

3

The climate along the Klamath River drive is generally moderate year-round. Summer temperatures vary from the upper nineties at the drive's desert origins on I–5 to seventies and eighties in the thick forests 100 miles downriver. Rain showers occasionally fall in summer at the lower elevations. The rainy season begins in October when the leaves change and continues through the winter. Expect cool, cloudy days with intermittent to heavy rainstorms. Snow sometimes falls along the highway but usually blankets the ridges and peaks above the river. The worst storm in recorded history occurred during the winter of 1964–65 when heavy rains and early snows saturated the Klamath Ranges. In mid-December 1964, moist tropical air that dashes against the coastal mountains further soaked the ground and melted the snowpack. The water, unable to soak into the sodden ground, ran into the already swollen Klamath and Eel Rivers. The rain continued unabated for days, and towns along the Klamath were evacuated as the river rose to record levels. Roadside signs today mark the river level, which reached a depth of 100 feet and washed out much of the highway.

YREKA TO HORSE CREEK

The drive begins 6 miles north of Yreka at the intersection of I-5 and CA 96. Turn west on CA 96. Yreka, the largest town in the area, nestles against rolling grassy hills along Yreka Creek. The town boasts a proud pioneer past that started, like many California settlements, with the discovery of gold. Miners en route to the Scott Bar gold fields from Oregon camped here in 1851. The next morning Abraham Thompson found flecks of gold clinging to the grass roots his pack mules were eating. The discovery brought more than 2,000 miners in just a few weeks and Thompson's Dry Diggins was born. The town underwent five name changes in the next year before settling on Yreka, a Shasta word meaning "north mountain." The town's numerous gold rush–era buildings, preserved on the National Register of Historic Places, can be toured with a free walking guide from the chamber of commerce. A display of gold nuggets at the Siskiyou County Courthouse and the Klamath National Forest Interpretative Museum are also worth seeing.

A roadside rest area is along the Klamath River immediately after you leave the interstate. The road swings down along the bottom of the river canyon, a position it will occupy for the next 128 miles to Weitchpec. Junipers and chaparral clot the dry grassy slopes above the highway, while oaks line the riverbank. At 2 miles, the Shasta River and California Highway 263 from Yreka join the drive. The highest elevation along the drive is here at 2,039 feet. The road wends westward, passing rocky crags and entering **Klamath National Forest.** The 1.7-million-acre forest offers five wilderness areas, four National Wild and Scenic Rivers, and lots of untrampled, remote space. Tree of Heaven Campground sits below the road on a bowknot river bend; it has twenty campsites. A mowed lawn, shaded by fruit and nut trees, spreads among the campsites.

The drive continues west past Cayuse and Gottville River access points, and at

18 miles goes through Klamath River, a small village on the river floodplain at 1,661 feet elevation; the town has limited services. A few miles beyond here, the canyon broadens and high forested ridges outline the Siskiyou Mountains to the north. This is California's northernmost mountain range, stretching across the Oregon border. The timbered slopes have been heavily logged. South of the road tower 4,173-foot Bearcat Mountain and 5,493-foot Bald Mountain. Oak Knoll Ranger Station and McKinney River Access lie along the 11-mile highway segment between Klamath River and Horse Creek. Just before Horse Creek, the road crosses the river on a girder bridge to the south bank. Tall pines mat the north-facing slopes while the warmer, grassy, south-facing slopes are sparsely sprinkled with oak and shrubs. As the road runs west, the canyon narrows and steep ridges rear up overhead.

HORSE CREEK TO SEIAD VALLEY

The 16 miles from Horse Creek to Seiad Valley are simply beautiful. The deep river swells through long placid pools before tumbling over water-worn boulders. Dense forest shades the banks and plentiful wildlife can be spotted from the road—including graceful, long-legged great blue herons and white egrets stalking the river shallows, beavers that attracted early trappers into these rugged canyons, and plentiful waterfowl such as pintail ducks, Canada geese, five species of grebes, and cormorants. Freshwater riparian habitats along rivers, streams, and lakes are California's most species-rich plant and animal communities. Riparian areas support 83 percent of the state's amphibian species, 40 percent of its reptiles, and 42 percent of its mammals. Common amphibians found here are the western toad, bullfrog, and Pacific giant salamander. Numerous reptiles also live in the forest, including sagebrush lizard, western skink, rubber boa, California mountain king snake, three types of garter snakes, and the western rattlesnake, commonly found in brushy, rocky areas along streams and rivers.

Five miles southwest of Horse Creek the Klamath River intersects the Scott River. This small river runs south from the Scott Bar Mountains and the Trinity Alps. Scott Bar, 3 miles south of the drive on County Road 7F01, is a dilapidated townsite where miners, including John Scott, panned for gold along the river's gravel bars in 1850. The Klamath River itself has also yielded gold from its river gravel. A prospecting party followed the river's length, panning gold from every promising bar along the way. Even now, weekend prospectors search for the elusive metal on placer claims along both rivers. A couple of good campgrounds sit along the Scott River farther south from Scott Bar.

SEIAD VALLEY TO HAPPY CAMP

Saran Totten Campground, with eight sites, is a mile down from the Scott River by the small town of Hamburg. Huge piles of tailings left by placer miners lie along the Klamath here. O'Neill Creek Campground lies another 5 miles downriver and

5 miles beyond is Seiad Valley, a small village on the river's north bank. A New York farmer settled in this wide valley in 1854 and made a small fortune by growing potatoes and selling them to prospectors for fifteen cents a pound. The Pacific Crest Trail drops north down Girder Creek and crosses the river just west of here; it then climbs steeply north over 6,011-foot Upper Devil's Peak before twisting along the Siskiyou crest into Oregon. Small Fort Goff Campground, with five sites, sits alongside the drive 4 miles west of Seiad Valley.

The drive and river begin a southward march just past Fort Goff. The forest thickens along the river, with towering Douglas fir and pines blanketing the surrounding mountain peaks. The river begins alternately cutting down into abrupt bedrock gorges and meandering across wide, grassy meadows lined with willows. The Klamath Ranges, composed primarily of ancient seafloor sediments like mudstone and sandstone that were recrystallized by heat and pressure into metamorphic rocks, are an extension of the Sierra Nevada. The two ranges separated some 140 million years ago. The best place to see the Klamath Ranges' old seafloor rocks is in the shallow gorges exposed by the Klamath River. Ten miles south of Fort Goff, the highway climbs away from the river, which winds below in entrenched meanders past Williams and Morgan points. After a couple of miles, the road drops down a steep, forest-lined corridor to a broad valley and Happy Camp.

Happy Camp, at 1,085 feet, calls itself the "Steelhead Capital of the World" for its excellent fishing opportunities. The town was once an isolated mining area. Now it is a base for many outfitters for fishing and rafting expeditions. Gold and jade are still mined here, and it also is a popular jumping-off spot for backcountry visitors to the Siskiyou and Marble Mountain wilderness areas. Fishermen flock to the Klamath River every fall for the steelhead and salmon run. More are caught in the Klamath River than in any other California stream. A joint project between the native Karuks and the California Department of Fish and Game is returning the Chinook salmon to the Klamath and its tributaries. The fish are reared in ponds, imprinted with water from various tributaries, and then released in the hope that they will return to spawn in their imprinted waters. Pristine lakes in the surrounding mountains yield great rainbow, brown, and brook trout fishing.

The Klamath River also is known as one of California's best rafting rivers. The river's relatively slow flow, lack of huge rapids, and warm water attracts flotillas of rafts, kayaks, and canoes. The easy access afforded by CA 96 allows numerous one- or two-day float trips of different lengths and difficulties. Happy Camp is a popular put-in for Class III runs that typically take three days. The river section from I–5 to Happy Camp is mostly flat water with occasional Class II riffles. River guides and rental boats are available in Happy Camp.

HAPPY CAMP TO WEITCHPEC

From Happy Camp to Weitchpec, a distance of 66 miles, the river plunges south through a deep gorge lined with steep, forested ridges that climb to lofty 4,000-

Morning sunlight glints off the Klamath River along California Highway 96.

foot peaks. The canyon is mostly a narrow V-shaped chasm that occasionally opens into a wide valley. The drive follows the river, sometime clinging shelflike to the steep slopes above. Numerous pullouts line the road, allowing easy access to the river below. Some good campgrounds lie along the road—Dillion Creek in Klamath National Forest, and Pearch Creek, Aikens Creek, and Bluff Creek Campgrounds in Six Rivers National Forest. Dillion Creek has twenty-one sites scattered along a forested bench above Dillion Creek and is an excellent stopover. A trail drops down from the campground to Dillion Creek and its fabulous, cliff-lined swimming holes, with deep, clear water.

Other points of interest along the drive include Somes Bar and the trailhead for the nearby 213,743-acre Marble Mountain Wilderness Area. Somes Bar is a small town located on the confluence of the Klamath and Salmon Rivers. The nearby Marble Mountain Wilderness Area has seventy-nine mountain lakes, several long limestone caves, verdant meadows, and glacier-polished peaks that climb to elevations of 7,000 feet. The town of Orleans lies another 11 miles downstream at an elevation of 400 feet. It offers all visitor services, including gas, food, lodging, and RV parks.

The rugged mountain country from Seiad Valley to Orleans is the ancestral homeland of the Karuks. The tribe, only recently recognized by the federal government as a distinct cultural group, still occupies the area and uses their sacred ceremonial grounds at "Kota-mein" near Somes Bar and "Inam" at Clear Creek. The Karuks traditionally lived in villages and harvested the land's rich game and plants.

Acorns, salmon, eels, deer, and ducks provided much of their diet. The Karuks are renowned for their exquisite basketry woven for food gathering and storage, carrying infants, and finely woven caps for ceremonies.

BIGFOOT COUNTRY

This remote land is also the home of Sasquatch or Bigfoot, the legendary man-ape who roams northern California. Numerous sightings here describe a creature 7 to 10 feet tall, weighing as much as 500 pounds, with thick fur, long arms, an erect posture, and huge footprints. A 1967 home movie captured the elusive animal on film, although biologists still argue about the film's veracity. Two young women from Happy Camp reportedly found a dead Sasquatch on a forest road in 1967, but they didn't report their grisly discovery until 1971 and were unable to relocate the exact site and remains that would have proven whether Bigfoot really exists.

Weitchpec sits on a bluff above the rocky confluence of the Klamath and Trinity Rivers. Here the drive leaves the Klamath River, which bends sharply northwest and flows to the Pacific. The road crosses the river on high bridge, passes through the small hamlet of Weitchpec, and begins a tortuous run southward above the precipitous gorge of the Trinity River. The road, carved into rock, hugs the steep mountainside for almost 4 miles before descending into the broad Hoopa and the Hoopa Indian Reservation. The 100-square-mile reservation was established in 1865 after twelve bloody years of war between the Hoopas and encroaching white settlers. The drive runs across broad meadows on the Trinity's floodplain and then past houses and businesses in the town of Hoopa, the reservation's administrative center.

The highway climbs over densely forested ridges out of the Hoopa Valley at its south end. **Ancient Indian Village Vista Point** is a good viewpoint that overlooks the valley to the north and the deep canyon of the Trinity River to the east. Tish Tang Campground, with forty sites, nestles in the forest here. The road drops back down along the river's gravel banks, swings through pastures studded with grazing cattle and horses, crosses Willow Creek, and climbs up to the town of Willow Creek and the drive's end at its intersection with CA 299. A turn west leads across the Coastal Range to Arcata and the scenic Redwood Coast. A turn east heads up the winding Trinity River to historic Weaverville and on to Redding at the north end of the Central Valley.

To Klamath Falls

OREGON
CALIFORNIA

CALIFORNIA

139

Tulelake

Tule
Lake

TULE LAKE
NATIONAL
WILDLIFE
REFUGE

10

Tule Lake

Petroglyph
Section

Gillem's
Camp

MODOC
NATIONAL
FOREST

Hospital
Rock

Captain Jack's
Stronghold

Devil's Homestead
Lava Flow

LAVA BEDS
WILDERNESS

Thomas-Wright
Battlefield

MODOC
NATIONAL
FOREST

Fleener
Chimneys

LAVA BEDS
NATIONAL
MONUMENT

Whitney
Butte
5,004 ft.

Schonchin Butte
5,253 ft.

Skull Cave

Indian Well
Campground

LAVA BEDS
WILDERNESS

Visitor
Center

Valentine Cave

To
US 97

Caldwell Butte
5,189 ft.

Cave
Loop
Road

Big Sand
Butte
4,661 ft.

139

(closed in winter)

Little Sand Butte

10

97

To
Canby

N

MODOC
NATIONAL
FOREST

Medicine
Lake

0   Kilometers   5

0   Miles   5

8

Lava Beds National Monument Scenic Drive

GENERAL DESCRIPTION: A 40-mile-long drive that makes an open loop through Lava Beds National Monument, passing cinder cones, vast lava flows, lava tube caves, the site of the Modoc Indian War, and the wetlands of Tule Lake National Wildlife Refuge.

SPECIAL ATTRACTIONS: Lava Beds National Monument, Lava Beds Wilderness Area, Cave Loop Road, lava tube caves, Devil's Homestead Lava Flow, Modoc War historic sites, Tule Lake National Wildlife Refuge, Modoc National Forest, wildlife, waterfowl, hiking, caving.

LOCATION: Far northeastern California, just south of the Oregon border.

DRIVE ROUTE NUMBERS AND NAMES: Modoc Forest Road 97 (Tionesta Road), Modoc For-est Road 10 (Lava Beds National Monument Road), Modoc County Road 111.

TRAVEL SEASON: Year-round. The drive is sometimes icy or snowy in winter.

CAMPING: Indian Well Campground, at the national monument, open year-round. Several campgrounds in adjoining Modoc National Forest.

SERVICES: All services available in Tulelake and Canby, California, and Merrill, Oregon.

NEARBY ATTRACTIONS: Clear Lake National Wildlife Refuge, Lower Klamath National Wildlife Refuge, Mount Shasta, Klamath National Forest, South Warner Wilderness Area, Cedar Pass–Fandango Pass scenic drive, Buckhorn Back Country Byway, Goose Lake, Glass Mountain Geologic Area.

THE DRIVE

The Lava Beds National Monument scenic drive traverses 40 miles of wild coun-try on the edge of the Modoc Plateau. It's a rare landscape of spreading lava flows studded with black cinder cones, a once-violent land filled with the silent fury of recent volcanism. The Modoc Plateau, covering all of northeastern California, is the southern part of the greater Columbia Plateau. This immense 200,000-square-mile area encompasses eastern Oregon and parts of Washington, Nevada, Utah, Idaho, Wyoming, as well as California. The Columbia Plateau built up over the last thirty million years as a long succession of lava flows, pouring out of surface vents and fis-sures. It flooded the land with thousands of feet of basalt and rhyolite and left only high peaks and volcanoes poking islandlike above the sea of lava. The flows varied from 10 to 200 feet in thickness. Geologists estimate that more than 100,000 cubic miles of lava formed the plateau. Although ancient stair-stepped lava plateaus sur-round Lava Beds National Monument, the flows and cones seen here are much more recent. The Callahan lava flow in the monument's southwestern corner is only 1,100 years old, while others formed in the last 100,000 years.

The climate at Lava Beds is generally dry, with temperatures ranging from a record low of minus 18 degrees to a high of 102 degrees. The monument receives just over 15 inches of precipitation annually and more than 41 inches of snow each winter. Elevations up to 5,600 feet ensure chilly weather any time of the year, and snow has been reported in every month except August. May through October is the best time to visit. Spring highs are in the fifties and sixties with cool nights and occasional showers. Summer can be hot, with temperatures approaching one hundred degrees. July, the warmest month, averages a high of eighty-two degrees daily, but be prepared for chilly nights. Heavy thunderstorms can douse the monument, even though it is usually dry. Winter highs hover around forty degrees, with nights in the low twenties. Tule fog often envelops the monument, riming junipers and sagebrush with a crystal coat of ice.

SAND BUTTES AND MEDICINE LAKE

The scenic drive begins 27 miles north of Canby on CA 139. Turn west from the highway onto FR 97. The turn is marked Lava Beds National Monument. The drive follows FR 97 for 2.5 miles before turning onto FR 10. The entire drive is a paved, two-lane roadway with numerous scenic and interpretive pullouts. For the next few miles, the road crosses a gently undulating landscape blanketed with sagebrush, grasses, junipers, and scattered ponderosa pines. After a few more miles, the road skirts the southern edge of a huge lava flow punctuated with rounded cinder cones. Watch for marked side roads that run north to East Sand Butte and 4,661-foot Big Sand Butte.

Southwest of the drive looms the Medicine Lake volcano, a huge blisterlike volcano spotted with numerous recent cinder cones. Recurrent eruptions over many millennia erected a rounded shield volcano here with gently sloping sides. The magma chamber under the summit later emptied through side vents, causing the peak to collapse inward and form a 6-mile-long, 500-foot-deep caldera. Medicine Lake, a popular fishing and boating lake, nestles its sparkling blue waters in the caldera's depths. Earthquakes under the mountain indicate to geologists that the volcano is not dead yet. Glass Mountain Geologic Area is another interesting point on the mountain. Sharp, glassy obsidian found here forms a 950-year-old lava flow on the volcano's east flank. The highlands are reached by Forest Road 49 along the drive. Three campgrounds surround Medicine Lake.

LAVA BEDS NATIONAL MONUMENT

At 9 miles from the beginning, the drive swings around Little Sand Butte and 3 miles later enters Lava Beds National Monument. The 46,559-acre monument, with more than 28,460 acres of established wilderness, preserves some of America's best volcanic features such as lava flows, lava tube caves, and cinder cones, as well as

The Lava Beds scenic drive crosses the recent Devil's Homestead Lava Flow in Lava Beds National Monument.

historic and archeological sites from the Modocs and plant and animal communities similar to those in the nearby Great Basin Desert. The national monument was established by presidential proclamation in 1933 and is literally blanketed by volcanic rock. The monument boasts the greatest concentration of lava tube caves in the United States, with more than 200 located so far. The longest, Catacombs Cave, stretches 6,900 feet underground. Other caves reach depths of 150 feet with several surveyed levels. Besides its geologic attractions, the monument offers a wealth of wildlife—including migrating birds on the Pacific Flyway that shelter over at nearby Tule Lake National Wildlife Refuge.

After entering the national monument, the drive runs northwest past 5,189-foot Caldwell Butte, Valentine Cave, and over an old lava flow sprinkled with western juniper and sagebrush on the way to the monument's visitor center. The center offers free information about the monument, as well as displays of natural history, geology, and history. Indian Well Campground, with forty sites, lies a half mile east of the visitor center. The sites, spread among junipers and cinders, have tables and grills. Water and flush toilets are available from May through September. In winter, all water is turned off, but camping is free. Nightly campfire programs occur in summer.

Mushpot Cave near the visitor center is a good introduction to the monument's caves. The cave is the only lighted one at Lava Beds and offers interpretive displays on the formation of lava tubes. Two basic cave types are found in the United States—limestone solution caves and lava tube caves. Lava tubes are caves that were once filled with flowing, molten lava. As lava advances downhill, the surface quickly cools and hardens into a thick crust. The rigid basalt surface acts as a good insulator, keeping underground lava fluid. The lava drains like a river down a tube or cavity toward the front edge of the flow. After the main volcanic vents stop spewing magma from the earth's mantle, the tube empties and leaves an open cavity beneath the surface. Some master tubes can run for miles, often branching to form distributary tubes.

The 2-mile-long **Cave Loop Road** west of the visitor center is an excellent place to discover the variety and beauty of the Lava Beds' caves. This area has the monument's largest concentration of caves, and many are easily accessible from numerous parking areas. Some caves have ladders or stairways that drop from the surface to the cave floor. Maps for many of the caves are available at the visitor center. Be sure to carry at least three sources of battery-powered light, as well as extra batteries. Carry a light for each explorer and never go alone. It's wise to wear a hardhat. There are many sharp and jagged lava chunks in the cave ceilings. The center also lends flashlights and bump hats to spelunkers. Dress warmly; the caves are cool and moist, even in summer. If you plan to go to undeveloped caves in the more remote parts of the monument, be sure to check in at the visitor center. It is unlawful to eat, smoke, or carry glass containers in the caves. The caves on the loop road include Catacombs Cave, the connected Hercules Leg and Juniper Caves, Golden Dome Cave, and Hopkins Chocolate Cave.

LAVA BEDS ECOLOGY

Past the visitor center, the drive swings around another cinder cone called Crescent Butte and then runs northwest through a sparse woodland of western juniper and mountain mahogany. Lava Beds sits on the boundary between two great ecosystems—the Great Basin Desert to the east and the Cascade Mountains to the west—and encompasses plants and animals characteristic of both. The monument at first glance appears somewhat barren. Life, however, has secured a firm foothold on the seemingly inhospitable lava beds. Lichen, the rock colonizer, covers the lava surface and slowly breaks the basalt down to soil. Sagebrush and grasses coat much of the monument's lower elevations, while woodlands of jumper and pine blanket the higher southern reaches. Six pine species, including ponderosa, knob cone, Jeffrey, and sugar, are found here as well as white fir and incense cedar. Spring and early summer bring a colorful display of wildflowers.

The monument's three main ecosystems—pine forests, sagebrush grasslands, and brushlands harbor an astonishing variety of life with more than 283 wildlife species. Mammal species total forty-eight. Mule deer are the most common large mammal, with hundreds migrating onto the monument during winter from the snowy Medicine Lake highlands. Other mammals at the monument include pronghorn, bobcat, porcupine, striped skunk, kangaroo rat, yellow-bellied marmot, pika, and twelve bat species.

Lava Beds National Monument and the surrounding Klamath Basin are renowned for large numbers of raptors, with twenty-five species recorded here. The area's plateaus and ridges, rimmed with basalt cliffs, make perfect aeries for hawks, owls, and eagles. More bald eagles winter along Tule Lake than anywhere else south of Alaska. Common raptors seen include turkey vultures, sharp-shinned hawks, red-tailed hawks, prairie falcons, barn owls, and great horned owls. The birds are often seen wheeling over the lava beds, looking for mice, rats, squirrels, and snakes. Eight different snake species live at Lava Beds. Some interesting snakes are the Rocky Mountain rubber boa, a type of boa constrictor; the rare ringneck snake; the semi-poisonous desert night snake; and the western rattlesnake. Rattlesnakes, while common here, are rarely seen. But visitors should use caution when hiking and when crawling into caves. Rattlesnakes are sometimes found on ledges near cave entrances.

SKULL CAVE TO DEVIL'S HOMESTEAD

The drive rolls northwest past cinder cones and old lava flows. Spectacular views unfold of high plateaus and the Warner Mountains to the east and Tule Lake to the north. A side road drops east to Skull Cave. This large cave, named for bighorn sheep skulls found inside, has a 75-foot-high chamber and a floor covered with ice year-round. Nearby is a 0.8-mile trail that leads to Big Painted Cave and Symbol Bridge. Outstanding pictographs painted by Native Americans, including the Modoc culture, adorn both sites. Unfortunately, vandalism has defaced many of them. Remember, look but don't touch. Finger oils transmitted to the delicate paintings hasten their ruin.

A mile and a half up the drive another road heads west to **Merrill Cave,** an excellent cave with perennial ice in its lower level. During winter beautiful icicles and ice crystals form on the cave walls and ceiling. The 3.4-mile Whitney Butte Trail begins at the cave parking area and travels west around 5,004-foot Whitney Butte. Schonchin Butte, a 5,253-foot cinder cone, looms north of the drive past the Merrill Cave turnoff. Another side road turns off the drive and leads to a hiking trail that climbs steeply to a fire lookout atop the peak. It offers marvelous 360-degree views of the surrounding lava fields and Tule Lake Basin. The side road is unsuitable for trailers.

Past the butte the drive runs onto a rolling sea of black lava, the crests frozen and twisted against the sky. A pull-off leads to the short trail to Balcony and Boulevard Caves. Another side road runs west to Fleener Chimneys. The chimneys are splatter cones that formed when lava spattered around a vent along a fissure. Magma, forced up through the vent, bubbled explosively and tossed molten rock onto the cone's steep sides. Rivers of lava also flowed out of vents here and meandered north for 3.5 miles, forming the Devil's Homestead Lava Flow. The **Fleener Chimneys,** one of the Lava Beds' first attractions, were more than 100 feet deep. Visitors, however, dropped rocks into the deepest hole and eventually filled it. The chimneys are slowly being restored to their former depth.

The drive drops northward, passes Black Crater and the trail to Thomas-Wright Battlefield, and dips down onto the **Devil's Homestead Lava Flow.** This flow looks almost new with only lichen and a scattering of juniper and rabbitbrush on the black lava. A pullout in the middle of the flow makes a good stop to look at a fairly recent flow. Both types of hardened lava—"aa" and "pahoehoe"—are seen here. Both words are Hawaiian. When the lava left the vents at Fleener Chimneys, the fluid pahoehoe lava ran north in the wide valley. By the time the lava reached today's drive, it had cooled, lost dissolved gases, and turned into viscous aa lava. Pahoehoe forms a ropy-textured surface when it cools, whereas aa is chunky, jagged, and heaped into loose ridges.

After crossing the half-mile-wide lava flow, the drive edges onto the east bank of Gillem Bluff, a long ridge striped with bands of basalt that stair-step upward. The road runs along a grassy bench above Devil's Homestead Lava Flow. A viewpoint on a cliff edge gives a great view of the tortuous lava landscape to the east. Three miles from the lava flow, the road bends east along the wildlife refuge border and follows old lava flows above Tule Lake. Several stops along here explain key historic sites of the Modoc Indian War.

THE MODOCS

The Modocs lived in the Klamath and Tule Lake Basins along the California-Oregon border for hundreds if not thousands of years. Archeological evidence suggests the area was inhabited as long ago as 11,500 years. The Modocs had a hunting and gathering society, following the deer and other game into the neighboring mountains in summer and coming back to more permanent camps around Tule, Lower Klamath, and Clear Lakes. Here were plentiful waterfowl, fish, roots, seeds, and tule reeds. But by the 1860s, American settlers came to the valley and asked the U.S. government to move the Modocs to a reservation. They were placed on the Klamath Reservation with the Klamaths and Snakes, their ancestral enemies. The arrangement was unsatisfactory and some of the Modocs, led by their young leader Kientpoos, nicknamed Captain Jack, left the reservation and went back to their homeland. On November 28, 1872, army troops were sent out to bring the Modocs, "by force if necessary," back to the reservation. Hostilities broke out and the war began.

The Modocs, after murdering some valley settlers in retribution, retreated into the lava beds and made their stand in a rugged area of lava trenches, shallow caves, and rough terrain now called Captain Jack's Stronghold. More than 300 troops made their way through thick fog on January 16, 1873, to capture the fifty Modoc men, women, and children. But the Modocs, using the natural fort to their advantage, routed the troops in the fog, killing nine, wounding twenty-eight, and capturing plenty of guns and ammunition. The government then decided to try to resolve the issue peacefully, and a peace commission was organized by Pres. Ulysses

Grant. Despite several meetings, the issue was unresolved. The Modocs wanted to live on their homeland and the U.S. government wanted them moved to the reservation. A militant Modoc faction, convinced that the army would leave if their leaders were killed, prodded Captain Jack into agreeing to help murder the commission. At an April meeting several Modocs opened fire on the four unarmed commissioners, killing Gen. Thomas Canby and Reverend Thomas. The army then began a siege of the stronghold, but upon capturing it a few days later on April 17, they found it deserted. The Modocs, under cover of night, had retreated across an unguarded lava plateau. On May 10 the Modocs attacked an army camp at Dry Lake, but were soundly defeated. The Modocs quarreled, split into several splinter groups, and headed out of the area. A group led by Hooker Jim was captured, and Hooker Jim agreed to track down Captain Jack. Captain Jack surrendered on June 1, and California's only major Indian war was over. Captain Jack and three other Modoc leaders were hanged in October 1873, and the surviving tribespeople were shipped to a reservation in Oklahoma. The Modoc tribe and culture virtually disappeared as many of them died of disease. About 200 Modocs live in Oklahoma today as descendants of the original 155 captured Indians. Some 300 people of Modoc ancestry also live in southern Oregon and northern California, descendants of those Modocs who never left the reservation during the war.

GILLEM'S CAMP TO TULE LAKE

The first of the drive's historic sites is located where the road bends east. This is Gillem's Camp, the 1873 site of army headquarters during the six-month Modoc War. A few small ruins with interpretive signs is all that remains. A mile farther lies Canby Cross, where General Canby was assassinated by Captain Jack. The drive runs across grass-covered lava flows to **Captain Jack's Stronghold.** Here, an interesting loop walk explores the natural lava battlements, stopping at various points of interest including shelter caves and firing positions. A small picnic area sheltered by junipers is located at the parking area. Two miles east lies Hospital Rock, site of a small army encampment during the Modoc War.

Two roadside wildlife turnouts overlook Tule Lake along the monument's northern border, offering views of ducks and geese bobbing on the lake surface. Tule Lake is known for its spectacular displays of birds, particularly waterfowl. The semiannual migrations of birds along the Pacific Flyway include lengthy stops at the Tule Lake National Wildlife Refuge, just north of the monument. The wetlands here support literally millions of birds. In autumn more than a million ducks and a half-million geese rest on their long journeys from the Arctic to winter's warmer climes. Springtime brings nesting waterfowl that dot the lake's placid water. The drive section along the Lava Beds' northern boundary skirts the edge of Tule Lake. The Tule Lake Refuge Tour Route is a dirt road that parallels the drive and gives great views of twenty duck species along with geese, pelicans, herons, cormorants, and others. A pair of binoculars is handy to help with species identifications. Good views of snowcapped Mount Shasta, a huge stratovolcano that looms in the west, are found along the drive here.

The drive dips down, leaves the Lava Beds, and runs across a dike next to Tule Lake. The lake, occasionally thick with waterfowl, is fringed by reeds and marsh, while irrigated fields spread to the south. Almost 2 miles later, the drive intersects 111. Turn north or left here. A short distance along the road, a turn leads to the **Petroglyph Section** of Lava Beds National Monument. A sand-colored volcanic cliff face here is etched with Native American petroglyphs or rock art. The drive continues north, skirting the east edge of the lake and passing wheat fields, grain elevators, egrets wading in a roadside canal, and red-winged blackbirds perched atop wavering tule reeds. The road ends on CA 139, 4 miles south of the town of Tulelake. A left turn heads to Tulelake and Oregon, and a right goes south on CA 139 to Canby.

Cedar Pass–Fandango Pass Scenic Drive

GENERAL DESCRIPTION: This 81-mile drive loops over the Warner Mountains via Cedar and Fandango Passes in northeastern California, passing ranch lands, rugged mountain scenery, a dried alkali lake bed, and Goose Lake.

SPECIAL ATTRACTIONS: Warner Mountains, Goose Lake, Cedar Pass, Fandango Pass, Cedarville, Modoc National Forest, hiking, camping.

LOCATION: Far northeastern California.

DRIVE ROUTE NUMBERS AND NAMES: California Highway 299, Surprise Valley Road, Modoc County Road 1, Fandango Pass Road, Forest Road 9, U.S Highway 395.

TRAVEL SEASON: Year-round. The paved highway sections on US 395 and CA 299 are open year-round. Watch for heavy snow and icy roads. The Fandango Pass Road closes in early winter and reopens in late spring.

CAMPING: Two national forest campgrounds near the Cedar Pass summit; low-impact, primitive camping in Modoc National Forest and BLM lands. Goose Lake State Park is just across the Oregon border.

SERVICES: All services in Alturas, California, and Lakeview, Oregon. Limited services in Cedarville and Fort Bidwell.

NEARBY ATTRACTIONS: Modoc National Forest, Barrel Springs Back Country Byway, Lava Beds National Monument, Klamath Basin National Wildlife Refuges, South Warner Wilderness Area, Buckhorn Back Country Byway, Goose Lake State Park (Oregon).

THE DRIVE

Northeastern California is a remote, hidden land, a place of broad volcanic plateaus, barren lava, cinder hills, fault-block mountains, wide valleys, and trickling creeks. The unpopulated region of California's outback forms a boundary between the state's fertile interior valleys and lush coastal ranges and the arid Great Basin Desert in Nevada. The area encompasses two of the state's geomorphic provinces—the Modoc Plateau, part of the greater Columbia Plateau, and the Basin and Range province. This 81-mile scenic drive explores the austere region's diversity, climbing over two passes in the Warner Mountains, traversing Surprise Valley, and passing Goose Lake. The drive offers stunning views—lofty mountains fringed with snow cornices, watery mirages that dance over desiccated lake beds, the dull-gray sheen of sagebrush blanketing rounded ridges and hillocks, and distant peaks that gleam with snow like alabaster towers. The US 395 and CA 299 road sections are part of

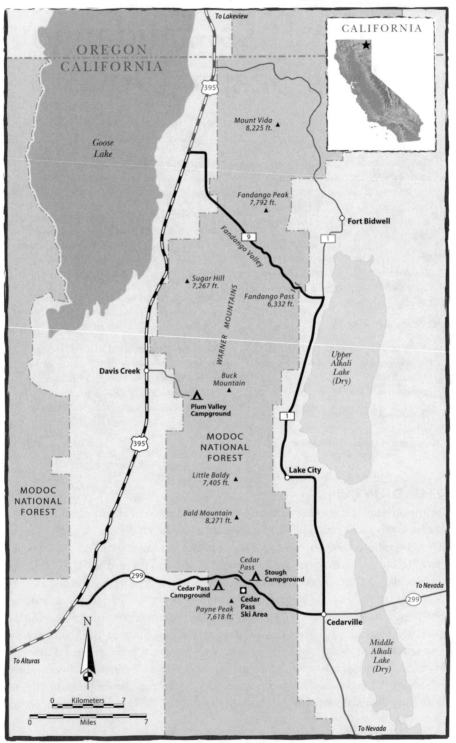

To Lakeview

CALIFORNIA

OREGON
CALIFORNIA

395

Mount Vida
8,225 ft.

Goose
Lake

Fandango Peak
7,792 ft.

Fort Bidwell

9

1

Fandango Valley

Sugar Hill
7,267 ft.

Fandango Pass
6,332 ft.

WARNER MOUNTAINS

Davis Creek

Buck
Mountain

Upper
Alkali
Lake
(Dry)

Plum Valley
Campground

1

MODOC
NATIONAL
FOREST

Little Baldy
7,405 ft.

Lake City

MODOC
NATIONAL
FOREST

Bald Mountain
8,271 ft.

395

Cedar
Pass

Stough
Campground

299

Cedar Pass
Campground

To Nevada

Cedar
Pass
Ski Area

Payne Peak
7,618 ft.

299

Cedarville

N

To Alturas

Middle
Alkali
Lake
(Dry)

0   Kilometers   7

0   Miles   7

To Nevada

the U.S. Forest Service's Emigrant Trails Scenic Byway, while Modoc County Road 1 is on the BLM's Surprise Valley-Barrel Springs Back County Byway.

Traffic along the drive's 71 paved miles and 10 gravel miles is light and mostly local. The 10-mile section over Fandango Pass is graded gravel and generally one-and-a-half lanes wide. This section is easily driven in a passenger car except after heavy rain when parts might be muddy and slick. Winter snow closes Fandango Pass, but the rest of the drive remains open.

Summer and autumn are the best times to drive the roads, with daily highs falling between seventy and one hundred degrees. The record high for the area is a sweltering 112 degrees. It is cooler in the Warner Mountains than the surrounding valleys. Rainfall is sporadic, with occasional thunderstorms crackling over the mountain crest. The area has severe winter weather with freezing temperatures and heavy snow atop the peaks. Temperatures can fall as low as minus thirty-five degrees, but daytime highs are usually in the thirties. Up to 8 inches of snow may fall on the valley floors, while up to 8 feet may blanket the higher elevations. Cold weather begins in November and often lasts until May. Spring tends to be short, with warm, breezy days.

ALTURAS

The scenic drive begins 6 miles north of Alturas where US 395 intersects CA 299. Turn east on CA 299. Alturas, the county seat of immense Modoc County, nestles among rolling hills along the Pit River on the gentle western flank of the Warner Mountains. Alturas means "valley on the mountaintop" in Spanish. It was settled in the early 1870s as ranchers and homesteaders took up residence in the grassy valley. The town, far from California's population centers, boasts an Old West ambience; it is surrounded by sheep and cattle ranches; its side streets are quiet and tree-lined; and it claims Modoc County's only two traffic lights.

OVER CEDAR PASS TO CEDARVILLE

The drive steadily climbs east from the North Fork of the Pit River over undulating basalt ridges. A forest of western juniper coats the rolling hillocks. After a couple of miles, the highway emerges onto a sagebrush-covered bench and reaches an elevation of 5,000 feet. The road drops into a shallow valley and follows Thomas Creek eastward. The trickling creek, densely lined with towering cottonwoods and willow thickets, is broken by wide grassy meadows and scattered ranches. Ponderosa pines crowd the hillsides south of the creek.

To the south and east looms the Warner Range, an impressive 80-mile-long sierra studded with rounded peaks seamed with deep canyons. These isolated mountains are a raised fault-block range of old volcanic rock. The Surprise Valley fault scarp forms a steep, precipitous face on the range's east side, while the western slope gently tilts upward to the range crest. Several Warner summits top 9,000 feet; Eagle Peak is the 9,892-foot high point. Much of the range's rugged character is protected in the 69,000-acre South Warner Wilderness Area with its wind-ruffled lakes, wildflower-strewn meadows, and abundant recreational opportunities. One of the best walks is the 26-mile Summit Trail along the range crest south of the scenic drive. Inquire at the Modoc National Forest office in Alturas for wilderness permits and hiking information.

The scenic drive follows the only highway over the Warner Range as it climbs alongside Thomas Creek. As it ascends, the climate cools. Pines and firs mat the moist north-facing slopes, while sagebrush and juniper are scattered across the slopes north of the asphalt. Cedar Pass Campground, its seventeen campsites shaded by tall conifers, sits just below the pass summit at 5,900 feet. Past the campground the canyon narrows. It is hemmed in by steep scree slopes and bold cliffs. Outcrops of breccia, a volcanic rock of ash and cinders, protrude out of the mountainside north of the highway. Almost 3 miles from the campground, the drive crests the top of 6,305-foot **Cedar Pass.** Bald and Cedar Mountains lift their rocky bulks to the north above Summit Canyon. The first road over the pass was built by pioneer John Bonner in 1869, and the modern road generally follows the same route.

The road drops steeply down Cedar Creek Canyon on the east side of the pass. Just below the summit, a short side road climbs to Stough/Stowe Reservoir and a fourteen-site national forest campground. Another turn leads south to Cedar Pass Ski Area, a small ski slope with a beginner hill, T-bar lift to advanced runs, and groomed cross-country trails. The highway twists down the canyon and empties onto the western side of the broad Surprise Valley and Cedarville, at 4,630 feet high.

Visiting **Cedarville** is like taking a big step back in time. It's a rural, friendly town that, except for a few modern amenities, looks like it just woke up to the twenty-first century. The town is the oldest in these parts; it got its start in 1865 when a Mr. Townsend built a cabin here. Indians killed him that same year, and his widow sold the place to John Bonner and William Cressler. They used it as a trading post and store, supplying passing emigrants on the Applegate-Lassen Trail and settlers in Surprise Valley. The old Cressler-Bonner Trading Post, a weatherworn log cabin with a shake roof, stands in a town park. Cedarville still serves as a supply center for neighboring ranches in the Surprise Valley and across the border in Nevada.

UP THE SURPRISE VALLEY

The drive turns in Cedarville on CR 1 (Surprise Valley Road). It then runs north along the sloping western edge of the huge valley. The Surprise Valley, so named because of the surprise registered by a party of 1861 emigrants on seeing the fertile, green valley floor after crossing the torturous Nevada desert, is a wide basin dotted with verdant hay fields, grazing cattle, and three dried lake beds—Upper, Middle, and Lower Alkali Lakes. The valley was formed as a down-faulted basin between two uplifted mountain ranges. It was an immense lake not long ago that stretched down the valley's 70-mile length. During the last ice age it filled with

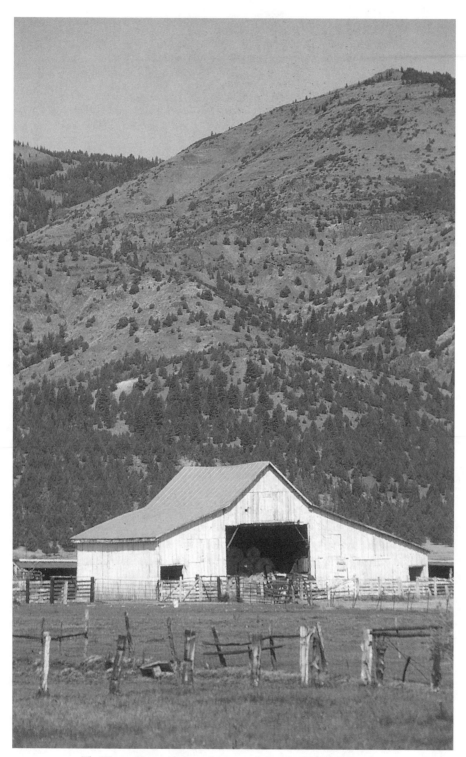

*The Warner Mountains loom above a ranch barn in Surprise Valley along
the Cedar Pass–Fandango Pass scenic drive in northeastern California.*

runoff, but over the succeeding 10,000 years the lake shrunk as the climate warmed and dried, leaving only these three huge sand pans. Water occasionally covers the lakes with a thin sheet that reflects the sky, clouds, and nearby peaks.

Just over 9 miles from Cedarville, the drive enters **Lake City,** another old settlement. Not much is left of the town now save a few clapboard homes surrounded by spreading cottonwood trees and orchards, but this site was once a busy town. Its first cabin was erected in 1864, and a sawmill began operations the next year. By 1868 Lake City offered a post office, saloon, hotel, log schoolhouse, and store.

The road runs north from Lake City on old shoreline terraces above Upper Alkali Lake. Green pastures dotted with cattle cover the gentle slopes between the lake and roadway. The Warner Mountains lift their lofty escarpment to the west with sagebrush and juniper on the lower slopes giving way to pine and fir forests up high. Snow cornices line the upper ridgelines against the cobalt sky.

Ten miles from Lake City the Surprise Valley Road intersects with FR 9 (Fandango Pass Road). Turn west on it. It's worth a side trip to continue north a few miles to Fort Bidwell at the head of the Surprise Valley. **Fort Bidwell** is the farthest northeast of any town in California. It was an important military site that provided protection from Indians for emigrant travelers and early settlers, beginning in 1866. The fort was abandoned in 1892 and used as an Indian school. The only remaining building is the fort hospital. The Fort Bidwell General Store exhibits some local military artifacts and serves as the community grapevine. The BLM's Surprise Valley–Barrel Springs Back Country Byway begins just east of Fort Bidwell and climbs east onto high mesas along the California and Nevada border. Several hot springs dot the area around Surprise Valley, including the Menlo Baths just south of Fort Bidwell. Ask at the Fort Bidwell General Store or the national forest office in Cedarville for directions.

FANDANGO PASS

The dirt Fandango Pass Road begins climbing immediately. Switchbacks steeply ascend slopes blanketed with gray sagebrush. A mixed pine and fir forest clings to the mountainside. After a couple of miles, the road enters Modoc National Forest. As the road climbs, climate and plant communities change, making the highlands a cool refuge from the hot valleys below. Groves of quaking aspen that turn gold in the autumn nestle in moist side canyons; forests of ponderosa, Jeffrey, white, and lodgepole pine, white fir, and mountain mahogany spread a patchwork carpet over the rolling mountains. Marvelous views of Surprise Valley and rugged Nevada ranges to the east spread out below the twisting road. Four miles and almost 2,000 vertical feet from the road's start at the valley floor, it crosses the summit of 6,332-foot Fandango Pass.

Fandango Pass is a significant site in California history. It was here, atop this lonely saddle, that two pioneer trails converged. The Applegate-Lassen Trail, established in 1846, traversed Nevada's barren northwestern corner from the Humboldt

River on the California Trail to this rugged highland. The Applegate Trail ran northwest from here across the lava beds near Tule Lake to the fertile Willamette Valley in the Oregon Territory; the Lassen Cutoff, established by guide Peter Lassen in 1848, turned south and meandered down to the northern gold mines in California. A historic marker atop the pass commemorates these two great emigrant trails.

The narrow road descends northwest through a pine and fir forest above the Fandango Valley, a flattish valley covered with sage and flanked by high ridges. Glimpses of Goose Lake appear through the trees. The drive quickly reaches the valley floor and runs along the ecotone where woodland and sagebrush meet. This valley edge is the tragic site of the **Fandango Pass Massacre.** In the early 1850s an emigrant party of men, women and children camped in this pretty valley, finding joy in its woodlands and flowing water after the arid tedium of northwestern Nevada. In their evening revelry, the group danced the Spanish fandango, unaware that hostile Indians had surrounded their camp. The warriors attacked the merrymakers without warning and killed all but two in a short, bloody struggle. News of the massacre quickly reached the military and a detachment of cavalry was sent to seek retribution. The attackers were surrounded and slain, and the valley and nearby pass were named for that last, ill-fated fandango.

GOOSE LAKE TO ALTURAS

After a few miles, the open valley narrows and the drive runs through pine woodlands broken with grassy meadows. At Buck Creek Fire Station, a national forest outpost, the road becomes paved. Heading northwest it crosses juniper-covered benches before turning abruptly west and dropping onto sloping pastureland above Goose Lake. Fourteen miles after leaving Surprise Valley, the road ends on US 395, eastern California's main north-south highway. The scenic drive turns south on US 395 toward Alturas. A right turn heads north past Goose Lake State Park on the Oregon side of the state line and runs to Lakeview, 19 miles north of the road junction.

The remaining 28 miles on the drive follow US 395 south back to its intersection with CA 299. The road traverses a wide sagebrush bench, part of an ancient wave terrace above Goose Lake. The lake, like the Alkali Lakes in Surprise Valley, sits in a fault-block valley. It too filled in prehistoric times with runoff from melting glaciers, forming a wide shallow lake. The drying climate as well as irrigation demands have shrunk Goose Lake to a fraction of its former size. The whole southern lake floor is a dusty playa below the roadway, although sagebrush and pastures have slowly reclaimed some of the lake bed. The lake has also shrunk away from its former outlets, including the North Fork of the Pit River; this makes the lake's water increasingly alkaline.

Heading south the road drops down through ranches and farmland on the old lake bed. The Warner Range forms a rugged eastern horizon. A turnoff at Davis Creek wends up Forest Road 11 to Plum Valley Campground and then over the range to Lake City. Davis Creek, a roadside stop, is named for an early prospector killed here in 1868. The area is famed for its obsidian mines, including the Rainbow Mine.

South of Davis Creek, the drive leaves the old lake bed, climbs over some low juniper-coated rises, and drops into the narrow, winding canyon of the Pit River. The river, usually a mere trickle in summer, meanders through willow-lined banks beneath the basalt cliffs of the canyon rim. West of the canyon stretches Devil's Garden. This high tableland of lava flows is covered with California's largest stand of western juniper, more than 300,000 acres. As the highway runs south, the valley slowly broadens and cattle graze on its fertile floor. Fanciful exposures of rhyolitic volcanic ash sculpted into pinnacles, tepees, and hoodoos line the road in places. The drive ends shortly afterward at the highway's junction with CA 299. Continue on to Alturas 6 miles ahead.

Lassen Volcanic National Park Scenic Drive

GENERAL DESCRIPTION: A 35-mile paved highway that twists around 10,457-foot Lassen Peak, passing numerous geothermal features and evidence of recent volcanism in Lassen Volcanic National Park.

SPECIAL ATTRACTIONS: Lassen Peak, Bumpass Hell, Lake Helen, Kings Creek, Summit Lake, Nobles Emigrant Trail, Manzanita Lake, Lassen Volcanic Wilderness Area, Pacific Crest Trail, hiking.

LOCATION: Northeastern California.

DRIVE ROUTE NUMBER AND NAME: California Highway 89 (Lassen Park Highway).

TRAVEL SEASON: Due to extremely heavy snowfall, as much as 50 feet a winter, the highway closes by the end of October and doesn't reopen until it is fully plowed in late May or early June. The road is open, however, to the Lassen Winter Sports Area on the volcano's southern slopes. Expect winds, chilly temperatures, and snow. Carry chains

and extra warm clothes. Occasional thunderstorms and even snow can make the pavement slick in summer.

CAMPING: Eleven campgrounds are in the national park.

SERVICES: Services are limited in Lassen Park at Southwest Entrance and Manzanita Lake. Gas is available only at Manzanita Lake in the park. The only lodging in the park is at Warner Valley near the park's southeast corner away from the drive. Full services are in Redding, Red Bluff, and Susanville.

NEARBY ATTRACTIONS: Lassen National Forest, Plumas National Forest, Feather River, Lake Almanor, Thousand Lakes Wilderness Area, Caribou Wilderness Area, Subway Cave and other lava tube caves in Hat Creek Valley, Eagle Lake, Susanville, Latour State Forest, McArthur-Burney Falls Memorial State Park, Ahjumawi Lava Springs State Park, Yuba Pass scenic drive.

THE DRIVE

Lassen Peak dominates northern California's skyline like no other peak except its sister volcano Mount Shasta, 70 miles to the northwest. Lassen's bulk lends to its conspicuousness. Lifting abruptly from surrounding forested ridges to its snow-capped 10,457-foot summit, Lassen Peak anchors the southern end of the Cascade Range. This mercurial mountain chain marches north from Lassen Peak into southern British Columbia, its crest endowed with majestic, symmetrical peaks, including Mount Rainier, Mount Hood, Mount Shasta, and Lassen Peak. These lofty

To Burney Falls

CALIFORNIA

89

LASSEN
NATIONAL
FOREST

Pacific
Crest
Trail

Nobles
Emigrant
Trail

*Reflection
Lake*

To
Redding

44

□ **Visitor
Center**

**Manzanita Lake
Campground**

▲ *Chaos Crags
8,503 ft.*

*Raker Peak
7,483 ft.*
▲

89

WILDERNESS
AREA

LASSEN
VOLCANIC
NATIONAL
PARK

*Emigrant
Pass*

Devastated Area

Summit Lake
North
Campground

*Loomis Peak
8,658 ft.*
▲

▲ *Lassen Peak
10,457 ft.*

*Summit
Lake*

Summit Lake
South
Campground

WILDERNESS
AREA

*Lake
Helen*

*Reading Peak
8,701 ft.*
▲

(closed in winter)

*Mount Diller
9,087 ft.* ▲

□ **Bumpass
Hell**

Kings Creek
Picnic Area

*Brokeoff
Mountain* ▲
9,235 ft.

**Sulphur
Works** □

**Lassen Winter
Sports Area** □

▲ **Southwest
Campground**

□ **Information
Station**

▲ *Mount Conrad
8,204 ft.*

N

0   Kilometers   2

0   Miles   2

89

LASSEN
NATIONAL
FOREST

To Quincy

mountains, all currently dormant volcanos, display the classic volcanic shape, with long graceful slopes that arc upward to the summit. The Cascades form the eastern boundary of some 300 active volcanoes that ring the Pacific Ocean. This is the only live volcanic area in the continental United States in the twentieth century, evidenced by the explosive 1980 eruption of Mount St. Helens and Lassen Peak's activity between 1914 and 1921.

The Lassen Park drive wends 35 miles through 106,372-acre Lassen Volcanic National Park on CA 89, traversing a spectacular mountain landscape. The mountain, raw with volcanic violence, dominates the drive, always towering above the twisted roadway. A host of bizarre and interesting volcanic features scatter along the highway, including mud pots, fumaroles, boiling lakes, and hot springs—a reminder that geology is not just exposures of rock but a living, dynamic force. Gentler touches of life soften the rugged landscape. Meadows, lush with summer wildflowers, and dense coniferous forests of pine and fir carpet roadside ridges. Tumbling creeks fed by melting snow rush over rounded boulders and pool in deep ponds. The park harbors eight distinct plant communities that are home to some 250 vertebrate species and is California's least known and visited national park. It also offers a host of outdoor recreation from hiking on Lassen Peak to fly-fishing in a pristine lake.

Lassen Park's climate can be summed up in one word—snow. As much as 700 inches of snow falls in the park, making an average 30-foot-deep snowpack. Severe winters characterize the area, with frigid temperatures, fierce winds, and unpredictable moisture-laden storms that blow off the Pacific Ocean. The scenic drive is closed by winter snow, generally from late October through May, although the southwest entrance remains open to the Lassen Winter Sports Area. After the road opens in early summer, it slices through deep drifts on the upper elevations. The park's summer weather is sunny and cool, with chilly nights. Daily highs generally rise to the sixties and seventies. Occasional thunderstorms or snow showers can make roads slick. Be prepared for adverse conditions, especially if hiking on the higher mountains. Autumn is pleasant here. Expect warm, clear days, cold nights, and few crowds.

LASSEN VOLCANIC NATIONAL PARK

The scenic drive, following CA 89, begins at the park's southwest entrance. CA 89 is a long highway that runs from Mount Shasta south through Truckee and South Lake Tahoe. It can be reached from Susanville and Red Bluff via CA 36. The drive runs north from its intersection with CA 36 along the edge of a high ridge. The road cuts through a lush red-fir forest as it climbs above 5,000 feet. The drive reaches the Lassen Volcanic National Park boundary after 4 miles.

The park was first protected as a national monument by Pres. Theodore Roosevelt in 1907 as part of the greater 1.5-million-acre Lassen Peak Forest Reserve. A bill was introduced in Congress in 1912 to make the area a national park, but little

Lassen Peak towers over Lake Helen and the Lassen Peak Highway.

happened until Lassen erupted on May 30, 1914. The national publicity accorded this geological phenomena led to the creation of Lassen Volcanic National Park in 1916. More than 80,000 acres of the park were designated wilderness in 1972.

A mile after entering the park, the road passes the entrance station. Beyond sit the **Southwest Information Station,** with park information and displays, and the Lassen Chalet, offering basic visitor services. Southwest Campground is nearby with twenty-one walk-in sites at an elevation of 6,700 feet. The campground is open in winter. The Lassen Winter Sports Area spreads across the ridges to the west. This small, friendly ski area, open from mid-November to April, is seldom crowded and offers lessons and a variety of runs for skiers. The southwest entrance also serves as a winter gateway for cross-country skiers and snowshoers. Some of the best Nordic tours follow the snow-covered highway to Lake Helen and Kings Creek Meadows. A spectacular tour ends at Bumpass Hell, with stunning views of the steaming thermal area surrounded by snow. Registration is required for all-day and overnight winter trips. Register at the ranger station.

SULPHUR WORKS

The two-lane highway edges north above the deep canyon of West Sulphur Creek and after a mile reaches Sulphur Works, the park's most accessible thermal area. A short trail leaves the roadside parking area and wanders past hot springs, bubbling mud pots, and fumaroles. As at all thermal areas in the park, stay on the trail. The water is extremely hot, in excess of 195 degrees Fahrenheit, and thin crusts and unstable footing around the springs can lead to disaster. The distinctive rotten eggs aroma of hydrogen sulphide permeates the air. The Sulphur Works is part of the central vent system of Mount Tehama, a massive volcano that stood here long before Lassen Peak.

The ring of peaks that surrounds Sulphur Works—9,235-foot Brokeoff Mountain, 9,087-foot Mount Diller, 8,886-foot Pilot Pinnacle, and 8,204-foot Mount Conrad—are all remnants of Mount Tehama, a stratovolcano that reached above 11,000 feet with an 11-mile-wide base. The peak built up some 600,000 years ago by long volcanic episodes. Tehama eventually wore away through thermal activity that allowed its soft slopes to be easily eroded by rain, runoff, and glaciation. A wide rim resembling a caldera was left behind.

Lassen Peak, considered the world's largest plug dome volcano, arose over 20,000 years ago, long after Tehama's collapse, when a giant mass of lava pushed up through a vent on Tehama's north side. The peak formed not by eruptions like other volcanos, but like a giant lava mushroom shoved up the vent. The thick, syrupy lava, instead of flowing downhill, solidified as it grew until the dome towered over the worn-down volcanos surrounding it and plugged the underground vent.

Past the Sulphur Works, the drive swings across the steep slopes of 7,968-foot Diamond Peak. The ragged peak, strewn with steep cliffs and crags, is the solidified remains of one of Mount Tehama's main vents, which carried magma from deep underground reservoirs to the surface. It was named for glittering quartz and calcite crystals that stud its rocks. On the east side of Diamond Peak and Pilot Pinnacle, the highway climbs above precipitous Little Hot Springs Valley. The road continues past this glacier-carved valley, and after a few miles passes Emerald Lake and Emerald Point. The emerald green lake, lying in a basin etched out by glaciers, is at an elevation of 8,000 feet. The forest here in the Hudsonian or subalpine life zone creeps upward to Lassen's 9,000-foot timberline. Life at this altitude is hardened by harsh conditions that prevail much of the year. Snow drifts as deep as 40 feet, and ferocious winds scour the open ridges. Dwarf forests of whitebark pine scatter across the drier slopes, while mountain hemlock thrive in sturdy clumps on moist, shaded slopes. Pioneer naturalist John Muir called the hemlock "singularly graceful in habit," and said "the finest groves I have yet found are on the southern slopes of Lassen's Butte." The nearby viewpoint offers superb views of the park's southern canyons and its volcanic peaks.

BUMPASS HELL

The trailhead to Bumpass Hell begins just past Emerald Lake at a large parking area about 11 miles north of the park entrance. The trail is a 3-mile round-trip that threads across the top of a glaciated cirque, passing striations etched into glacial polished rock. Glacial erratics or large glacier-deposited boulders balance on bedrock along the trail. After winding through groves of whitebark pine and mountain hemlock, the trail emerges on the western rim of a steaming ten-acre basin—Bumpass Hell. This spectacular thermal area, Lassen Park's largest, is named for Kendall Vanhook Bumpass, who discovered it and subsequently lost a leg by accidently stepping into one of the boiling springs while showing the area to visiting reporters. The trail drops steeply down to a series of boardwalks that explore the area. Stay on the trail and avoid having a Bumpass accident. The crust is fragile around the springs and will break under body weight.

Bumpass Hell is a seething cauldron of bubbling mud pots, boiling hot springs, sulphur vents, and mineral-stained water. The area, which lies outside of Tehama's caldera, is heated by cooling magma deep underground. Surface water from melting snow and rain percolates down until it turns into steam from the heat of the magma chamber and returns to the surface. Water at this altitude boils at 198 degrees, rather than the 212 degrees at sea level. Much of the water, however, is hotter because of underground superheating under pressure. The circulating hot water deposits dissolved minerals around the springs. More valuable ores such as gold are often deposited by hot water at great depths underground.

LAKE HELEN TO KINGS CREEK MEADOWS

From the Bumpass Hell parking lot, the drive skirts the edge of Lake Helen, a spectacular glacial lake that lies at 8,164 feet. Lassen Peak looms north over the lake, which remains frozen up to eight months of the year. The water temperature is a chilly thirty-nine degrees even in late summer. The lake was named for Helen Tanner Brodt, who, in 1864, was the first woman to ascend Lassen Peak. The peak's first recorded ascent was in 1851 by Grover Godfrey. A picnic area is on the lake's eastern shore.

The **Lassen Peak Trail** lies another mile up the road. The 2.5-mile-long trail switchbacks 2,000 feet up steep rocky slopes to the peak's lofty 10,457-foot-summit. All northern California unfolds below. To the east lie dark, forested ridges, and in the far distance stretch shadowy ranges in Nevada. Northward spreads the dark Modoc Plateau broken by the snowcapped Warner Range. Mount Shasta gleams to the northwest, its shoulders capped with brilliant snow. Westward lies the Sacramento Valley with the Klamath Ranges standing above the haze. The long ridge of the Sierra Nevada marches southeastward. Late summer or early fall is the best time to climb the mountain; otherwise, heavy snow covers the trail. Early-season climbers should carry an ice ax. The round-trip ascent takes about four hours. Be prepared for strong winds and inclement weather. Carry a raincoat, suntan lotion, sunglasses, water, and a hat.

The drive reaches its 8,512-foot high point just beyond the Lassen Peak parking area and drops over the mountain's southeastern flank. Magnificent views down the Warner Valley toward broad Lake Almanor and of the rough volcanic peaks in the park's eastern half stretch out below the winding highway. Prospect Peak, a prominent peak to the northeast, is an 8,338-foot shield volcano in the park's northeast corner. At its base is the perfectly symmetrical Cinder Cone, a 700-foot-high cone built by violent eruptions that tossed ash and cinders from its central vent. A sea of lava surrounds the cone. Argonauts on the Nobles Emigrant Trail in 1850 and 1851 reported the cone's eruptions, although scientists now say it erupted around one hundred years earlier. The road descends and passes from woodlands inhabited by whitebark pine and mountain hemlock into dense stands of stately red fir broken by meadows strewn with wildflowers in summer.

The **Kings Creek Meadows,** about 4 miles below the road summit, are the largest of these mountain meadows. The highway skirts the Upper Meadow. Kings Creek meanders placidly in wide curves across the damp grassland, while steep ridges cloaked in red fir surround the bucolic valley. The meadow was once a lake, but waterborne debris and silt carried by Kings Creek slowly filled it. The summer floral display includes alpine gentian, fawn lily, false hellebore, and lupine. Nearby is Kings Creek Picnic Area with cool sites scattered through the forest. A trail heads south from here to Cold Boiling Lake, a bubbling clear lake, and around Bumpass Mountain to Bumpass Hell; a turn-off trail twists 5 miles to the southwest park entrance. Another trail begins below the Upper Meadow and drops 1.5 miles to Kings Creek Falls, a rushing cascade in a narrow volcanic gorge. Lassen Volcanic National Park offers more than 150 miles of trails, including 17 miles of the famed Pacific Crest Trail.

SUMMIT LAKE TO THE DEVASTATED AREA

The drive bends northeast from the meadows and runs along the southern flank of Reading Peak, an 8,701-foot plug volcano formed in the same way as Lassen Peak. The peak is named for Major Pierson Reading, first settler in Shasta County and leader of the third recorded ascent of Lassen Peak. The road gradually loses elevation as it runs northward, and 4 miles from Kings Meadows it reaches picturesque 6,695-foot Summit Lake. The small lake, surrounded by a dense forest of red fir, lodgepole pine, and whitebark pine, sits atop the summit or divide between the north-flowing Pit River drainage and the south-flowing Feather River drainage. Two popular campgrounds, North Summit Lake with forty-six sites and South Summit Lake with forty-eight sites, sit on the lakeshore. A nearby ranger station provides trail information and backcountry permits for the adjoining Lassen Volcanic Wilderness Area to the east.

The road turns northwest at Summit Lake and crosses 2-mile-long Dersch Meadows along the East Fork of Hat Creek. After 2.5 miles, the drive dips down over Hat Creek's west fork, a lively creek draining Lassen Peak's eastern slope. A parking area allows access to shallow Hat Lake, a shrinking lake that formed when a mud flow unleashed on Lassen Peak blocked the creek's path on May 19, 1915. Volcanic sediment carried by Hat Creek has quickly filled the lake, leaving this small remnant that will soon become a meadow like Kings Meadows.

From Hat Lake to the park's northwest entrance, the drive crosses destructive evidence of Lassen Peak's last violent eruptions. The peak, until Mount St. Helens' activity, was the only active volcano in the continental United States in the twentieth century. Even today, despite Lassen's deceptively calm demeanor, geologists consider it an active volcano that could erupt sooner rather than later. Early settlers considered the peak an extinct volcano, so it was somewhat surprising when on May 30, 1914, the mountain belched forth a gaseous column and ejected lava and debris onto its upper slopes. A new vent opened in the summit crater and Lassen erupted 150 times over the next year. In May 1915 lava overflowed the crater rim and seeped down its slopes. The molten rock melted the peak's heavy snowpack, sending an avalanche followed by devastating mud flows down into Hat and Lost Creeks. The next day the peak exploded a mushroom cloud of ash and steam over 25,000 feet into the air, a frightening sight visible as far away as Sacramento. An avalanche of steam and gas rocketed down Lassen's northeastern slopes, decimating forests like mere matchsticks. This swath of destruction, the **Devastated Area,** borders the drive just north of Hat Lake. The fallen trees along the mud flow's edge lie facing downhill from the volcano, and the great pines standing along the edge still retain scars where their bark was shredded off that violent day. Today, young stands of lodgepole pine and quaking aspen slowly fill in the Devastated Area. After this eruption, Lassen's fury abated and by 1917 most volcanic activity had ceased.

ALONG THE NOBLES EMIGRANT TRAIL

The drive follows the old Nobles Emigrant Trail from Hat Creek to the park's northwest corner. The Nobles Trail was laid out as an alternative to the longer Lassen Trail, which ran from Fandango Pass to the northern end of the Sacramento Valley in the early 1850s. The Nobles Trail traversed the rough country from Black Rock in Nevada to Fort Reading, now Redding, California. This shortcut proved popular and its ruts are still visible today. Parts of the trail were used as recently as 1931 when the present highway was completed. William Nobles laid out the trail and sold the route to Shasta City businessmen for $2,000 in 1852. The Lassen Trail and Lassen Peak were named for Peter Lassen, a Danish pioneer who guided parties along his trail beginning in 1848.

Northwest of the Devastated Area, the road passes west of 7,483-foot Raker Peak, a 1,200-foot-high shield volcano named for John Raker, the state representative who pushed passage of the 1916 bill that created Lassen Volcanic National Park. Hot Rock, alongside the drive, is a large lava boulder carried down by the 1915 mud flow. Mature forests of white fir, incense cedar (not a true cedar), sugar pine, and ponderosa pine, untouched by the volcanic devastation, cover the hillsides above the drive. One of the nation's largest white firs, measuring 168 feet high, grows on the roadside.

Past Hot Rock, the drive leaves Lost Creek and swings around the northern end of **Chaos Crags.** These rumpled mountains are a group of four smaller, more recent lava plug domes than neighboring Lassen Peak. Geologists say they are about

1,000 years old, with their last activity reported in 1850. When the crags arose, steam blasts undermined their northern flank and scattered a massive landslide of boulders northward. The drive crosses this area of broken talus, called the Chaos Jumbles. A pygmy forest grows on porous soil patches among the boulders.

REFLECTION AND MANZANITA LAKES

The highway descends east from Chaos Jumbles and quickly reaches Reflection Lake and Manzanita Lake. Reflection Lake, at 5,880 feet, offers a perfect reflection of Lassen Peak and Chaos Crags on peaceful summer evenings. Manzanita Lake is named for the manzanita bushes that clot its shores. The wide lake gives a spectacular view of Lassen's bold, bulky outline that looms to the south, rising 4,625 feet above the peaceful lake. In summer, fishermen line its shores and swimmers cool off in its clear water; waterfowl rest on its waters during fall migrations. Manzanita Lake Campground, with 179 sites, sits in thick forest above the lake's eastern shore. This pleasant campground offers private sites, and a nearby concessionaire sells groceries, gas, and showers. From Manzanita Lake the drive turns northwest, passes the park entrance station, and reaches the park boundary at CA 89's junction with CA 44. A left turn on CA 44 drops through pine forests to Redding at the head of the Sacramento Valley. CA 89 continues north, dropping down along Hat Creek and passing numerous forest campgrounds (ranging in size from six to seventy-five campsites) and a huge lava flow pockmarked with lava tube caves, including Subway Cave. The highway continues north to Burney.

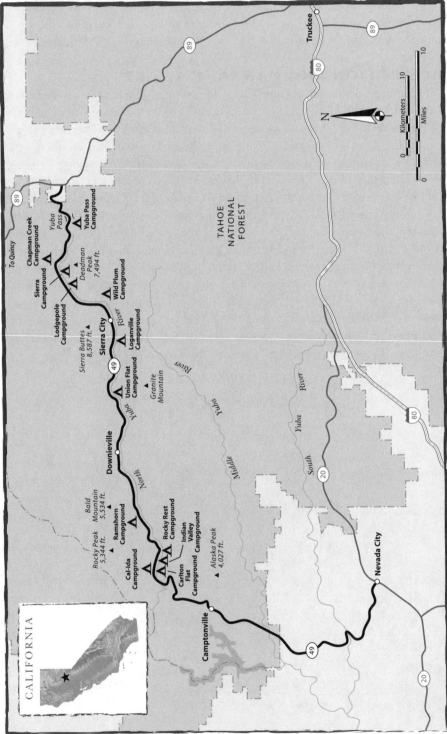

CALIFORNIA

To Quincy

89

Chapman Creek
Campground

Yuba
Pass

Yuba Pass
Campground

Sierra
Campground

Deadman
Peak
7,494 ft.

Lodgepole
Campground

Wild Plum
Campground

Sierra Buttes
8,587 ft.

Sierra City

River

Loganville
Campground

49

Union Flat
Campground

Granite
Mountain

Yuba

Downieville

North

Bald
Mountain
5,534 ft.

Ramshorn
Campground

Rocky Rest
Campground

Rocky Peak
5,344 ft.

Indian
Valley
Campground

Cal-Ida
Campground

Carlton
Flat
Campground

Alaska Peak
4,027 ft.

Camptonville

Middle

Yuba

River

South

Yuba

River

20

TAHOE
NATIONAL
FOREST

89

80

Truckee

89

N

Kilometers   10

Miles

0

0   10

80

Nevada City

49

20

Yuba Pass Scenic Drive

NEVADA CITY TO CA 89

GENERAL DESCRIPTION: A 75-mile highway that begins in Nevada City, crosses the South and Middle Forks of the Yuba River, and follows the North Fork of the Yuba River to the 6,701-foot summit of Yuba Pass.

SPECIAL ATTRACTIONS: Nevada City, Yuba River forks, Tahoe National Forest, Downieville, Sierra City, Yuba Pass, hiking, fishing.

LOCATION: East-central California.

DRIVE ROUTE NUMBER: California Highway 89.

TRAVEL SEASON: Year-round. The drive receives heavy snow in winter and may be temporarily closed. Adequate snow tires and chains are advised.

CAMPING: Thirteen Tahoe National Forest campgrounds are along the drive. Those at a lower elevation along the river tend to fill up early in summer. Numerous other forest campgrounds are on side roads.

SERVICES: All services in Nevada City, Downieville, and Sierra City; limited services at North San Juan and Camptonville.

NEARBY ATTRACTIONS: South Yuba Trail, Malakoff Diggins State Historic Park, Donner Pass, Donner Lake, Donner Memorial State Park, Truckee, Lake Tahoe, Desolation Wilderness Area, Plumas Eureka State Park, Empire Mine State Historic Park.

THE DRIVE

The Yuba Pass Scenic Drive follows CA 49 for 75 miles from Nevada City to the North Fork of the Yuba River. It parallels the river through several historic mining towns before climbing over 6,701-foot Yuba Pass on the crest of the Sierra Nevada. The road dips through deep river gorges, traverses high wooded ridges, passes the remains of California's gold rush days, and offers numerous recreational opportunities from camping and fishing to snowmobiling and cross-country skiing. The winding, paved highway, part of the larger 160-mile Yuba Donner Scenic Byway loop, has numerous turnouts for sightseeing and takes at least three hours to drive.

The weather along the drive is typical Sierran, with hot summers in the low canyons and cool temperatures in the higher elevations. Expect summer highs in the nineties in the lowlands and seventies atop the pass. Occasional thunderstorms build over the mountains, dropping a curtain of rain across the peaks. Autumns are pleasant, with warm clear days and chilly nights. Winter brings severe storms that dump deep snow across the high country. Be prepared when driving in winter by bringing extra warm clothes, a sleeping bag, food, and tire chains. The highway may be closed after harsh storms. Spring brings warmer temperatures and rivers full of runoff. The lower elevations begin turning green by April.

NEVADA CITY

The drive begins in 2,520-foot-high Nevada City at the intersection of CA 20 and CA 49. Turn north on CA 49. Nevada City lies 5 miles northeast of Grass Valley and 28 miles north of I–80. Nevada City, one of California's most picturesque gold rush towns, sprawls along the wooded hills above Deer Creek. The town arose when miners began probing rich placer deposits along Deer Creek in 1849. It ran through a succession of names—Caldwell's Upper Store, Deer Creek Dry Diggin's, and Coyoteville—before settling on Nevada after the severe winter of 1850; Nevada is Spanish for "snow-covered." When the neighboring state stole its name a few years later, City was added.

The town quickly grew and soon almost every square foot around Nevada City and nearby Grass Valley was being mined. Much of the gold excavated came from underground mines that followed gold-quartz veins along the contact of granite and metamorphosed sedimentary rocks. By 1856 the town had burned down three times. Eventually, more than $400 million in gold was extracted, with the last mine closing in the early 1950s. Nevada City today is one of the gold country's prettiest towns, with white-steepled churches, narrow winding streets lined with shops, and lovely autumn colors when the surrounding sugar maples and oaks blaze with color. It's a good place to explore on foot. The chamber of commerce offers a brochure for walkers to discover the town's historic attractions—including Firehouse Number 1, the Nevada Theatre, and the National Hotel, which has operated continuously since 1856 and claims to be the oldest operating hotel west of the Rockies.

ALONG THE SOUTH YUBA RIVER

The highway runs north from Nevada City and drops down through a mixed forest of oak and gray pine into the steep canyon of the South Yuba River, one of the river's three forks that drain the northern Sierra Nevadas. The river, named by the Spanish *Rio de las Uvas* or River of Grapes for the tangled vines along its banks, supposedly yielded more gold in its thick gravel deposits than any other American river system. Almost 7 miles north of Nevada City, the drive sweeps across the river and its narrow granite gorge on a concrete bridge. The Independence Trail, along Rush Creek a mile before the river crossing, is the nation's first wheelchair-accessible wilderness trail. It follows the abandoned Excelsior Canal flume for 7 miles into the South Yuba River canyon and allows physically challenged visitors to enjoy the Sierra foothills.

After crossing the river, the highway quickly climbs away from the river over chaparral- and oak-covered ridges and swings around rounded Bunker Hill. Four miles from the river, the drive passes a side road that heads east to **Malakoff**

The Yuba River along California Highway 49 is a good place to take a break from driving.

Diggins State Historic Park, a monument to the destruction that mining can cause. The diggings were thick gravel deposits filled with low-grade gold ore on San Juan Ridge, a long ridge that was once an ancient river bed. To get at the ore required a large hydraulic mining operation that washed the gravel into long sluice boxes and yielded only ten cents a cubic yard. From 1866 until 1884, the Malakoff Diggins were the site of the world's largest hydraulic mine and employed hundreds of men who literally resculpted the ridge in search of gold. The mine was an ecological disaster, even by the lax mining standards of that era. The land was laid waste with eroded ravines, mountains of gravel, and a countryside denuded of forest. Silt swept down the Yuba River, choking waterways in the Central Valley, damming irrigation canals, burying crops and fields, and muddying San Francisco Bay almost 200 miles away. Public outrage led by farmers and landowners led to passage of the Federal Anti-Debris Act in 1883, which almost overnight closed down the Malakoff mine. Travelers today can walk on trails that wander across the Bryce Canyon-like bluffs above the mine and explore the remains of this destructive mine. Water has filled the bottom of the 7,000-foot-long pit, creating a huge lake. The 3,400-acre park is also used for picnicking, fishing, and camping.

The drive continues across the rolling San Juan Ridge under a canopy of pine, fir, and oak. On its north side lies the town of **North San Juan,** another gold rush village. It was named by Mexican War veteran Christian Kientz, who thought a hill where he found gold in 1853 resembled a hill with a prison in Mexico called San Juan de Ulloa. The town boasted a population of 10,000 when it headquartered the nearby Malakoff Diggins. Now the town has a population of about 125.

The highway drops down from North San Juan, enters the immense Tahoe National Forest, and crosses the Middle Fork of the Yuba River. On the river's north side is a turn to the **Oregon Creek Day Use Area,** a pleasant picnic site and swimming hole along the riverbank. The river is flanked by dense Sierran forest of oak, pine, and incense cedar. The river winds west through a shallow, rocky canyon.

The road climbs alongside Oregon Creek from the river and reaches an intersection with the Marysville Road after 3 miles. A Tahoe National Forest ranger station sits at the junction. A turn down the side road leads to New Bullards Bar Reservoir and several forest campgrounds. The narrow, twisting highway steadily rises through a tree-lined corridor to Camptonville, another sleepy mining town that's home to a small number of residents. A national forest office here provides camping, hiking, and fishing information. After a few miles, the road crosses into Sierra County, crests a hilltop, and begins spiraling around Indian Hill to the North Fork of the Yuba River. The highway is extremely narrow and winding through here, with a maximum speed of 20 miles per hour. The drive crosses the Yuba River on a wide concrete bridge span. A couple of pullouts here allow access to the river below and excellent late-summer swimming.

NORTH FORK OF THE YUBA RIVER

The North Fork headwaters arise to the east atop Yuba Pass on the Sierra divide and run swiftly westward to a confluence with its other forks before draining into the Central Valley at Marysville. The scenic drive along CA 49 parallels the river through its wooded canyon for 37 miles to the pass summit. Numerous national forest campgrounds, a couple of historic towns, and spectacular scenery line the highway. Yuba's North Fork, the most active placer stream in California, is famed for its rich gold deposits. Mining dredges scatter along the river from Shenanigan Flat to Downieville, floating in deep pools below tumbling rapids. Most of the river is worked by legal mining claims. Amateur prospectors can search the river for their own pot of gold, but be sure to do it legally. Although hanging claim-jumpers from the nearest oak is out of the question these days, claim-jumping is not fondly looked upon. Check at the ranger station in Camptonville for maps detailing where recreational gold-panning is allowed.

On the river's north bank, a succession of fine campgrounds line the highway—Carlton Flat Cal-Ida, Indian Flat, Rocky Rest, and Ramshorn. All make good summer base camps to swim, fish, hike, pan for gold, or relax under shady trees. The river and road, heading east, follow the bottom of a deep V-shaped gorge. The river sliced the canyon into the firm bedrock over the last few million years as the Sierras rose. Thick forests of oak and pine blanket the canyon walls. The ancient sedimentary and volcanic rocks of the canyon floor were altered by intense heat and pressure, while volcanic crags from primeval eruptions punctuate the craggy ridge lines silhouetted against the turquoise sky.

DOWNIEVILLE TO SIERRA CITY

Downieville, the next historic point of interest along the route, sits astride the confluence of the Downie and Yuba Rivers. The town was founded in 1849 and was first called The Forks. It was later renamed for Major William Downie, who supposedly said he would toss a pan of gold dust into the street if the town was named for him. By 1852 Downieville's population had swollen to more than 3,000. Miners flocked in to dig the rich gravels, some yielding as much as $300 a pan. The Tincup Diggings were named because its owners worked each day until a tin cup was filled with the precious metal. Other stories include miner Jim Crow finding gold flecks in a cooking pot after boiling a fourteen-pound salmon and Frank Anderson, the first miner to pan here, taking $12,900 out of a 60-square-foot claim in eleven days. In the 1850s the North Yuba River was diverted from its channel so the riverbed gravel could be laboriously processed. After a few years the placer gold ran out, and miners began hard-rock mining on a few gold-quartz veins. But another mother lode was never found. The town also saw its share of disastrous fires and floods. The great 1938 flood wiped out most of the original buildings, except for scattered houses clinging to hillsides above the river. It's a quiet, restful place these days. California's only original gallows, now a state historic monument, stands outside the Sierra County Courthouse. Another worthwhile sight is the Downieville Museum, with an informative collection of gold rush artifacts, including mining tools, household items, and Native American artifacts.

The drive continues above the river for 13 miles to Sierra City. The road traverses on south-facing slopes through a forest of pine, incense cedar, and oak, and then passes Union Flat and Loganville Campgrounds. **Sierra City**, another old mining town, sits below the 8,587-foot Sierra Buttes, which lift their ragged, snow-capped crowns to the north. In 1850 it got its start, like neighboring Downieville, from placer gold deposits in the Yuba River. Over the next twenty years, miners honeycombed the Sierra Buttes with tunnels and dug out a fortune in gold ore. The Monumental Mine yielded a hundred-pound nugget worth $25,000 in 1860. But tough times lay ahead as avalanches from the buttes wiped out the town in 1852, 1888, and 1889. Sierra City now offers several informative attractions. Best is the Sierra County Historical Park at the Kentucky Mine. The mine, preserved as a historical site, boasts its original machinery and offers tours of the mine and stamp mill. Haypress and Wild Plum forest campgrounds lie just east of Sierra City along Haypress Creek.

OVER YUBA PASS

The drive swings north from Sierra City, paralleling the river, and steadily climbs into a broad valley. Sierra City is the western limit of glaciation in this part of the Sierra Nevada. The highway follows a wide U-shaped valley to Yuba Pass, in contrast to the abrupt V-shaped gorge to the west carved by the river. As the road climbs, it passes through lateral moraines, huge piles of boulders and gravels pushed to the side as ancient glaciers crept down valley. The road climbs above 5,000 feet and passes small waterfalls, including Loves Falls, and cascades along the tumbling river. About 5 miles from Sierra City at Bassetts, a gravel side road called the Gold Lakes Highway heads north to some forest campgrounds and several excellent lakes formed from glaciation. Sand Lake, Sardine Lake, Goose Lake, and Gold Lake offer fishing, boating, and swimming. Sand Pond, near twenty-nine-site Sardine Campground just off the drive, is considered one of the Sierra's best swimming holes. The area is part of Sierra Buttes Recreation Area, which also is popular in winter for cross-country skiing and snowmobiling.

Past Bassetts the highway meanders east along the river, rapidly climbing toward the pass summit. Some quiet campgrounds scatter along the drive, offering great overnight stays among the lodgepole pine and red fir forest. The best campground, however, is the last—Yuba Pass Campground. This twenty-site campground sits atop the broad 6,701-foot summit of Yuba Pass by a wide grassy meadow flanked with quaking aspen and towering red fir. The 6,708-foot **Yuba Pass Summit** is a popular cross-country ski area in winter. The word Yuba was first applied to the river by Captain Sutter in 1840 after a Maidu village that sat at the river's mouth.

The highway descends the east slope of the pass through a thick fir forest that changes to pine and cedar in the warmer climes of lower elevations. The abrupt escarpment here is a fault scarp that forms the eastern face of the Sierra Nevada. Three miles from the summit, the road leaves Tahoe National Forest. A lofty viewpoint lies a mile farther, providing a stunning vista of Sierra Valley to the east. The valley, like Lake Tahoe, is a down-dropped graben flanked by faults. The Middle Fork of the Feather River empties the broad valley that was once the bottom of a great mountain lake. Sierra Valley was discovered by black explorer and mountain man James Beckwourth in 1851 while searching for a feasible wagon route over the northern Sierras. The following year he established a trading post and hotel in the valley. The lush valley provided livestock, hay, and timber to the gold boom at Sierra City and Downieville over the range and later to the silver rush at Nevada's Virginia City. The valley's wetlands today are a popular stopover for migrating waterfowl. Large deer herds also winter over here away from the deep mountain snow. Sierra Valley sits astride two great North American ecosystems—the High Sierra woodlands of pine and fir and the Great Basin Desert with its characteristic sagebrush and juniper communities.

CA 49 ends a few miles later at its junction with CA 89 on the valley's western edge at a lumber mill. Truckee and I–80 lie 30 miles south on CA 89. Quincy and Lassen Volcanic National Park sit in rough, wooded country a couple of hours to the north.

Lake Tahoe Scenic Drive

SOUTH LAKE TAHOE TO TRUCKEE

GENERAL DESCRIPTION: A 42-mile, two-lane paved highway that traverses the scenic west shore of Lake Tahoe and follows the Truckee River Canyon.

SPECIAL ATTRACTIONS: Lake Tahoe, Fallen Leaf Lake, Emerald Bay, D. L. Bliss State Park, Sugar Pine State Park, Squaw Valley, Tahoe National Forest, hiking, boating, skiing.

LOCATION: East-central California near the Nevada border.

DRIVE ROUTE NUMBER AND NAME: California Highway 89 (Emerald Bay Road).

TRAVEL SEASON: The highway is open year-round. Heavy snow and ice can make the road dangerous in winter. Use proper snow tires and chains, and carry extra clothing.

CAMPING: The numerous campgrounds along the drive offer tent, RV, family, and group campsites. Some are on a first-come, first-served basis.

SERVICES: All services are at South Lake Tahoe, Tahoe City, and Truckee.

NEARBY ATTRACTIONS: Desolation Wilderness Area, Carson Pass, Donner Summit, Lake Tahoe State Park (NV), Donner Memorial State Park, Yuba Pass, Carson City, Fort Churchill to Wellington Back Country Byway (NV).

THE DRIVE

This forty-two-mile drive between South Lake Tahoe and Truckee traverses some of the state's best scenery. The road runs along Lake Tahoe's west shore and then north through the Truckee River Canyon to I–80. Lake Tahoe itself is unsurpassed—a glistening jewel cupped in a wide basin surrounded by snowcapped mountains. The lake is 22 miles long and 12 miles wide, with a shoreline of 72 miles; it is 1,645 feet deep, which makes it the tenth-deepest lake in the world and third-deepest in North America after Canada's Great Slave Lake and Oregon's Crater Lake. The lake's deepest point lies 92 feet lower than Carson City. Sixty-three streams and rivers flow into the lake, but only one, the Truckee River, drains it. Because of its depth, the lake never freezes and is famed for its extreme clarity. The lake contains so much water that it could cover California with a 14-inch layer.

The Tahoe Basin offers an excellent year-round climate with an average of 307 days of sunshine annually. Summers are mild and warm, with highs usually in the seventies and eighties and occasional afternoon thunderstorms. Spring is cool and

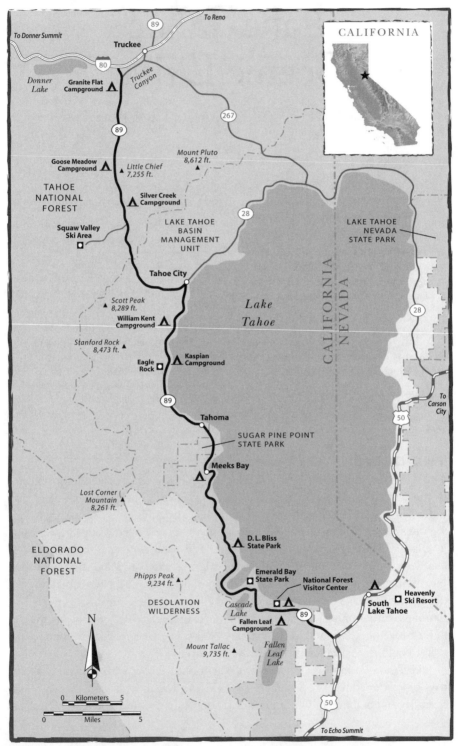

To Reno

89

To Donner Summit

Truckee

80

Donner
Lake

Granite Flat
Campground

Truckee Canyon

267

89

TAHOE
NATIONAL
FOREST

Goose Meadow
Campground

Little Chief
7,255 ft.

Mount Pluto
8,612 ft.

Silver Creek
Campground

LAKE TAHOE
BASIN
MANAGEMENT
UNIT

28

LAKE TAHOE
NEVADA
STATE PARK

Squaw Valley
Ski Area

CALIFORNIA

Tahoe City

Scott Peak
8,289 ft.

William Kent
Campground

Lake
Tahoe

CALIFORNIA
NEVADA

28

Stanford Rock
8,473 ft.

Eagle
Rock

Kaspian
Campground

89

Tahoma

To
Carson
City

50

SUGAR PINE POINT
STATE PARK

Meeks Bay

Lost Corner
Mountain
8,261 ft.

ELDORADO
NATIONAL
FOREST

Phipps Peak
9,234 ft.

DESOLATION
WILDERNESS

D. L. Bliss
State Park

Emerald Bay
State Park

National Forest
Visitor Center

Cascade
Lake

Fallen Leaf
Campground

89

South
Lake Tahoe

Heavenly
Ski Resort

Mount Tallac
9,735 ft.

Fallen
Leaf
Lake

50

N

0   Kilometers   5

0   Miles   5

To Echo Summit

CALIFORNIA

★

breezy. Falls are gorgeous, with warm Indian summer days, golden aspen leaves, and chilly nights. Winter brings an average of 213 inches of snow a year along the lakeshore. The area is famed for its Sierra ski resorts, including Squaw Valley, site of the 1960 Winter Olympics. In winter expect cold days and colder nights. The drive is regularly plowed and sanded after snowstorms, but be prepared for adverse conditions by carrying tire chains and warm clothing.

SOUTH LAKE TAHOE

The scenic drive begins at the intersection of CA 89 and US Highway 50 in South Lake Tahoe, just a few miles over the state line. Turn north on CA 89. South Lake Tahoe, the largest town on the lakeshore with a population of 23,000, attracts more than 2.5 million visitors annually. Many come in winter to sample neighboring ski areas like Heavenly Ski Resort. The area is one of California's most popular vacation spots. In summer, tourists marvel at the lake, enjoy the cool climate, play golf, mountain bike and hike the myriad trails, and relax on the town's three beaches. Besides gaming in South Lake Tahoe's Nevada-side casinos, popular activities include riding the mile-long Heavenly Gondola for a spectacular panoramic vista of the lake and the Sierra Nevada and cruising across the lake on a stern-wheel paddleboat. The Lake Tahoe Museum, along US 50 in town, acquaints visitors with the area's colorful past.

The highway quickly leaves South Lake Tahoe's suburban developments and enters the U.S. Forest Service's Lake Tahoe Basin Management Unit, which administers all forest lands in the Tahoe Basin. Upon entering the forest, the Pope-Baldwin Recreation Area is immediately encountered. This area, now managed by the Forest Service, was once the summer home of many of California's affluent elite. Elias J. Baldwin built the opulent Tallac Hotel and Tallac House casino here in the pine woods in 1879. The lavish hotel boasted a ballroom, string orchestra, tennis courts, and boat rides. After Baldwin's death in 1909, the hotel's fortunes declined, and his widow had it razed. Wealthy San Franciscans Emanuel Heller, George Pope, and Lloyd Tevis bought the land and erected grand summer cottages. Their heirs donated the property to the federal government because of maintenance costs and high taxes. The area is now the center of the Forest Service's Lake Tahoe interpretative programs.

TALLAC HISTORIC SITE

Tallac Historic Site is 3 miles from the highway junction with US 50. The historic site preserves 150 acres with the scattered remains of the Tallac Resort along with the three summer estates. The Tallac Museum serves as the site's interpretative center with ranger-led tours that explore the lake's rich turn-of-the-century past. Many special events and programs occur here throughout the summer, including the Valhalla Summer Festival of Arts and Music. A schedule is available from the nearby Forest Service Visitor Center.

Fannette Island, in Emerald Bay, is Lake Tahoe's only island.

The visitor center, just off the drive 3 miles north of South Lake Tahoe, offers a wide range of activities, displays, trails, and information. The center's six interpretative trails give a broad overview of the natural history and history of the Lake Tahoe area. The half-mile Rainbow Trail passes through pine forest and meadow. Along the way is the interesting Stream Profile Chamber. The underground, plate-glassed chamber peers into the stream ecology of Taylor Creek, exploring the life cycle of trout and the importance of marshes and meadows that filter and preserve Tahoe's clear water. Autumn visitors can also witness the spawning run of crimson-colored kokanee salmon digging and defending their egg nests. The half-mile-long Lake of the Sky Trail provides an easy stroll to Tahoe's south shore, offering interpretative displays on the impressions of the area's first explorers. The Trail of the Washoe discovers the culture of the ancient Washoes, who journeyed from the Carson Valley to this area, a favorite summering spot rich in game and fish. The other trails—Tallac Historic Site Trail, Forest Tree Trail, and Smokey's Trail—all reward the inquisitive hiker. Other visitor activities include ranger-led programs, regular campfire programs at the center's amphitheater, bicycling, and fishing. Pope and Baldwin Beaches and the Kiva Beach Picnic Area complete the area's opportunities.

Campers flock to popular Camp Richardson, a private resort with more than 300 RV and tent sites, and the 205-site Fallen Leaf Campground. Camp Richardson is operated by a concessionaire on a nonreservation basis; Fallen Leaf Campground is a pleasant, well-spaced campground surrounded by towering sugar and Jeffrey pines. Fallen Leaf Lake was formed by a glacial moraine and sits just south of the campground. Rugged 9,735-foot Mount Tallac looms west of the lake. At the end of the Fallen Leaf Road is a popular trailhead for visitors venturing into

63,469-acre Desolation Wilderness Area, the single most visited wilderness in the United States. Permits are required to hike and camp in this spectacular section of the Sierras to minimize human impact on the area's fragile ecosystems. The permits are free and available from the Forest Service.

EMERALD BAY STATE PARK

The drive runs northwest, passing Cascade Lake, another pretty glacial moraine lake nestled in a hollow above Lake Tahoe. The road switchbacks away from the lake onto a high ridge and enters scenic Emerald Bay State Park, which, coupled with adjoining D. L. Bliss State Park, protects 6 miles of Lake Tahoe's magnificent shoreline.

Emerald Bay is the real heart of today's Lake Tahoe. It's a beautiful sparkling bay gouged out by ancient glaciers that spilled eastward from the Sierra crest. This watery jewel is surrounded by thick forest and is one of California's most photographed and seen natural wonders. Inspiration Point sits high above the bay's southwest edge. It gives a spectacular view and offers interpretive displays on the area's unique history. Far below lies Fannette Island, the lake's only island. At the head of the bay hides Vikingsholm Castle, a Scandinavian-style mansion built in 1928 by heiress Lora Knight and fashioned after an eleventh-century Norse fortress. Vikingsholm is part of the state park now. A mile-long trail drops down from Emerald Bay Overlook on the bay's west end to the mansion. Tours are scheduled throughout the summer. The **Emerald Bay Overlook** is a good place to park and explore the surrounding mountains. Glacier-polished granite east of the road offers great viewpoints to sit and meditate on the lake's subtle grandeur. A short hike heads west from the parking area to Eagle Falls on the edge of the Desolation Wilderness Area. The area also offers excellent rock climbing on the many buttresses and small crags above the parking area.

LAKE TAHOE NATURAL HISTORY

Lake Tahoe has long attracted visitors. First the Washoes summered along the lakeshore, finding the cool climate and abundant game to their liking. Tahoe itself is a Washoe word meaning "lake of the sky." The first Anglo-Americans to see the lake were John C. Fremont and his expedition cartographer Charles Preuss from atop Red Lake Peak just north of Carson Pass on February 14, 1844. Fremont noted in his journal, "We had a beautiful view of a mountain lake at our feet, about fifteen miles in length, and so entirely surrounded by mountains that we could not discover an outlet." The discovery of the Comstock silver lode in Nevada brought waves of emigrants and miners through the Tahoe Basin, beginning in 1859. Then young Samuel Clemens, not yet Mark Twain, visited the area in 1861. He wrote in his best seller *Roughing It:* "The lake burst upon us—a noble sheet of blue water lifted six thousand three hundred feet above the level of the sea, and walled in by a rim of snow-clad mountain peaks. . . . I thought it must surely be the fairest picture the whole earth affords."

The mining era's history was not all so rosy. The silver rush decimated the forests of the Tahoe Basin between 1860 and 1900, with entire stands stripped to stumps and shipped via flumes and narrow-gauge railroads to Virginia City for mine timbers and building construction and for firewood to drive machinery. More than 2 billion board feet of timber was cut in the Tahoe Basin by 1881. By the turn of the century the land was so overlogged that one Bureau of Forestry official wrote, ". . . the forest is much reduced in density . . . the sugar pine has disappeared almost entirely . . . the finest of Jeffrey and yellow pine and white fir has been removed." Today, a second-generation forest coats the mountain slopes above Lake Tahoe. The common trees include Jeffrey, ponderosa, sugar, lodgepole, and pinyon pines, incense cedar, Sierra juniper, white fir, quaking aspen, willow, and alder.

Wildlife abounds in the woodlands along the drive, particularly on the lake's west shore, which butts up against the Desolation Wilderness. Beavers dam creeks that meander across meadows. Mule deer, which migrate down to the warmer Carson Valley in winter, often graze in the early evening near Baldwin Beach. Black bears roam the highlands, dropping down to forage in residential areas and campgrounds. As with other areas in the Sierras, store all food in your car or hang it from a tree to avoid bear problems. Other animals include the ubiquitous coyote, raccoon, porcupine, pine marten, marmot, and golden-mantled ground squirrel. Commonly seen birds are the mountain chickadee, Canada goose, western tanager, yellow-headed blackbird, Steller's jay, and hairy woodpecker. Bald eagles occasionally winter at the lake. California gulls scavenge along Tahoe's beaches.

Lake Tahoe, contrary to what early visitors thought, is not the interior of a collapsed volcano like Crater Lake. Rather, the lake lies in a down-faulted basin, between two uplifted fault blocks that form the Sierra Nevada on the west and the Carson Range on the east. Lava later spilled from Mount Pluto, a volcano north of the lake, and blocked the path of the ancestral Truckee River. Streams and rivers swollen with runoff, especially in postglacial periods, filled the basin. Today's Lower Truckee River eventually wore an outlet through the lava dam and dropped down steep canyons to Reno and the Carson Sink in the Nevada desert.

EMERALD BAY TO TAHOE CITY

The narrow, winding highway runs north around Emerald Bay and into **D. L. Bliss State Park.** The 1,237-acre park offers almost 4 miles of mostly pristine coastline at Lester Beach, 4 miles of trails, a picnic area, and a 168-site campground. A short nature trail winds through the forest and passes a huge balanced boulder.

Continuing north, the road passes through **Meeks Bay,** a popular summer recreation area managed by the Forest Service. Visitors flock to the bay's huge white sand beach to sunbathe, swim, and boat. Nearby is forty-site Meek's Bay Campground. Just north of Meeks Bay lies **Sugar Pine Point State Park,** a 2,000-acre park with hiking trails, picnicking, and General Creek Campground, which has ninety-nine family sites and seventy-five group sites. The park is named for a stand of towering sugar pines that were not logged on a 160-acre homestead here. The historic Ehrman Mansion, built by banker I. W. Hellman, was acquired by the state in 1965. In summer tours explore the three-story estate. From Meeks Bay to Tahoe City, a distance of about 15 miles, the drive meanders along the lakeshore. Views of its blue water glimmer through open pine woodlands. This road section is lined with summer cabins and rustic retreats. Also, many homes line the shore with piers jutting into the water. Homewood Mountain Resort offers great views and many intermediate ski runs. It sits north of Meeks Bay. Just past Tahoe Pines and Eagle Rock lies **Kaspian Recreation Area,** with a nine-site campground, a pier, and public beach. Eagle Rock, lying alongside the road, is also worth a stop. Scramble up the west side for a spectacular view of Lake Tahoe and the surrounding Sierra peaks. William Kent Campground has ninety-one sites and is reached just before Tahoe City.

DOWN TRUCKEE CANYON

The drive turns away from the lake at Tahoe City, the largest town on the lake's north shore. For the next 13 miles, the highway runs alongside the Lower Truckee River to Truckee. Three national forest campgrounds—twenty-eight-site Silver Creek, twenty-five-site Goose Meadows, and seventy-five-site Granite Flat—scatter through this placid gorge. Rafting, once a popular activity, has declined because the river is low after many drought years. The river, however, offers excellent trout fishing in its deep clear pools. A 4-mile bike path runs along the Truckee from Tahoe City to Midway Bridge, offering a gentle, but scenic ride. Rock climbers are exploring the volcanic crags above the river, putting in many excellent routes.

The Truckee Canyon is best known for its two world-class ski resorts—Alpine Meadows and Squaw Valley—tucked into side canyons west of the river. Alpine Meadows offers excellent skiing in steep gullies and chutes with names like Our Father and Promised Land. The area usually remains open until July Fourth. Squaw Valley, site of the 1960 Winter Olympics, is justly famous. It boasts 8,300 acres of ski terrain serviced by twenty-seven lifts.

Truckee lies astride I–80 at the end of the scenic drive. The town grew up along the tracks of the transcontinental railroad at the east base of Donner Pass and Donner Lake. Donner Lake is the site of one of the greatest gold rush tragedies. In the harsh winter of 1846–47, a number of families en route to California, including George and Jacob Donner, were caught by winter storms at the foot of the pass. The travelers constructed rough lean-tos, including one against a granite boulder where the smoke marks are still visible. Severe winter weather stranded them. Food ran out, and one by one they perished. A relief party that arrived in March found survivors lying among half-eaten human remains. **Donner Memorial State Park,** just west of Truckee, interprets the party's tragic story and the construction of the Central Pacific Railroad through the Sierras in the park's Emigrant Trail Museum. The park also offers camping, fishing, hiking, and boating.

To US 395

To Nevada

88

Woodfords

89

Kit Carson Campground

Crystal Springs Campground

TOIYABE NATIONAL FOREST

Snowshoe Springs Campground

Hawkins Peak

88

Red Lake Peak 10,061 ft.

Luther Pass

Red Lake

Elephant's Back

To Lake Tahoe

89

Waterhouse Peak 9,497 ft.

Stevens Peak

Carson Pass 8,573 ft.

Caples Lake

Woods Lake Campground

STANISLAUS NATIONAL FOREST

Pacific Crest Trail

Kirkwood

Kirkwood Ski Area

Silver Lake

Devil's Garden Vista

SQUAW RIDGE

Silver Lake Campground

Silver Lake West Campground

Tragedy Spring Picnic Area

Shot Rock Vista

Bear River Reservoir

4

Peddler Hill Overlook

Lumber Yard Campground

ELDORADO NATIONAL FOREST

50

88

Pioneer

Volcano

FARNHAM RIDGE

Indian Grinding Rocks State Park

Pine Grove

To Angels Camp

Placerville

49

Jackson

88

49

CALIFORNIA

N

Kilometers 10

Miles 10

13

Carson Pass
Scenic Byway

JACKSON TO WOODFORDS

GENERAL DESCRIPTION: A 75-mile highway that climbs over 8,573-foot Carson Pass in the central Sierra Nevada.

SPECIAL ATTRACTIONS: Carson Pass, Emigrant Trail, Hope Valley, Silver Lake, Caples Lake, Mokelumne Wilderness Area, Indian Grinding Rocks State Historic Park.

LOCATION: East-central California almost to the Nevada border.

DRIVE ROUTE NUMBER: California Highway 88.

TRAVEL SEASON: Year-round. The road's upper elevations receive heavy winter snowfall; be prepared for adverse conditions by

checking weather reports and carrying chains and survival equipment. The road may be closed or chains may be required in winter.

CAMPING: Many Eldorado and Toiyabe National Forest campgrounds are on or just off the drive.

SERVICES: All services at Jackson and several resort areas.

NEARBY ATTRACTIONS: Grover Hot Springs State Park, Lake Tahoe, Yosemite National Park, Mono Lake, Ebbetts Pass, Sonora Pass, Desolation Wilderness Area, Donner Summit, Tahoe ski areas, Placerville, Calaveras Big Trees State Park.

THE DRIVE

This 75-mile-long drive ascends the gentle western slope of the Sierra Nevada from Jackson, crosses 8,573-foot Carson Pass on the range crest, and drops steeply through Hope Valley and Carson Canyon to Woodfords near the Nevada border. The drive traverses diverse terrain, including oak-shrouded foothills, dense forests, rocky peaks, and a deep canyon. Marvelous views unfold along the highway, particularly in the upper elevations. The two-lane, paved highway also offers interesting historical sites from a Native American grinding area and gold rush towns to the path of John C. Fremont's ill-fated 1844 expedition and the Emigrant Trail over Carson Pass.

Expect a variety of climates along the drive. As the road ascends to higher elevations, the temperature cools and precipitation increases. Summer offers the mildest weather. Expect hot temperatures above ninety degrees in the western foothills. Above 5,000 feet, temperatures are more moderate with warm days and cool nights. Occasional severe thunderstorms occur on summer afternoons.

101

Autumns are delightful, with warm Indian summer days and cloudless skies. Winter is generally frigid in the high elevations, with heavy snowfall and below-freezing temperatures. Be prepared for adverse conditions by carrying tire chains and adequate clothing.

JACKSON TO INDIAN GRINDING ROCKS

The scenic drive, following CA 88, begins in the historic town of Jackson at the highway junction with CA 49. Jackson is an old gold rush town that was originally named Bottileas, a misspelling of the Spanish *botellas* or bottles, by Chilean miners who noted many bottles left around a nearby spring. The town was later renamed for Indian fighter Col. Alden Jackson. Much of Jackson's wealth came from the hard-rock Kennedy and Argonaut Mines, both famed gold producers. The Kennedy Mine operated from 1850 to 1942 and boasted a straight-down shaft of 4,600 feet, more than 150 miles of tunnels, and a yield of more than thirty-two million dollars in gold. The Argonaut Mine, west of town, was the site of one of California's worst mine disasters. Forty-seven men died from poisonous gas during a 1922 fire. The Amador County Museum, in an 1850s brick house, details Jackson's colorful history and explains local gold-mining operations. Jackson, with its historic buildings, narrow streets, and wooden sidewalks, is a perfect place to explore on foot. The chamber of commerce offers a walking tour map.

The highway runs northeast from Jackson up Jackson Creek past undulating foothills covered with grass and open oak woodlands. After 9 miles the road climbs onto a ridge at the small hamlet of Pine Grove. A side trip on Pine Grove–Volcano Road leads a few miles north to a couple of interesting sites—Volcano and Indian Grinding Rocks State Historic Park.

The sleepy village of **Volcano** is worth visiting today because it was once one of the gold rush country's richest towns. Volcano sits in a cup-shaped crater rimmed by forested hills mistaken for a volcanic crater. In 1848 Gen. John Sutter mined on Sutlers Creek here. The following year Col. J. D. Stevenson's New York Volunteer Regiment found rich gold deposits in Soldier's Gulch and a town of 5,000 instantly arose. By 1850 Volcano was a leading California city, producing millions of dollars in gold annually. The town also became a cultural haven, with the state's first public library, first astronomical observatory with a 3-inch refractor telescope on nearby Observatory Hill, and first literary and debating society. It also boasted seventeen hotels, three breweries, four bakeries, thirty-five saloons, two temperance societies, and a Chinatown.

Indian Grinding Rocks State Historic Park lies on the road to Volcano 1.5 miles north of Pine Grove and the highway. The park preserves a grassy meadow broken by flat outcrops of limestone and groves of oaks. The bedrock is covered with 1,185 *chaw'ses* or mortar cups, shallow holes used by Miwok women to grind acorns and seeds into flour. This grinding site is California's largest. The acorns, ground with stone pestles, yielded a palatable meal that was eaten as mush or baked as small cakes

The Mokelumne Wilderness Area lies south of the Carson Pass Scenic Byway.

on hot rocks. Petroglyphs (stone carvings) cover the main grinding rock. A reconstructed Miwok village with a roundhouse, bark tepees, and ball field helps visitors understand and experience village life. The **Chaw'se Regional Indian Museum** displays Miwok and other local Native American artifacts. The park has two short hiking trails and a twenty-one-site campground.

INTO ELDORADO NATIONAL FOREST

The drive follows rounded ridgelines coated with dense forest northeastward, slowly climbing up the gentle western slope of the Sierra fault block. The roadside forest changes as the road gains elevation from oak woodlands to mixed conifer forests filled with towering ponderosa and sugar pines, Douglas and white fir, and incense cedar. Azalea and California dogwood add colorful blossoms to the forest in springtime. By 32 miles, the road is at 6,000 feet and enters Eldorado National Forest, a 586,000-acre mountain playground that spreads north from the North Fork of the Mokelumne River to Lake Tahoe. The forest includes little-used, 50,400-acre Mokelumne Wilderness Area and 63,469-acre Desolation Wilderness Area west of Lake Tahoe, the nation's most visited wilderness.

Lumberyard Campground, with five sites, sits at the turn to Salt Springs Reservoir, a popular recreation site on the Mokelumne River. A 19-mile paved road leads to the lake. Three campgrounds—eight-site Mokelumne River, eight-site Moore Creek, and six-site White Azalea—are found along the road on the river's North

Fork below the dam. Two miles farther up the highway is the turn to Bear River Reservoir, a long lake surrounded by forest that lies in the broad valley south of the road. South Shore Campground, with twenty-two campsites, sits on the lakeshore. The lake offers good fishing as well as waterskiing and swimming before the water level drops in late summer and fall.

Past the reservoir turn, the drive edges across Peddler Hill on a high ridge that separates the Mokelumne and American Rivers. An overlook here gives one of the road's best vistas. The Sierra crest spreads across the eastern skyline with high peaks poking above glistening snowfields. Granite domes and crags break the dense green forest that spreads southward into the Mokelumne River drainage.

ALONG THE MORMON EMIGRANT TRAIL

Almost 7 miles later, the highway joins the Mormon Emigrant Trail. This was the first wagon road to traverse the lofty Sierras. The original trail ran up the divide between the American and Consumnes Rivers from Placerville and climbed over Carson Pass, sometimes called Mormon Pass. Men in the Mormon Battalion—soldiers organized by Brigham Young to fight in the Mexican War—axed the road out of the thick forest on their way home to Utah in 1848. Much of the early gold rush traffic followed this route in 1849 and the early 1850s. It became a toll road in the 1860s and is roughly paralleled today by CA 88. In the late 1850s much of the road's business was usurped by the Placerville Road over Echo Summit to the north.

After the road junction, the highway enters the high Sierra country. An uplifted block of granite some 350 miles long and 50 miles wide forms the Sierra bedrock. Above that lie dark volcanic deposits of mud and ash left by violent eruptions twenty million years ago. The deep volcanic deposits sit atop the range crest above Carson Pass and CA 88. Glaciation did the final sculpting of the range, gouging deep U-shaped valleys, sharpening peaks and arêtes, and leaving crystal lakes nestled behind moraines left by melting glaciers. The Sierra's geology is visible from a couple of good overlooks—Shot Rock Vista and Devil's Garden Vista Point—beyond the intersection with the Mormon Emigrant Trail.

Tragedy Spring is a little more than a mile past Devil's Garden Vista. This lovely spot hides a sad history. In 1848, as the Mormon Battalion hacked their way up the western slope of Carson Pass, an advance party of three men was sent ahead to scout the trail. On July 18 party member Henry William Bigler told of a gruesome discovery: "As we were returning to camp we found the place where we supposed our three pioneers had camped by a large spring. Near where they had their fire, was the appearance of a fresh grave. Some of us thought it might be an Indian grave . . . but the more we looked at it, the more we felt there lay our three men. Determining to satisfy ourselves, it was soon opened. We were shocked at the sight. There lay the three murdered men robbed of every stitch of clothing, lying promiscuously in one hole about two feet deep . . . We called this place Tragedy Spring." The massacre was blamed on Indians, but further investigations revealed the perpetrators were probably white men seeking gold. A three-site picnic area sits among the firs and pines near the spring.

SILVER LAKE TO CARSON PASS

The highway drops from Tragedy Spring to Silver Lake Recreation Area, a popular boating, fishing, and camping spot in a broad valley above the Silver Fork of the American River. Silver Lake East with sixty-two campsites and Silver Lake West with thirty-five campsites lie on the lake's northern edge. Plasse's Resort is a private campground operated here since 1853; several other resorts nearby offer additional accommodation choices. A subalpine forest of lodgepole pine, Jeffrey pine, mountain hemlock, and California juniper spreads a green mantle over surrounding mountain ridges.

The drive swings north and then east above Caples Creek and climbs into an alpine valley. In spring and summer, this serene valley's meadows are clad with wildflowers. The area's forests of pine and aspen and the snowy peaks of the high Sierras offer popular getaways. The lake, one of the largest in the central Sierras, bustles with activity. Fishing here is superb for rainbow, cutthroat, and brook trout, as well as trophy-size mackinaw and brown trout. Boaters, swimmers, and windsurfers enjoy the mountain water. Kirkwood Campground at tiny Kirkwood Lake offers twelve campsites, while nearby Caples Lake Campground has thirty-five sites and a boat ramp. A few miles south of the lake are Kirkwood Mountain Resort and Kirkwood Cross Country Center, with 80 kilometers of groomed track.

The highway runs along the north shore of Caples Lake and then begins its final ascent to Carson Pass up Woods Creek. A turn leads to Woods Lake and a twenty-five-site forest campground. The **Pacific Crest National Scenic Trail** passes the lake, crosses the highway, and runs north toward Echo Summit. It offers excellent day hikes and backpacking trips to a number of alpine lakes like Round Top, Winnemucca, and Upper Blue, as well as into the popular northern section of the Mokelumne Wilderness Area.

The summit of 8,573-foot **Carson Pass** lies almost 2 miles east of the turn to Woods Lake. A monument atop the pass honors famed scout Kit Carson, who, with celebrated pathfinder and gold and land speculator John C. Fremont, blazed a trail over this pass in February 1844. Fremont, an officer in the army's Topographical Engineers, was charged with exploring possible rail and overland routes to California. His detailed geographic information was later used in the conquest of California. Fremont's party had floundered through deep snow up the East Carson River and then encountered even deeper drifts over the pass. Scanty food and frigid temperatures forced the men to eat their mules and pet dog Tlamath. Fremont and Charles Preuss, the expedition cartographer, climbed Red Lake Peak north of the pass and became the first Anglo-Americans to see Lake Tahoe. That same day Kit Carson carved the only words he could spell—his name—into a tree trunk atop the pass named after him. A replica of his engraving is on the pass summit today.

Another monument atop the pass honors Snowshoe Thompson, a skiing mailman who carried mail over the Sierra in the 1850s and 1860s. A national forest information station is maintained on the pass during the summer.

From Carson Pass the drive drops down the abrupt east face of the Sierra escarpment on a steep 8 percent grade, swinging north around Red Lake nestled in a valley below. **Red Lake Vista Point** provides great views of the lake, 10,061-foot Red Lake Peak to the north, and 9,635-foot Elephant's Back to the south. The route of the old Mormon Emigrant Trail is visible on the steep slopes above the lake. This abrupt section, called Devil's Ladder, was the final steep pull to the Sierra crest for California-bound forty-niners. Ropes and chains, along with triple-teamed oxen and mules, pulled the pioneers' wagons up the rocky trail. A careful examination of rocks and trees along the pitch reveal marks left by their efforts.

HOPE VALLEY TO WOODFORDS

The highway quickly loses elevation and enters Hope Valley, a broad, grassy valley carved by the meandering West Fork of the Carson River. This 7,000-foot-high valley, one of the prettiest in all the Sierras, was named by the Mormon road builders. Emigrant chronicler Bigler wrote, ". . . camped at the head of what we called Hope Valley, as we began to have hope." The handsome valley, edged by lodgepole pine and aspen forest, blazes with wildflower colors in summer. On the valley's east end, the drive merges with California Highway 89, which runs north over Luther Pass to Lake Tahoe. Just east of the road junction are twelve-site Kit Carson and thirteen-site Snowshoe Springs Campgrounds in Humboldt-Toiyabe National Forest.

The river and the highway make a mad dash down steep Carson Canyon east of Hope Valley. The river through here offers Class II and III runs in May and June. The rocky canyon slopes are studded with granite crags and sharp boulders. As the highway drops, the climate dries and the plant communities change from the Sierran forest to the scrubby Great Basin flora. A forest fire decimated the lower canyon's slopes in 1987, but the area was reforested in 1988. Near the canyon's east mouth, the drive passes twenty-site Crystal Springs Campground, a pleasant overnight spot along the river sheltered by sugar and Jeffrey pines.

Woodfords, the end of the scenic drive, sits at the yawning canyon mouth. Steep, rock-ribbed slopes tower above and the broad Diamond Valley stretches northwest into Nevada. Woodfords, a stop on the old Emigrant Trail, was named for Daniel Woodford, who opened the Sign of the Elephant Hotel here in 1849. A small monument commemorates the town's Pony Express Trail station. Limited services are available. CA 89 turns south at Woodfords and goes to Markleeville and over Monitor Pass. CA 88 continues northeast across gravel benches above the Carson River, past hayfields and paddocks filled with grazing cattle, before turning north and entering Nevada and the wide Carson Valley.

Sonora Pass Scenic Drive

SONORA TO US 395

GENERAL DESCRIPTION: An 80-mile-long paved highway between Sonora and U.S. Highway 395 that climbs the gradual western slope of the Sierra Nevada to the summit of 9,624-foot Sonora Pass.

SPECIAL ATTRACTIONS: Sonora Pass, Stanislaus National Forest, Humboldt-Toiyabe National Forest, Columns of the Giants, Donnell Vista, Strawberry, Emigrant Wilderness Area, Carson-Iceberg Wilderness Area, Sonora, hiking, fishing, winter sports.

LOCATION: East-central California, from Sonora to near the Nevada border.

DRIVE ROUTE NUMBER: California Highway 108.

TRAVEL SEASON: The highway past

Pinecrest closes in winter, generally from November to early May. Call the forest service office for information on road closure.

CAMPING: Hundreds of campsites in national forest campgrounds are found on or just off the highway.

SERVICES: All services at Sonora and Bridgeport; limited services at Pinecrest and Strawberry.

NEARBY ATTRACTIONS: Ebbetts Pass, Carson Pass Scenic Byway, Yosemite National Park, Moaning Caves, Columbia State Historic Park, Railtown 1897 State Historic Park, Calaveras Big Trees State Park, Hoover Wilderness Area, Mono Lake.

THE DRIVE

The 80-mile-long Sonora Pass scenic drive twists up forested ridges on the gentle western slope of California's mountain backbone, the Sierra Nevada, to the airy summit of Sonora Pass, one of the highest automobile roads in the state. The drive follows paved CA 108 and offers a wealth of scenic vistas and recreational opportunities. The road's upper reaches from Kennedy Meadows on the west to Leavitt Meadow on the east are unsuitable for large RVs and trailers. The winding road has no shoulder, narrow lanes, and grades as steep as 15 percent.

The drive, like other Sierra routes, boasts a wide variety of climates. The elevation difference between 1,826-foot-high Sonora and 9,624-foot Sonora Pass is almost 8,000 feet. The area experiences relatively dry summers and wet, snowy winters. Summers in the foothills around Sonora are hot and dry, with temperatures often above ninety degrees. As the highway climbs, temperatures decrease and pre-

cipitation increases. Summer days along the drive's upper elevations are usually between sixty and seventy degrees with occasional afternoon thunderstorms. Winters can be severe, closing the highway beyond Pinecrest. As much as 30 feet of snow fall in the high valleys along the range crest. Deep snowdrifts remain well into the summer in sheltered ravines along the highway edge.

SONORA AND COLUMBIA

The drive begins in downtown Sonora at the intersection of California Highway 49 and CA 108. Head south and then east on CA 108 via Washington Street (town's main street) and then Mono Way. Sonora is a picturesque mining town that was originally built on seven rounded hills in 1848 by miners from the state of Sonora in northern Mexico. A year later the town boasted a population of more than 5,000, but in 1850 the town government slapped a twenty dollar tax on all foreign-born miners. Almost overnight the town's population dropped to 2,000. In 1851 the tax was repealed and Sonora again began to prosper. Millions of dollars worth of gold was extracted from the ore-rich gravels under Sonora and Columbia to the north. One of the richest lodes was Big Bonanza, discovered by Chilean miners in 1851. Besides its impressive old buildings, Sonora's Tuolumne County Museum, in an old jailhouse, displays the area's colorful history.

Columbia was Sonora's main rival in the 1850s and lies just to the north. Once nicknamed "Gem of the Southern Mines," it is perhaps the best-preserved gold-country town in California. The entire downtown district is preserved in Columbia State Historic Park. The town lost the state capital to Sacramento by just two votes in 1854. Columbia is a good place to investigate history. Through its buildings and artifacts, the roaring 1850s come alive.

SONORA TO STRAWBERRY

The highway heads northeast from Sonora and immediately begins climbing high ridges covered with oak groves and grass, and then a thick, mixed Sierra forest. By 6 miles, the four-lane road is at 3,000 feet and a couple of miles later passes the turn to Twain Harte, a small suburban town named in the 1920s for the gold country's two most famous writers—Mark Twain and Bret Harte. Past Twain Harte, the highway drops back to two lanes and reaches Mi-Wok Ranger Station on the edge of Stanislaus National Forest.

The ranger station is a good place to get camping and visitor information. The forest stretches across 1,090,039 acres between the Merced and Mokelumne Rivers on the western slope of the Sierra Nevada. The Stanislaus River and the forest are named for Estanisalo, a Miwok leader who resisted Spanish efforts to capture and colonize the Indians. The river's name was anglicized to its present spelling. Its three forks drain most of the land in the Stanislaus forest.

The road continues climbing along ridgelines, with occasional views through breaks in the thick forest. After 26 miles the drive reaches Summit Ranger Station and the turnoff to Pinecrest Lake, a popular boating, fishing, and swimming reservoir on the South Fork of the Stanislaus River. Two large national forest campgrounds, Pinecrest (200 sites) and Meadowview (100 sites), sit on the lake's south shore. The Shadow of the Me-Wuk Trail begins at Summit Ranger Station. The quarter-mile walk offers interpretations of Miwok life and traditions. The easy Pinecrest Lake National Recreation Trail encircles the lake, offering good views of the lake nestled in its shallow granite basin. A thick forest of ponderosa pine and red fir lines the trail along the south shore. The forest service offers a variety of interpretative walks, tours, and campfire programs in summer. Dodge Ridge Ski Resort, with beginner to advanced downhill skiing, sits on the hills east of the lake.

From the ranger station, the highway drops down to Strawberry, crosses the South Fork of the Stanislaus River, and winds northeast onto high forested ridges. The drive passes twelve-site Cascade Creek Campground, 9 miles from Strawberry. Three miles farther lies primitive nineteen-site Mill Creek Campground. Acorn grinding holes left by summering Miwok are found on flat boulders alongside the creek. Small, ten-site Niagara Creek Campground sits 2 miles up the road in a stand of tall Jeffrey pines. Nearby is the half-mile-long **Trail of the Ancient Dwarfs.** This excellent path explores a dwarf tree grove stunted by poor soil. A 10-mile dirt road, Forest Road 5N01, threads up Niagara Creek and across Eagle Creek to the gnarled Bennett juniper, the largest-known western juniper. The tree, named for naturalist Clarence Bennett, stands 80 feet tall and is thought to be over 3,000 years old.

DONNELL VISTA TO KENNEDY MEADOWS

Donnell Vista, one of the road's best viewpoints, is just past the campground. A short trail drops down from the parking lot through granite bedrock to the lofty 6,400-foot viewpoint. Donnell Lake is a long reservoir along the Middle Fork of the Stanislaus River that tucks into the steep canyon far below. Rock buttresses and cliffs soar above the glassy water. The reservoir was built for electricity generation and irrigation diversion. There is no public access or recreational development. The Dardenelles, named by the Whitney Survey party after the strait in Turkey, lift their craggy volcanic summits above the river to the north. These flat-topped buttes were formed when 1,000-foot-thick lava flows spread across the land over nine million years ago. This 8,875-foot mountain stands above the forested 77,993-acre Carson-Iceberg Wilderness Area.

The road drops away from Donnell Vista, skirting the north flank of Double Dome Rock, and reaches the Middle Fork of the Stanislaus River after 4 miles. A side road heads north up the river's Clark Fork, allowing access to the Carson-Iceberg Wilderness, the Dardenelles, excellent trout fishing, and several placid campgrounds.

For the next 10 miles, the highway parallels the Stanislaus River as it tumbles over worn boulders in the bottom of a deep, glaciated valley. Seven campgrounds—Boulder Flat, Brightman Flat, Dardanelle, Pigeon Flat, Eureka Valley, Baker, and

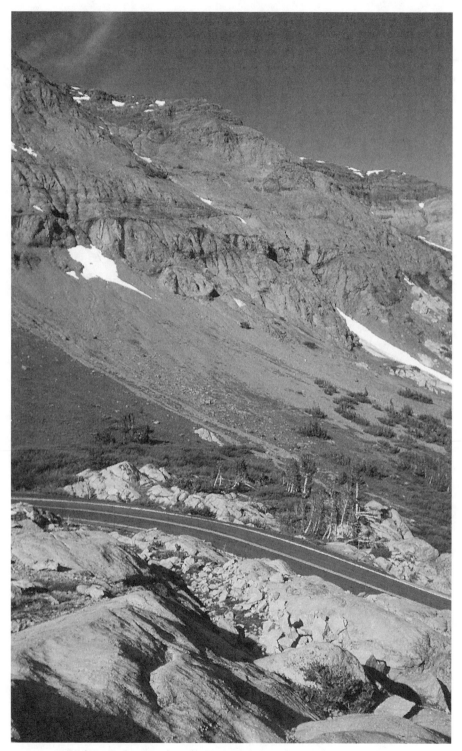

Nightcap Peak towers above the Sonora Pass scenic drive in the Sierra Nevada.

Deadman, which range in size from seven sites to forty-four, scatter along the river-banks. The campgrounds, deservedly popular for their magnificent scenery and great fishing, usually fill up early in the day.

Some good stops lie along this scenic road stretch. The world's largest Jeffrey pine sits at the end of a mile-long hike that begins at Brightman Flat. At Dardanelle are a store, gas, lodging, and RV park. A sign claims the town's population is two. The **Columns of the Giants** geologic site, reached by a quarter-mile trail from Pigeon Flat Campground, is a miniature replica of famed Devils Postpile. Fluted basalt columns, deposited by ancient lava flows, tower above the river's south bank. Eureka Flat was the site of an early stage stop on the old Sonora–Mono Toll Road. A roadside marker tells of Dave Hays' log roadhouse. A few posts, fallen logs, and foundation pieces are all that remain.

Kennedy Meadows spreads across the far eastern end of the canyon. Steep forested slopes climb away from the river, broken by granite crags. A side road passes Baker and Deadman Campgrounds and ends at the northern trailhead for the 112,277-acre Emigrant Wilderness Area. The popular trail wends south across the grassy meadows toward Relief Reservoir and the wilderness backcountry. Soaring Sierra Mountains—Leavitt Peak, Relief Peak, and Granite Dome—lift their snowy ridges high above the trail. A rustic resort lures visitors to Kennedy Meadows to enjoy horseback riding and fishing.

OVER SONORA PASS

The drive effectively ends at Kennedy Meadows for large RVs or vehicles pulling trailers. Beyond the meadows, the highway climbs steeply away from the river valley, winding shelflike across boulder-strewn slopes. For the next 20 miles, the road twists, turns, switchbacks, and ascends grades as steep as 15 percent. The road climbs more than 3,000 feet in 10 miles from Kennedy Meadows to the crest of Sonora Pass. A shoulder is lacking most of the way. Drive carefully, stay in your lane, and pull off to enjoy the scenery.

As the road climbs, it bends east into Deadman Canyon. A couple of viewpoints, Que de Porka and East Flange, offer majestic views south into the Emigrant Wilderness. The original pioneer road is visible below the second overlook. Past East Flange the highway climbs into Deadman Canyon. This deep U-shaped valley was excavated by ancient glaciers. It is now thinly forested with cedars, white fir, and streamside willows. A spectacular waterfall slices through granite bedrock just past Chipmunk Flat. A small primitive campground is located here. South of the road, granite arêtes and buttresses, separated by steep snow couloirs, sweep up to the 10,641-foot summit of Night Cap Peak. North of the drive, glacier-polished slabs, broken by vertical cracks, are popular with rock climbers.

The drive follows Deadman Creek to the pass summit, paralleling the old Sonora–Mono Toll Road. When gold was discovered near Mono Lake in 1860, a road was needed to haul supplies and equipment from the bustling Sonora area to the new mines. The wagon road was completed in 1865. A round-trip from Sonora to Bridgeport by six-mule team took up to three weeks. The same year the road was completed, Deadman Creek received its morbid name. In early spring a man attempted to cross the snowbound Sierras on snowshoes. Trapped by a storm, he froze to death just west of the summit. The owners of Douglas Station found his rigid corpse the next day and named the valley. Traces of the old road can be seen past Chipmunk Flat.

After a couple more miles, the drive climbs out of the granite gorge and enters a gentle, shallow valley surrounded by peaks. Two miles later the highway crests the summit of 9,624-foot **Sonora Pass,** the second-highest road crossing of the Sierras. A small picnic area lies among stunted pines on the ridge. A panorama of peaks and valleys surrounds the pass. Northward looms broad 11,459-foot Sonora Peak; to the south towers 11,570-foot Leavitt Peak. The Pacific Crest Trail, accessed by a trailhead on Sonora Pass, closely follows the range crest here.

Sonora Pass is one of the oldest trans-Sierra emigrant trails. The Bartleson-Bidwell party, the first pioneers to follow an overland route to California, crossed the pass on October 18, 1841. The pass was not attempted by wagons again until 1852. Grizzly Adams traversed it in April of 1854 and noted, "On all sides lay old axle trees and wheels . . . melancholy evidence of the last season's disasters."

DOWN THE WEST WALKER RIVER

From the pass summit, the highway plunges down a 15 percent grade for 1 mile. The road loses 2,500 feet in the next 7 miles in a series of steep grades, curves, and switchbacks. Great views unfold from the drive southward to the rugged heart of the Emigrant Wilderness. As the road drops, the flora changes from the high Sierra fir forest to the pine forest and sagebrush typical of the upper Great Basin Desert.

The road eventually reaches broad, grassy 7,200-foot-high Leavitt Meadow. The West Walker River uncoils across the wide valley. Leavitt Meadow Campground, with sixteen sites, sits on the riverbank among boulders and pines. A side road leads south to a trailhead. The trail goes south from here, following the historic Emigrant Trail up the river, past a string of high mountain lakes that offer excellent trout fishing.

Running northeast above the river, the highway continues losing elevation and drops into sagebrush-covered Picket Meadow, the site of the U.S. Marine Corps Mountain Warfare Training Center. The road swings around 8,084-foot Pickel Mountain, enters the Walker River Canyon, and passes Sonora Bridge Campground. Three miles later, in grassy meadows and beaver ponds, the drive dead-ends at US 395. A right turn leads to Bridgeport and a left heads north to Nevada and Carson City.

To Bishop

Mono Lake

395

To CA 49

Lee Vining

Lee Vining Canyon

Mono Dome
10,613 ft.

△ **Lee Vining Campground**

120

INYO NATIONAL FOREST

Saddlebag Lake

△ **Saddlebag Lake Campground**

△ **Ellery Lake Campground**

Mount Dana
13,053 ft.

Mount Gibbs
12,764 ft.

Donohue Peak
12,024 ft.

N

△ **Tioga Lake Campground**

INYO NATIONAL FOREST

△ **Tioga Junction Campground**

Tioga Pass
9,945 ft.

Dana Fork

Dana Meadows

Lyell Fork

Pacific Crest Trail

Mammoth Peak
12,116 ft.

Mount Conness
12,630 ft.

Lambert Dome

TUOLUMNE MEADOWS

Johnson Peak
11,069 ft.

CATHEDRAL RANGE

△ **Tuolumne Campground**

Pacific Crest Trail

River

Fairview Dome

Cathedral Peak
10,940 ft.

Tenaya Peak
10,302 ft.

YOSEMITE NATIONAL PARK

Polly Dome

Tenaya Lake

□ **Olmsted Point**

May Lake

Mount Hoffman
10,850 ft.

Clouds Rest
9,926 ft.

Mount Watkins

△ **Porcupine Flat Campground**

△ **Yosemite Creek Campground**

Yosemite Village

YOSEMITE VALLEY

Tuolumne

△ **White Wolf Campground**

120

Gin Flat

Tamarack Flat

Big Oak Flat Road

STANISLAUS NATIONAL FOREST

Hetch Hetchy Reservoir

YOSEMITE NATIONAL PARK

Crane Flat

CALIFORNIA

Kilometers 5

Miles 5

0

0

Tioga Pass Scenic Drive

BIG OAK FLAT ROAD TO LEE VINING

GENERAL DESCRIPTION: A 55-mile drive that traverses spectacular mountains, domes, meadows, and forests between Big Oak Flat Road west of Yosemite Valley and Lee Vining at the eastern base of the Sierra Nevada.

SPECIAL ATTRACTIONS: Tioga Pass, Ellery Lake, Tioga Lake, Yosemite National Park, Tuolumne Meadows, Tenaya Lake, Olmsted Point, sequoia grove, hiking, fishing, rock climbing.

LOCATION: East-central California.

DRIVE ROUTE NUMBER AND NAME: California Highway 120 (Tioga Pass Road).

TRAVEL SEASON: May or June through October. The highway usually opens sometime in late May and is closed after the first severe snowstorm around November 1. Check with Yosemite National Park or Inyo National Forest for information on road closure.

CAMPING: Yosemite has four campgrounds along the drive (some need reservations). Four forest campgrounds are on the east side of Tioga Pass; two lie north at Saddlebag Lake; nearby is Lower Vining Campground.

SERVICES: All services in Lee Vining; limited services in Tuolumne Meadows.

NEARBY ATTRACTIONS: Yosemite National Park scenic drive, Mono Lake, Ansel Adams Wilderness Area, Hoover Wilderness Area, Devil's Postpile National Monument.

THE DRIVE

This 55-mile-long scenic drive twists across the southern Sierra Nevada mountains in Yosemite National Park and Inyo National Forest. The highway climbs through steep canyons, crosses grassy Tuolumne Meadows, passes under soaring granite domes etched by glaciers, offers one of California's best views at Olmsted Point, and drops through a thick forest to Yosemite Valley. The drive's last 12 miles follow the U. S. Forest Service's Lee Vining Canyon Scenic Byway.

The Sierra Nevada, called "the range of light" by pioneer naturalist John Muir, forms California's backbone. This immense sawtooth escarpment stretches 430 miles from Bakersfield to Lassen Peak. It is a range of awesome beauty that includes three national parks, eight national forests, and eleven 14,000-foot peaks. The Sierra Nevada, a fault-block range, is a tilted and uplifted block of granite with a steep east face and a gentle western slope. Giant glaciers a mile thick gouged out the mountains, excavating deep valleys and carving sharp peaks as recently as 12,000 years ago. Small glaciers still nestle in north-facing cirques, echoes of the great Ice Age glaciers.

Temperatures along the drive vary greatly from the sagebrush desert at Lee Vining to the summit of Tioga Pass, a 3,200-foot elevation difference. Summer daytime temperatures reach into the nineties in the lower elevations, while temperatures in the subalpine zone at Tuolumne Meadows seldom climb above eighty degrees. Nights are cooler, sometimes dropping into the thirties. Afternoon thunderstorms occur in July and August, while snow can line the road in any month. Fall is chilly in the upper elevations, while the climate is more moderate around Lee Vining and the drive's west end. The highway closes after the first heavy snowfall, which occurs anytime from mid-October to early December. The road seldom opens before mid-May.

BIG OAK FLAT ROAD

The Tioga Pass Road follows CA 120. It turns north at Crane Flat off the Big Oak Flat Road between Big Oak Flat Entrance Station and Yosemite Valley in western Yosemite National Park. Big Oak Flat Road, which drops west into the Central Valley, was completed in 1874; it was the second road built into Yosemite Valley. Just past its intersection with the Tioga Pass Road is a junction with the Old Big Oak Flat Road, a steep, one-way road that runs west to the entrance station. A short drive down this one-way spur road leads to the **Tuolumne Grove,** one of Yosemite's three groves of giant sequoia trees. Return to Tioga Pass Road via Big Oak Flat Road. A self-guided nature trail loops through the grove. Hikers should stay on the trail to protect fragile sequoia roots.

Historians believe this grove of twenty-five sequoia or the nearby Merced Grove was the first stand of big trees discovered by Anglo-Americans. In 1833 a party of trappers led by Joseph Walker crossed the Sierra crest somewhere north of Tioga Pass and followed this high forested ridge between the Merced and Tuolumne Rivers west to the San Joaquin Valley. En route they happened upon these forest giants. On October 30 trapper Zenas Leonard noted in his journal, ". . . we have found some trees of the Redwood species, incredibly large." *Sequoia gigantea* lives 3,000 years, weighs more than two million pounds, and is the world's largest living thing. The trees have thick cinnamon-colored bark and grow in isolated groves on the western slopes of the central and southern Sierra Nevada. A walk among these immense trees is a fitting start to one of California's best scenic drives.

CRANE FLAT TO MOUNT HOFFMAN

The highway threads east from the meadows at 6,200-foot Crane Flat, climbing along the high divide between the Merced and Tuolumne Rivers. A dense forest of mixed conifer—incense cedar (not a true cedar), ponderosa pine, and sugar pine—hems in the road. After a few miles the drive runs northeast and climbs up along the South Fork of the Tuolumne River. As the road ascends, the forest changes and

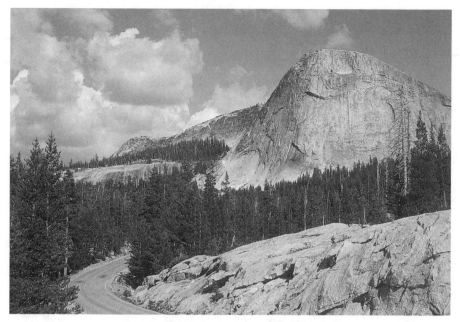

Fairview Dome looms over the Tioga Pass Road.

becomes an almost pure stand of California red fir. This handsome tree, growing to heights of 120 feet, thrives at an elevation of 6,000 to 9,000 feet along the Sierra's west slope, with its dry summers and heavy snows. Here, as in most Sierra stands, lodgepole pine mingles with the red fir. Lodgepole pine is perhaps the most ubiquitous tree of the Yosemite highlands. It grows straight in thick stands as well as twisted and bent over at timberline.

After 13 miles the road passes Siesta Lake, a lake that formed when a terminal moraine at the end of a small glacier south of the lake blocked the stream's course. **White Wolf,** supposedly named for an Indian chief, lies a mile north of the highway on the Old Tioga Road. The original road was built by Chinese laborers in 1883 by the Great Sierra Consolidated Silver Company to haul ore from the old Tioga Mine on the east side of the pass. Facilities here include eighty-seven-site White Wolf Campground (first-come, first-served), dining, lodging in tent cabins, and stables. A popular hike goes north to Harden Lake.

Past White Wolf the drive swings into the Yosemite Creek drainage and the white granite characteristic of the high Sierra peaks. Yosemite Creek, fed by melting snow on Mount Hoffman and Tuolumne Peak, tumbles southward over boulders and glacier-polished slabs before dropping 2,425 feet into Yosemite Valley as three-tiered Yosemite Falls (North America's highest waterfall). A 5-mile spur road, not suitable for trailers and large vehicles, drops down to pleasant seventy-five-site Yosemite Creek Campground. A 6-mile-long trail follows the creek down to the waterfall and switchbacks another 3.6 miles to the valley floor.

The drive turns south above Yosemite Creek and bends east around the forested shoulder of 10,850-foot Mount Hoffman, a rocky peak at the geographic center of Yosemite National Park. Past fifty-two-site Porcupine Flat Campground, the road enters the magical world of the upper Sierras. Views open around every corner; the Clark Range lifts its ragged crest to the southeast. Ancient granite, chiseled and smoothed by glaciers, dominates the roadside. Hardy western junipers nestle among the rock outcrops. These gnarled evergreens reach ages of 2,000 years and trunk diameters of 16 feet. John Muir described them as ". . . a sturdy storm-enduring mountaineer of a tree, living on sunshine and snow, maintaining tough health on this diet."

The North Dome Trail begins about a mile east of Porcupine Flat. This 3.7-mile path drops south from the road and climbs to the rounded summit of North Dome perched above Yosemite Valley. Farther east a spur road leads north toward May Lake, site of one of Yosemite's five High Sierra camps. A 1.2-mile trail heads up to this backcountry camp, which offers meals and rustic accommodations. Reservations are required. Mount Hoffman towers above May Lake to the west.

OLMSTED POINT AND TENAYA LAKE

Olmsted Point is the next stop that offers a superlative view. This overlook provides an unsurpassed panorama of the Sierra crest and the upper reaches of Yosemite Valley. The point is named for Frederick Law Olmsted, who chaired the Board of Commissioners that managed the Yosemite Grant as the world's first natural parkland. To the south above glacier-polished slabs towers 9,926-foot Clouds Rest, a rocky peak often wreathed in gray clouds. Beyond looms the rounded granite bulk of 8,842-foot Half Dome, one of Yosemite's most famous and beloved landmarks. Half Dome's sheer 2,000-foot-high northwest face was quarried by the thick Tenaya Branch of the Tuolumne Glacier, which spread from the Sierra crest into today's Yosemite Valley. A short walk south from the parking lot to a low dome yields a spectacular view down Tenaya Canyon to Half Dome.

Tenaya Lake nestles east of Olmsted Point in a broad trough surrounded by massive granite domes. This glorious alpine lake is named for Chief Tenaya of the Yosemite tribe. State militiamen captured Yosemites at the picturesque lake in June of 1851. A few years later John Muir wrote, "A fine monument the old man has in this bright lake, and likely to last a long time, though lakes die as well as Indians." The Indians called the lake "Pywiak" or shining rocks, a more fitting name. The highway wends down over granite benches to Tenaya Lake and skirts its northern shore. Picnic sites lie along the road. Trout fishing and boating (motors not permitted) are popular lake uses. A strenuous 7-mile hike begins at Tenaya Lake and scales Clouds Rest, offering lofty views of the Yosemite backcountry.

Superb rock climbs scale the gray granite domes surrounding Tenaya Lake. Most popular are Stately Pleasure Dome's gentle slabs north of the lake and Pywiak Dome just east of the lake. A roadside pull-off allows visitors to watch climbers edge their way up Pywiak Dome's classic Dike Route. The climbing here and at Tuolumne Meadows to the east is among the best in the United States, with steep, glacier-polished slabs, knobby bolt-protected faces, and long crack routes up Fairview Dome, Lembert Dome, Daff Dome, and others. The Yosemite Mountaineering School at Tuolumne Meadows provides daily lessons and guided climbs for novices.

The drive climbs away from Tenaya Lake through upper Tenaya Canyon, crossing a low divide into the Cathedral Creek drainage and running east past soaring granite domes. Geologists note that Tuolumne Meadows boasts the largest concentration of granite domes in the world. **Fairview Dome,** the largest, towers almost 2,000 feet south of the highway. Daff Dome, its letters standing for "Dome across from Fairview," squats north of the forest-lined drive. The domes formed when glacial ice buried and scoured the rock. Exfoliation of granite slabs gives the unique dome shape when surface rock peels off like thick onion layers. Also note the shiny glacial polish on domes where ice scraped the featureless rock surface smooth.

TUOLUMNE MEADOWS

The road threads through the domes, their roadside flanks coated in hemlocks and pines, and enters Tuolumne Meadows. They form the largest subalpine meadow in the Sierras, sprawling along the meandering course of the upper Tuolumne River at 8,600 feet. The Dana and Lyell Forks of the river arise from deep snows along the range crest and flow down through the Grand Canyon of the Tuolumne River into Hetch Hetchy Reservoir, where much of the river's water is diverted to the San Francisco area.

The drive runs across the meadows, which provide an open panorama of jagged peaks poking above snowbound cirques to the east. The pastoral meadows are one of Yosemite's best scenic features. The rolling grassland spreads eastward to the mountain wall, broken by forested humpbacked ridges and rounded rock domes. An immense 2,000-foot-thick glacier once divided in the meadows; one branch dropped into Yosemite Valley and the other down the Grand Canyon of the Tuolumne River. The last glacier melted away some 10,000 years ago, leaving a bog studded with shallow ponds. The meadows are covered with short grasses such as beaked sedges, Sierra ricegrass, tufted hairgrass, and shorthair reedgrass. Summer brings wildflowers that carpet the ground with blazes of color. The meadow's wetness halts an advancing forest of lodgepole pine along the flattened valley edges. The pines, preferring a drier mineral soil, are slowly encroaching on the meadows, particularly on the south edge where the highway blocks runoff.

John Muir described the meadows on his first visit in 1869 as "... the most spacious and delightful high pleasure-ground I have yet seen. The air is keen and bracing, yet warm during the day; and though lying high in the sky, the surrounding mountains are so much higher, one feels protected as if in a grand hall." Most visitors today agree with Muir's assessment. The meadows, besides being a place of great beauty, are a recreational playground.

A network of excellent trails fan out from the **Tuolumne Meadows Visitors Center.** The Pacific Crest Trail runs across the meadows from Lyell Canyon and down to the High Sierra camp of Glen Aulin. Other good paths include the trail to Elizabeth Lake and the John Muir Trail to Cathedral Lakes. Climbers, besides scaling the polished slabs of Lembert Dome north of the campground, ascend the sharp horn of 10,940-foot Cathedral Peak. An excellent 304-site campground (half reservations and half first-come, first-served) hides in a thick lodgepole pine forest. A small museum with interpretive exhibits, a grocery store, and a gas station complete the meadow's visitor services.

Past bulky Lembert Dome, the road ascends through glacial moraines—huge boulder piles left by retreating glaciers—above the Dana Fork of the Tuolumne River. Lembert Dome is a water-streaked granite crag named for 1885 homesteader Jean Baptiste Lembert. After a few more miles, the drive turns northeast into Dana Meadows, a broad swath of grassland broken by islands of granite and small tarns that mirror the rounded ridges of 13,053-foot Mount Dana and 12,764-foot Mount Gibbs. James Dana was a nineteenth-century Yale geologist and Wolcott Gibbs a Harvard chemist.

OVER TIOGA PASS

Eight miles from Tuolumne Meadows, the highway crosses 9,945-foot Tioga Pass, the highest highway pass in the Sierra Nevada. Yosemite National Park's east entrance station sits on the pass summit. A forest of whitebark pine stretches beyond the meadow edge atop the pass and climbs to timberline on surrounding peaks. Whitebark pine is a characteristic high-altitude tree in the Sierra. Timberline, the uppermost limit of the subalpine forest, occurs at about 10,500 feet in Yosemite. The high mountains along the range crest lie in the Arctic-Alpine life zone, a windswept, barren land of harsh winters, rock fields and talus slopes, dwarfed shrubs, and delicate tundra flowers—alpine sorrel, elephant's head, saxifrage, rock primrose, and alpine paintbrush.

A mile-long trail climbs north from the pass summit to Gaylor Lakes on the west flank of Gaylor Peak and the derelict site of the Tioga Mine. Another short, rough trail at the end of the old Tioga Pass Road begins on the east side of the pass and leads to the ghost town of Bennettville, former headquarters of the Great Sierra Consolidated Silver Company. The company tunneled into the mountain in search of the Sheepherder Lode, a supposedly wealthy silver vein. The old Tioga Pass Road reached the town in 1883 before the company and Bennettville closed down. Tioga, an Iroquois word meaning "where it forks," was probably attached by a pioneer from New York's Tioga County.

From the Tioga Pass summit, the highway begins dropping eastward. The drive's last 12 miles follow Lee Vining Canyon Scenic Byway, a designated U.S. Forest Service scenic drive. A couple of good fishing lakes, Tioga and Ellery, lie along the roadside. Three Inyo National Forest Campgrounds—Tioga Lake, Junction, and Ellery Lake—offer first-come, first-served sites. They fill up early in summer. A side trip heads up Forest Road 1N04 to two more campgrounds and Saddlebag Lake, a large reservoir on the southern edge of the Hoover Wilderness Area.

DOWN LEE VINING CANYON

Past Ellery Lake the road sweeps around 11,513-foot Tioga Peak and begins spiraling down steep grades on rocky talus slopes above abrupt Lee Vining Canyon. The road falls almost 4,000 feet in less than 6 miles on the eastern escarpment of the Sierras, from Tioga Pass to the sagebrush desert at Lee Vining. A huge glacier once spilled down this canyon, shoving its icy snout into an immense lake at the range base. The upper part of the canyon below the Tioga Pass summit is a hanging valley left by the glacier. Lateral moraines—rock ridges left by the retreating glacier—line the edges of the broad lower canyon.

Spectacular views spread out below the road as it descends. To the south loom the peaks and arêtes of 230,258-acre Ansel Adams Wilderness Area, and to the east stretch the snowcapped Inyo and White ranges, glassy Mono Lake, and the dark volcanic plug domes of Mono Craters. Lee Vining Creek, offering trout fishing, meanders across the cobbled canyon floor. Lower Lee Vining Campground has sixty-two sites. Seventeen-site Big Bend Campground sits just south of the drive. Forests of Jeffrey pine, sprinkled with intermittent aspen groves, blanket the hillsides above the creek.

An Inyo National Forest ranger station sits at the drive's eastern terminus, with national forest information, maps, and wilderness area permits. Beyond the station, the drive ends at US 395, the major north-south highway on the eastern slope of the Sierra Nevada. Lee Vining, a small town named for an 1852 prospector, is immediately north of the junction and has all traveler services.

Ancient **Mono Lake,** one of California's most unusual natural features, straddles the wide basin to the northeast. The million-year-old lake, surrounded by volcanic domes, lava flows, and sagebrush-covered benches, is the drying remnant of what was in glacial times a 900-foot-deep lake. The lake is known for the bizarre and exquisite tufa formations that scatter along its shoreline. Mono Lake is also alive with birds. About 85 percent of the California gull population nests here in spring, while more than 300 other bird species have been identified. But the lake has come under siege by water-hungry Los Angeles. Water is taken from Mono Lake's four feeder streams in the Sierra, leaving nothing to replenish water that disappears through evaporation. Since 1941, when water was first diverted from Mono Lake, the lake's level has dropped 45 feet or an average of 18 inches a year.

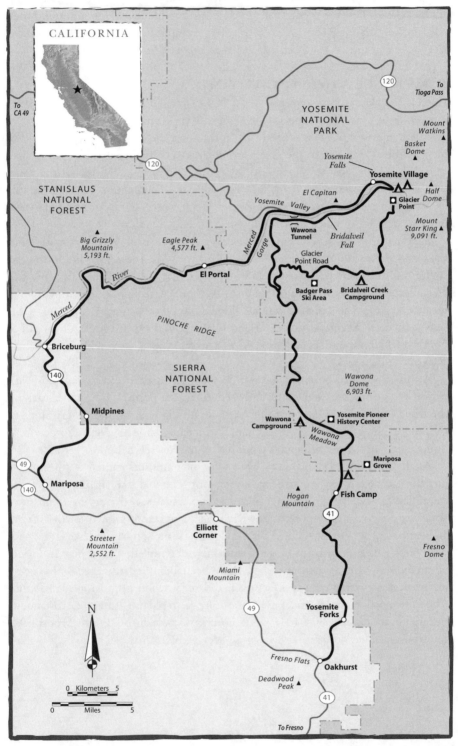

CALIFORNIA

To
CA 49

120

YOSEMITE
NATIONAL
PARK

To
Tioga Pass

Mount
Watkins ▲

Basket
Dome ▲

Yosemite
Falls

Yosemite Village

El Capitan

Half
Dome ▲

□ **Glacier
Point**

Yosemite Valley

El Capitan ▲

Mount
Starr King ▲
9,091 ft.

STANISLAUS
NATIONAL
FOREST

120

Big Grizzly
Mountain
5,193 ft. ▲

Eagle Peak
4,577 ft. ▲

Merced Gorge

**Wawona
Tunnel**

*Bridalveil
Fall*

Glacier
Point Road

River

El Portal ○

□ **Badger Pass
Ski Area**

△ **Bridalveil Creek
Campground**

Merced

PINOCHE RIDGE

Briceburg ○

140

SIERRA
NATIONAL
FOREST

*Wawona
Dome
6,903 ft.*
▲

Midpines ○

**Wawona
Campground** △

□ **Yosemite Pioneer
History Center**

*Wawona
Meadow*

49

Mariposa ○

140

□ **Mariposa
Grove**

△

*Streeter
Mountain
2,552 ft.* ▲

**Elliott
Corner** ○

*Hogan
Mountain* ▲

Fish Camp ○

41

*Fresno
Dome* ▲

*Miami
Mountain* ▲

49

**Yosemite
Forks**

N

Fresno Flats

Oakhurst ○

*Deadwood
Peak* ▲

0 Kilometers 5

0   Miles   5

41

To Fresno

Yosemite National Park Scenic Drive

OAKHURST TO MARIPOSA

GENERAL DESCRIPTION: Two California highways form this 105-mile-long scenic loop from Oakhurst to Mariposa. The drive crosses high ridges cloaked in mixed Sierra forests, traverses the incomparable Yosemite Valley, and drops down the abrupt Merced River Gorge.

SPECIAL ATTRACTIONS: Yosemite National Park, Yosemite Valley, Glacier Point Road, Glacier Point, Taft Point, Bridalveil Fall, Sentinel Rock, Half Dome, Yosemite Falls, El Capitan, Merced River, Mariposa Grove Big Trees, Pioneer Yosemite History Center, Wawona, Badger Pass Ski Area, Yosemite Mountain Sugar Pine Railroad, historic Mariposa, hiking, rock climbing.

LOCATION: East-central California. The drive lies on the western flank of the Sierra Nevada range east of Merced and the Central Valley.

DRIVE ROUTE NUMBERS AND NAMES: California Highway 41 (Wawona Road), California Highway 140 (Merced Road), Glacier Point Road.

TRAVEL SEASON: Year-round. Winter driving can be hazardous, especially on the Wawona Road; use snow tires or carry tire chains. The Glacier Point Road closes in winter.

CAMPING: Four campgrounds with 414 sites in Yosemite Valley; two are open year-round. Check the National Park Service's Yosemite Web site for details. Two park campgrounds are outside the valley; one is open year-round. Private campgrounds in the Oakhurst and Mariposa areas.

SERVICES: All services available in Yosemite Valley, Oakhurst, and Mariposa.

NEARBY ATTRACTIONS: Tioga Pass scenic drive, Tuolumne Meadows, Sierra Nevada crest, Pacific Crest Trail, Sequoia-Kings Canyon National Parks, Millerton Lake State Recreation Area, Wassama Round House State Historic Park, Sonora, Columbia State Historic Park, Railtown 1897 State Historic Park.

THE DRIVE

Yosemite Valley, an astounding spectacle, is a place of exquisite beauty and grandeur, a place that inspires reverence and awe. John Muir, its poet laureate and ardent admirer, wrote: "God always seems to be doing his best here." The dramatic valley, molded and sculpted by great rivers of ice, sits like a giant, open-air cathedral on the western slope of the Sierra Nevada. Its granite walls soar upward to merge with a roof of turquoise sky and diaphanous clouds. In spring and early summer, water-falls plunge in frothy veils over the valley rim. Thick forests and verdant meadows cloak the valley floor and line the gravel banks of the Merced River. Yosemite Valley, the centerpiece of 761,266-acre Yosemite National Park, remains the enduring heart of California. It remains, despite its popularity, a place touched with the timeless magic and mystery of planet Earth.

The Yosemite scenic drive, following CA 41 and CA 140, makes an open 105-mile loop that begins in Oakhurst in the Sierran foothills, climbs into Yosemite National Park, makes a side trip to Glacier Point, explores Yosemite Valley's floor, and follows the Merced River down a deep gorge to Mariposa. Every California visitor and resident needs to drive this route—it's simply the best the state offers.

This is a land of distinct seasons, with each bringing its own voice to the year's rhythm. Summers are hot on the valley floor and along the drive, with daily high temperatures often climbing into the nineties and even to one hundred degrees. July and August highs average eighty-nine degrees on the valley floor, with an average low of fifty. Cooler weather is found at the higher elevations along the Glacier Point Road. It's generally dry, but occasional thunderstorms dampen the mountains. Hikers should wear a hat and use suntan lotion. Autumn is crisp and clear, with warm days and chilly nights. Early snows whiten the peaks and provide contrast to colorful fall foliage, which climaxes in late October. Winters are generally mild in the lower foothills and the valley floor. As much as 90 percent, however, of the valley's annual 37 inches of precipitation falls between November and March. December, the wettest month, averages 7.10 inches of precipitation and an average high of forty-nine degrees. Be prepared for snowy road conditions in winter. Carry chains and warm clothing. The Glacier Point Road closes in winter. The lower elevations are mild and rainy in winter. Spring, a season of transition, brings both warm and cool days as well as extended wet periods. The park's famous waterfalls peak in May and early June as the high country's blanket of snow melts away.

OAKHURST TO YOSEMITE NATIONAL PARK

The drive begins at the intersection of CA 41 and CA 49 in 2,290-foot Oakhurst, 47 miles north of Fresno. Oakhurst lies in the bottom of a broad valley called Fresno Flats along the Fresno River. The town, originally named Fresno Flats, was renamed for the luxuriant groves of oaks that scatter across the scrubby foothills above town. Oakhurst, Yosemite's southern gateway, offers all visitor services as well as the **Fresno Flats Historical Park,** with several historic buildings, and nearby Bass Lake, a popular fishing, motorboating, and waterskiing reservoir southeast of town. Five forest campgrounds lie along its shores. **Wassama Round House State Historic Park,** a ceremonial round house maintained by the local Miwok tribe, sits northwest of town off CA 49.

Head north on CA 41 from Oakhurst. This drive section from Oakhurst to its junction with CA 140 in Yosemite Valley is 45 miles long. The road begins climbing immediately, winding up grass- and oak-covered hillsides above the Lewis Fork of the Fresno River. The Yosemite-Sierra Visitors Bureau provides information and maps and is just over a mile up the highway. The road enters the national forest 4.5 miles north of Oakhurst. As the highway ascends, the surrounding woodland changes to a mixed Sierra forest dominated by pine, oak, manzanita, and incense cedar. The rounded foothills here form a transition zone between the oak, gray or "digger" pine, and chaparral woodland on the east side of the Central Valley and the pine belt of the lower Sierra Nevada.

At 6 miles the highway reaches an elevation of 4,000 feet. West Fall Picnic Area, 3 miles farther, sits along the roadside in a shady cedar and pine forest with a thick fern understory. The **Yosemite Mountain Sugar Pine Railroad,** operating from mid-April through October, makes a delightful stop. The forty-five-minute ride twists down a 4 percent grade into Lewis Creek Canyon on the narrow-gauge tracks of the old Madera Sugar Pine Lumber Company Railroad. The railroad operated from 1899 to 1931, hauling some 1.5 billion board feet of lumber from the surrounding forests. Two massive Lima Shay locomotives transport tourists on old logging cars with sectioned log benches around the tracks.

Past the railroad the highway climbs to 5,000 feet, crosses a divide, and drops into Fish Camp. This small town, a popular summer stop, offers food and lodging. A mile up the road sits thirty-site Summerdale Campground, a good overnight stop for visitors touring southern Yosemite.

MARIPOSA GROVE TO WAWONA

Fourteen miles from Oakhurst the drive enters Yosemite National Park. An entrance fee of $20 per vehicle (which is good for seven days) is required. Just past the entrance, a 2-mile side road wiggles east to the Mariposa Grove of Giant Sequoias. This grove, Yosemite's largest, contains more than 500 mature sequoias on a 250-acre tract ranging from 5,500 to 7,000 feet in elevation. The giant sequoia, *Sequoiadendron giganteum,* is the world's largest living thing. The trees are found only in isolated stands on the western slope of California's Sierra Nevada and grow as tall as 310 feet, measure more than 40 feet in diameter, and live as long as 3,000 years. These giants grow from tiny seeds that are the size of an oat flake. The trees scatter billions of seeds on the forest floor, yet few sprout. As John Muir wrote, ". . . not one seed in a million shall germinate at all, and of those that do perhaps not one in ten thousand is suffered to live through the vicissitudes of storm, drought, fire and snow-crushing that beset their youth." The Mariposa Grove, discovered in 1849, is explored by a tram system that runs through the grove to the Mariposa Grove Museum and by a loop trail. The Grizzly Giant, the grove's largest sequoia, grows about a half mile back. The huge tree is the largest in Yosemite and fifth largest in the world; it is at least 2,700 years old. Note its side limbs—some are bigger than most other tree species. The Mariposa Grove was protected along with Yosemite Valley by the 1864 act signed by Pres. Abraham Lincoln.

The drive twists north from the Mariposa Grove and drops to Wawona Meadow in the broad valley of the South Fork of the Merced River. Wawona, an Indian word meaning "big tree," is a surprising oasis of civilization in the wild Sierran forest. Originally called Clark's Station after Yosemite pioneer Galen Clark, Wawona was a popular stopover on the old stage route to Yosemite. Today manicured lawns spread up from the highway to the elegant Wawona Hotel, a gleaming white, two-story structure built in the 1800s for wealthy visitors. The hotel offers a spacious veranda, swimming pool, and tennis courts. A nine-hole golf course stretches alongside the road across from the hotel. Make reservations through DNC Park's & Resorts at Yosemite, Inc., the park's concessionaire.

Wawona is also home to the **Pioneer Yosemite History Center,** an interesting living history program that recreates historic Yosemite National Park and its horse era. The center includes furnished buildings and cabins, an 1858 covered bridge, and educational exhibits. A stagecoach ride gives greater appreciation for the ease of today's transportation. The ninety-three-site Wawona Campground, open all year on a first-come basis, is nestled among pine trees above the Merced River. The site was originally used by the U.S. Army, which administered the park, as a camp and headquarters from 1881 to 1906.

Past Wawona the highway leaves the Merced River, swings around Turner Ridge, and begins contouring across steep, forested hillsides and crossing shallow, tumbling creeks. Ten miles later the road climbs to 6,000 feet and a mile later reaches Chinquapin, the junction of CA 41 and the Glacier Point Road. The site is named for the common evergreen chinquapin, a low shrub that scatters across the dry hillsides here. The 16-mile-long Glacier Point Road begins here. Turn east on it for some of the scenic drive's most spectacular views.

GLACIER POINT ROAD

The two-lane, paved Glacier Point Road climbs east from Wawona Road, crossing steep slopes densely forested with red fir, lodgepole pine, and sugar pine. At 3 miles the **El Portal View** offers a view westward down the Merced River gorge to the chaparral-covered Sierra foothills and beyond to the San Joaquin Valley, California's agricultural breadbasket. On clear days look for the hazy outline of the coastal ranges 125 miles away. Badger Pass Ski Area is 2 miles farther up the drive. It offers 700 feet of vertical drop, 300 inches of annual snowfall, and great beginner and intermediate skiing on the state's first ski slopes. The area opened in 1935. In winter the Glacier Point Road is open only to the ski area. Beyond lies a white wilderness that beckons cross-country skiers. This backcountry yields fabulous skiing. Most popular is the long, groomed track out to Glacier Point itself. The park offers more than 350 miles of signed cross-country ski trails. The Yosemite Cross-Country Ski School is based at Badger Pass. Skiers are advised to take a free shuttle from the valley floor to the ski area, especially on weekends, to avoid the parking crunch, to save gas, and to limit air pollution in the area.

Yosemite Falls, one of the world's tallest waterfalls, plunges over a sheer granite cliff into Yosemite Valley.

The road crests a hill just past the ski area and descends to meadows, which are sprinkled with wildflowers in summer. Deer often graze along the forest edge. Just before crossing Bridalveil Creek, a side road that is a quarter mile long leads to the 110-site Bridalveil Creek Campground. This campground is open July through mid-September on a first-come basis; it lies at a cool 7,200 feet. At Mono Meadow the drive bends north and alternately plunges through dense forests and crosses open meadows. At Sentinel Dome a short trail scrambles over bedrock to its rounded 8,122-foot summit. Jeffrey pines, stunted by fierce winds, twist out of granite fissures. The rocky top gives a splendid view into Yosemite Valley. Three-tiered Yosemite Falls and the sweeping nose of El Capitan lie opposite. Another rewarding trail begins at the parking area and goes 1 mile to Taft Point, an isolated lookout with another marvelous view.

For the last 2 miles, the narrow road switchbacks steeply down to **Glacier Point.** A short walk from the parking lot leads to the 7,214-foot overlook. This viewpoint, some 3,000 feet above the valley floor, yields one of the premier views in a park of superlative views. Immediately below the railing is a thousand-foot vertical cliff atop the sloping Glacier Point Apron. The floor of Yosemite Valley, broken by forests and meadows and laced with roads, stretches out below. Half Dome's vertical face lifts a rocky brow to the east. Little Yosemite Valley, Vernal Fall, and Nevada Fall are nestled south of Half Dome. The lofty crest of the Sierra Nevada rims the eastern horizon; its tall peaks—11,522-foot Mount Clark, 13,114-foot Mount Lyell, and 10,850-foot Mount Hoffman—pierce the sky. Facilities at Glacier Point include restrooms, limited food service, and ranger-led activities. Retrace the road back to the Wawona Road to continue the scenic drive.

YOSEMITE VALLEY

From Chinquapin, CA 41 edges north across wooded slopes that dip into shallow ravines. Six miles later the drive crosses exfoliated granite layers on Turtleback Dome and enters Wawona Tunnel, a 0.8-mile-long passage chiseled in granite to avoid an unsightly roadcut. The traveler's first dramatic view of Yosemite Valley lies on the other side. Watch for the pull-off on the road's north side but it may be full of vehicles in summer. This is the classic Yosemite view. Towering cliffs of white granite form a wall around the flat valley floor, with 8,842-foot Half Dome lording over the rocky domain. The white plume of Bridalveil Fall plunges 620 feet from a hanging valley between Cathedral Rocks and the Leaning Tower. A 1.25-mile trail climbs south to Inspiration Point, a lookout on the old road into Yosemite. Be careful pulling on and off the highway, and be wary of heavy traffic during summer months.

The road descends steeply down the valley's south slope and 1.5 miles later reaches a parking area with a short trail that leads to a view of **Bridalveil Fall.** The waterfall is particularly spectacular in late spring when snow melts and swells its stream. The water leaps off the rim, exploding into filmy mists and draperies at its base. The area below Bridalveil is treacherous, with slick boulders and a roaring creek. Just past the parking area, the route joins the one-way Southside Drive on the valley floor. Continue east on the road into Yosemite Valley.

Some legends say Yosemite was named from the southern Miwok word *yo'hemiteh,* meaning grizzly bear, by members of the Mariposa Battalion. This ragtag band of militia found the valley in 1851 while searching for its native inhabitants, who had raided several stores in retribution for incursions by miners into their territory. The Indians called themselves *Ahwahneechee* or "dwellers in Ahwahnee," their name for the magnificent valley.

Philosopher Ralph Waldo Emerson called Yosemite Valley "the only place that comes up to the brag about it, and exceeds it." Horace Greeley wrote in the *New York Tribune* in 1859 that Yosemite was "the greatest marvel of the continent." In 1860 travel writer Thomas Starr King proclaimed, "Great is granite, and the Yo-Semite is its prophet." Lafayette Bunnell, a doctor with the Mariposa Battalion and among the first whites to enter the valley, wrote that on seeing the spectacle for the first time ". . . a peculiar exalted sensation seemed to fill my whole being, and I found my eyes in tears with emotion."

John Muir, however, was the greatest chronicler of Yosemite's wonders. In his classic book *The Yosemite* he wrote: "No temple made with hands can compare with Yosemite. Every rock in its walls seems to glow with life. Some lean back in majestic repose; others, absolutely sheer or nearly so for thousands of feet, advance beyond their companions in thoughtful attitudes, giving welcome to storms and calms alike, seemingly conscious, yet heedless of everything going on about them. Awful in stern, immovable majesty, how softly these mountain rocks are adorned and how fine and reassuring the company they keep."

Yosemite Valley, as John Muir ascertained through his ramblings in the high Sierra, formed not from earthquakes and uplifts but from massive glaciers that gouged and excavated the deep Merced River canyon, beginning about one million years ago. Several glacial advances filled the valley to the brim and chiseled the park's familiar topographic features—Half Dome, El Capitan, and Sentinel Dome—from the valley's granite walls during this long era of periodic glaciation. By 10,000 years ago the last glacier retreated from the Valley, leaving a long lake dammed by a terminal moraine, or pile of eroded glacial debris, near El Capitan's base. Sediments eventually filled the lake, forming a flat floor.

LOOPING THROUGH YOSEMITE VALLEY

The drive tours the loop road through Yosemite Valley, paralleling the serpentine Merced River and passing numerous visitor services scattered through what is called Yosemite Village. About 3.5 million annual visitors flood the park. In summer, crowded trails, stressed interpretive services, full campgrounds, smog from auto emissions and campfires, and crunched parking lots await park visitors. To alleviate parking problems, the Park Service offers free shuttle buses around the valley's eastern end and 8 miles of paved bike paths. Buses run to Glacier Point and Tuolumne Meadows in summer. The park is much less congested during the off-season.

North Pines, Upper Pines, Lower Pines, and Sunnyside Walk-in Campgrounds, with 414 total campsites, sit in the eastern valley. Camp 4 Campground still attracts climbers to its first-come, first-served sites. Campers need to be aware of black bears in the park. Keep a clean camp, do not leave food unattended, and cover all food, food containers, and ice chests in unattended vehicles. The bears will recognize the food and break the car windows. It's best to keep all food in the bear-proof storage lockers at each campsite.

A wealth of outdoor adventures greet the Yosemite visitor. Many hiking trails lace the valley. Some of the best include the 5-mile walk up Four-Mile trail to Glacier Point, the 1-mile round-trip to Mirror Lake, the 7-mile round-trip to Upper Yosemite Falls, and the hike up the rushing Merced River to Vernal and Nevada Falls. Swimmers and tubers cool off in summer in the Merced's placid valley waters. Rock climbers scale all the cliffs. Climbs range from one-pitch sport routes near Camp 4 Campground and the Chapel Wall to difficult, multipitch free climbs like Astroman on Washington Column to ascending the valley's famed big walls of Half Dome and El Capitan. Most popular are the Nose and Salathe Wall on El Capitan and Half Dome's Northwest Face. At El Cap Meadows visitors crane their necks and peer through binoculars and telescopes to spot climbers clinging to El Capitan's 3,000-foot-high face, the world's single largest piece of exposed granite. Numerous interpretive programs, including ranger-led hikes, evening programs, and nature talks, are held daily. Inquire at the visitor center for information and schedules and consult the Yosemite Guide issued at the park entrances.

At the gas station just beyond the Yosemite Lodge, the drive turns onto one-way Northside Drive and runs west. **Yosemite Falls,** the world's third-highest waterfall at 2,425 feet, plunges over the canyon rim, stair-stepping down over three separate falls to the valley floor. The Lower Fall itself is twice the height of Niagara Falls. The road bends through a pine forest, skirts the Three Brothers, and enters **El Capitan Meadow.** This broad grassland, flanked by towering oaks and tall pines, lies beneath El Capitan. Southward, in the shade, towers bulky Middle Cathedral Rock. Past the meadow the road crosses a low, hummocky ridge of glacial rubble, left as a terminal moraine at the far western edge of the Yosemite Valley. A pull-off down the road gives the famed valley view through the portals of Yosemite. El Cap on the north and the Cathedral Rocks and Bridalveil Fall on the south frame this postcard-perfect view. A half mile farther west is the junction with Southside Drive. Turn here to head back into the valley, or take the Wawona Road out of the park to CA 41 and Wawona. The scenic drive continues west on El Portal Road. Another road junction lies just downriver. The Big Oak Flat Road climbs up to Tuolumne Meadows and Tioga Pass on the scenic Tioga Road.

ALONG THE MERCED RIVER

For the next 7 miles, the road descends sharply down the Merced River's abrupt V-shaped canyon, dropping from 4,000-foot Yosemite Valley to 2,100 feet at El Portal just outside the park. As the drive descends it passes from the mixed Sierra forest of conifers and deciduous trees through chaparral to the dry Upper Sonoran life zone with its blue oaks and gray pines. The highway passes several points of interest. **Cascade Fall** plunges through a granite-encased box canyon north of the road. Farther west the highway intersects the old Coulterville Road, a wagon route that was used from 1874 until a landslide blocked it in 1982. The frothy river rushes over huge boulders alongside the highway, until reaching the Arch Rock Entrance Station 5 miles from the valley. The station is named for the two immense boulders that form an arch over the eastbound traffic lane. The park boundary is 2 miles west of Arch Rock.

El Portal sits just outside the park and serves as home for many of Yosemite's employees. The town, once the terminal station on the Yosemite Valley Railroad, offers an informative display that includes a locomotive and train cars. From here, early visitors climbed aboard stagecoaches for the journey's final leg to the fabled valley.

The drive edges the Merced River for the next 18 miles to Briceburg. The river begins at snowfields on the Sierra crest, tumbles clear and cold down Nevada and Vernal Falls, meanders peacefully through Yosemite Valley, and foams fiercely through its canyon above El Portal. The river was named *El Rio Nuestra Senora de la Merced* or "the River of Our Lady of Mercy," by Mexican Army Lieutenant

Gabriel Moraga after a hot, 40-mile march to its banks in 1806. Miners plied its banks in the 1850s, finding rich gold deposits. Between 1907 and 1945 the railroad toted passengers up the river canyon to El Portal. The level, abandoned railbed follows the north bank across the Merced from the highway. Much of the river, one of California's outstanding, free-flowing streams, is protected as a National Wild and Scenic River.

The Merced River, managed by the Bureau of Land Management and U.S. Forest Service, offers superb rafting and kayaking on its rough waters. Stand on its banks and listen to the flow. Its racing waves sing as they roar over boulders and churn through rapids. In spring, when the river swells with runoff from melting snow, it is full of white-water dreams for the river runner. The Merced's first 9 miles from Rose Bud just west of El Portal to Emory boasts several difficult and scary Class III and IV rapids. Stark Reality and Ned's Gulch rapids can flip a 16-foot raft at high water levels. The 7-mile section from Emory to Split Rock below Briceburg is easier, with deep pools and shallow Class II and III riffles. Local outfitters offer Merced River trips. The best time to float the river's white water is spring and early summer.

Fishing is decent along the Merced, with the section around Red Bud Picnic Area designated as wild trout water. Good hiking is also found in the canyon. The abandoned rail grade is popular; two bridges allow access on the river's north bank. A superb hike follows the river's South Fork in Sierra National Forest west of El Portal. The wildflower display on the grassy hillsides above the sparkling river is simply breathtaking in April and May, when more than fifty flower species carpet the hills. Campers stay overnight at fourteen-site Indian Flat Campground near El Portal, and three primitive BLM campgrounds—fourteen-site McCabe Flat, eight-site Willow Placer, and nine-site Railroad Flat—downriver from Briceburg in the BLM's Merced River Recreation Area. The Bureau of Land Management also manages an information station at 1,441-foot Briceburg, offering nature guides, maps, and river information.

The drive swings inland at Briceburg and leaves the Merced River behind. It climbs steeply up Bear Creek canyon, its slopes coated with brushy chaparral, and 4 miles later reaches a pine forest in Midpines at 2,962 feet. **Mariposa** straddles oak-covered hills a couple of miles farther west. It is near the southern tip of California's gold country and was named by Spanish explorers in 1806 for the area's multitude of butterflies. The town was established by trailblazer and mapmaker John C. Fremont, who acquired some 40,000 acres of seemingly worthless land here. Gold was later discovered and his Las Mariposas Land Grant was worth a fortune. Mariposa offers California's oldest courthouse, built in 1854, and the excellent Mariposa Museum and History Center with mining and Miwok displays. The California Mining and Mineral Museum exhibits one of the nation's best rock collections, including placer gold nuggets, meteorites, gems, and stunning minerals.

Mist Falls

Zumwalt Meadows

The Sphinx 9,146 ft.

North Dome 8,719 ft.

Grand Sentinel 8,504 ft.

Moraine Campground

Wren Peak 9,450 ft.

Sheep Creek Campground Sentinel

Cedar Grove

Canyon View Campground

KINGS CANYON NATIONAL PARK

SEQUOIA NATIONAL PARK

Cold Springs Campground

Alta Peak 11,204 ft.

Atwell Mill Campground

Lookout Peak 8,531 ft.

Kings Canyon

South Fork

Lodgepole Visitor Center

Lodgepole Campground

General Sherman Tree

Castle Rocks 9,180 ft.

Middle Fork

Hume Lake Campground

KINGS CANYON NATIONAL PARK

Stony Creek Campground

Lost Grove

Giant Forest

Moro Rock 6,725 ft.

Buckeye Flat Campground

Mineral King Road

Crystal Cave

Potwisha Campground

Kaweah River

Three Rivers

Redwood Canyon

198

Hammond

Kings River

Visitor Center

General Grant Tree

SEQUOIA NATIONAL FOREST

Shepherd Peak 3,570 ft.

Lake Kaweah

Pinehurst

Lemon Cove

198

To Visalia

180

Squaw Valley

Bear Mountain

245

Woodlake

N

Jesse Morrow Mountain 2,109 ft.

Campbell Mountain

63

Kilometers 10

Miles

0

Pine Flat Reservoir

Reedley

Kings River

Minkler

CALIFORNIA

180

To Fresno

Sequoia and Kings Canyon Scenic Drive

MINKLER TO LEMON COVE

GENERAL DESCRIPTION: This 160-mile open-loop drive begins in Minkler on the eastern edge of the San Joaquin Valley, climbs into the western Sierra, visits the spectacular gorge at Kings Canyon National Park, traverses towering stands of giant sequoia trees in Sequoia National Park, and descends sharply down the Kaweah River to Lemon Cove.

SPECIAL ATTRACTIONS: Kings Canyon National Park, General Grant Tree and Grove, Kings Canyon, Zumwalt Meadow, Redwood Canyon, Sequoia National Park, Giant Forest, General Sherman Tree, Moro Rock, hiking.

LOCATION: East-central California, 20 miles east of Fresno to 20 miles east of Visalia.

DRIVE ROUTE NUMBERS AND NAMES: California Highway 180 (Kings Canyon Highway), California Highway 198 (Generals Highway).

TRAVEL SEASON: Most of the route is open year-round. The section on CA 180 from Grant Grove to Cedar Grove in Kings Canyon National Park closes in winter from November until May. Check with the park office for information. The Generals Highway is open in winter, although it may temporarily be closed during periods of heavy snow and for plowing. Be prepared for adverse conditions by carrying adequate clothing and food. Have proper snow tires, carry chains, and drive with extra care.

CAMPING: Ten excellent National Park campgrounds lie along the drives, a few of which are open year-round.

SERVICES: All services at Fresno, Visalia, Grant Grove, Cedar Grove, and Lodgepole.

NEARBY ATTRACTIONS: Kings Canyon and Sequoia National Parks, Mount Whitney, Sierra crest, Kern Canyon, Mineral King area, Lake Kaweah, Fresno, Yosemite National Park, John Muir Wilderness Area.

THE DRIVE

The Kings Canyon Highway and Generals Highway drive forms a 160-mile long open loop across the western foothills and mountains of the southern Sierra Nevada. The highways traverse both Sequoia and Kings Canyon National Parks, passing groves of huge sequoia trees and dipping into deep canyons. The scenery along the drive is on a grand scale. Here lies evidence of the power and complexity of the changing earth, the raising and erosion of a great mountain range, and the passage of different lives. Along the drive grow the largest groves of giant sequoias, the world's biggest living things, and Kings Canyon, one of North America's deepest canyons.

The weather along the highway, as with most mountain areas, is unpredictable and variable. Temperatures generally fall about one degree for every 300 feet gained in elevation. Summer temperatures in the western part of the San Joaquin Valley and the low foothills are often in the nineties and occasionally over one hundred degrees, while in the Giant Forest at 6,500 feet the daily high ranges from fifty to eighty degrees, with a July average of seventy-six degrees. Summers are generally dry, although occasional thunderstorms drop a curtain of rain across the high country. Autumns are pleasant, with warm days and cool nights. Snow can fall in the upper elevations as early as October. More than 250 inches of snow seal the parks by late November. Most of the area's 40 or so inches of precipitation falls as rain in the lowlands and snow in the mountains between October and May. Expect heavy snow that may temporarily close the Generals Highway. The Kings Canyon Highway closes because of rock slides and doesn't reopen until late spring. Carry chains and warm clothing in winter. In the lowlands, spring begins in December, when luxuriant greenery coats the foothills, and lasts until May. On the drive's upper elevations, however, spring doesn't arrive until April, when the snow melts.

The Kings Canyon Scenic Byway, a designated U.S. National Forest scenic drive following CA 180, begins in Minkler 20 miles east of Fresno, the "Raisin Capital of the World," on the eastern edge of the broad San Joaquin Valley. The Kings River drains out of the mountains north of Minkler, feeding irrigation ditches and watering the vast fields of California's salad bowl. The gentle western slope of the Sierra Nevada, the state's mountainous backbone, stair-steps up from the valley here through rounded grassy foothills to steep forested ridges. Beyond and out of sight lies the sawtooth crest of the middle Sierras, a wild range of cirques and peaks that includes Mount Whitney, the highest point in the lower forty-eight states.

MINKLER TO KINGS CANYON

Minkler, a pleasant little farm town, sits along the Blossom Trail, a Fresno County back-road tour that explores verdant fruit orchards. The scenic drive heads east on CA 180 from Minkler through a broad gap between rounded Jesse Morrow Mountain on the north and Campbell Mountain on the south. Orange and plum orchards and irrigated fields line the Frant-Kern Canal along the valley floor, while wavering grass among dark boulders blankets the smooth hillsides. After 6 miles, the drive enters low foothills and climbs above 1,000 feet. Granite crags, oak trees, and golden grass spread over the hills. The highway crests a ridgeline below Bear Mountain and drops into broad Squaw Valley. The city of Squaw Valley lies on the valley's northern edge at 1,700 feet. Sequoia National Forest's Hume Lake Ranger Station dispenses visitor information and maps 5 miles up the road.

Past the ranger station, the drive begins seriously climbing upward, edging shelflike above Mill Creek and its broad valley to the south. At 21 miles, the road enters Sequoia National Forest and reaches 3,000 feet. The road, as it ascends, crosses a foothills transition zone from what is left of the great open savannas of the San

Joaquin Valley to the Sierran forests in the national parks. This terrain ranges from the valley edge to about 5,000 feet in elevation. It is a two-season land of mild winters with moderate rainfall and dry, hot summers. The plants that clothe the slopes have correspondingly adapted to these conditions by growing vigorously in the wet season and lying dormant during the dry periods. Chaparral, a stunted drought-resistant forest, covers the driest slopes with a dense, ragged brush that includes manzanita and chamise. Oak groves interspersed with grassland and stands of California buckeye range across moist hillsides. At 25 miles, the road passes the 4,000-foot level, and ponderosa pines and incense cedars appear in the forest. Precipitation on the Sierra's western slope increases 8 to 10 inches for every 1,000 feet of elevation up to about 7,000 feet. As the drive continues edging upward, great views of the rolling foothills, the San Joaquin Valley, and the Coast Ranges unfold to the west. At 30 miles, the elevation is over 5,000 feet, and the drive intersects California Highway 245. Three miles later, it leaves the national forest and enters Kings Canyon National Park.

KINGS CANYON NATIONAL PARK

Kings Canyon and Sequoia National Parks together preserve more than 863,000 acres of the pristine southern Sierra Nevada. The two parks harbor an incredible diversity of life zones, plants, and topography. The elevation range itself begins at 1,700 feet at Sequoia's park headquarters at Ash Mountain and tops out on 14,494-foot Mount Whitney. The rugged parks are seamed by abrupt river canyons, lorded over by glacier-carved peaks, and blanketed by the world's most unique forest.

After several miles CA 180 intersects the Generals Highway. Turn north on CA 180, the **Kings Canyon Highway.** The highway is a twisting, narrow ribbon that ends 39 miles ahead at Copper Creek in Kings Canyon.

A couple of miles up from the highway junction, the drive reaches General Grant Grove Village. The 6,500-acre area, once the headquarters of former General Grant National Park, offers numerous visitor services, including a visitor center, lodging, food service, and gas. The small Grant Grove section of Kings Canyon National Park became a national park in 1890, one week after Sequoia National Park was established. The park status preserves the area's pristine sequoia forests from logging. In 1940 the grove was combined with Kings Canyon and the rugged Sierra wilderness to form Kings Canyon National Park. Three campgrounds are found at Grant Grove—113 site Azalea, 200-site Sunset, and 63-site Crystal Springs.

The **Grant Grove** is a spectacular forest of giant sequoias perched atop a broad ridge. A side road drops down to the **General Grant Tree,** the third-largest tree in the world and a designated National Shrine honoring American servicemen and the nation's Christmas tree. It towers 267 feet above the forest floor, boasts a base diameter of 40 feet, and is over 2,000 years old. Another side road begins opposite the General Grant road and winds 2.3 miles to **Panoramic Point.** The view overlooks a maze of canyons and peaks in the high Sierra.

Numerous trails wend through the Grant Grove section. An excellent path begins near the General Grant Tree and threads among the North Grove's mature sequoias. The mile-long **Big Stump Basin Trail,** near the park entrance, loops through a sequoia grove destroyed by 1880s lumbering. Sequoia cutting here and north of Grant Grove led to the rapid protection of remaining sequoia stands throughout the Sierras. Timber companies in the late nineteenth century dreamed of huge profits from these forest giants, but, fortunately for the sequoia, the wood was brittle and tended to splinter when the tree toppled. More than 60 percent of virgin sequoia forest remains scattered in some seventy-five groves on the western flank of the Sierra Nevada today, whereas over 95 percent of the original coast redwood forest has been harvested.

INTO SEQUOIA NATIONAL FOREST

The Kings Canyon Highway runs north from Grant Grove and enters Sequoia National Forest, a 1.1-million-acre forest that includes more than 264,000 acres of designated wilderness and 135 National Wild and Scenic River miles. The next 25 miles of highway cross national forest lands. McGee Vista Point lies a couple of miles up the road at 6,800-foot Cherry Gap on Park Ridge. A major forest fire devastated this area in the summer of 1955 when a rancher lost control of a fire in the foothills below. The fire, fanned by dry winds, engulfed the forest. More than four million trees were later planted on the burned hillsides. The point offers good views west across the foothills to the San Joaquin Valley.

Past the overlook, the highway begins steeply descending down the east side of Park Ridge, passing the remains of the Indian Basin and Converse Basin sequoia groves. A lumber company decimated both groves one hundred years ago. The Converse Basin was reputed to be the largest sequoia grove in the Sierra. All that remains of its majesty are immense stumps and the solitary Boole Tree, ironically named for the timber foreman who oversaw the forest's destruction. A 2-mile loop trail leads to the tree through a maze of stumps.

The drive descends through a dry forest of ponderosa pine and incense cedar. A side road runs 3 miles east to eighty-seven-acre Hume Lake, a popular forest recreation site with fishing, boating, and a seventy-four-site campground. A few miles past the Hume Lake turnoff, the highway swings around a corner and enters the abrupt defile of Kings Canyon. The road edges the steep mountainside and 3 miles later reaches Junction View at 4,500 feet.

This view is one of California's grandest sights. It overlooks deep gorges carved by the Middle and South Forks of the Kings River. The Middle Fork originates high on 13,361-foot Mount Powell and plunges down steep canyons, including Tehipite Valley, before draining into the South Fork far below the overlook. The South Fork begins with melting snow on Taboose Pass on the Sierra crest and empties down Paradise Valley into Kings Canyon. The canyon below Junction View reaches its greatest depth with a vertical relief of 7,891 feet from the river bottom just west of the two forks' confluence to the summit of 10,051-foot Spanish Mountain north of the gorge. The canyon's depth exceeds both Idaho's Hells Canyon and Arizona's Grand Canyon. The canyon was chiseled out of bedrock by the relentless cutting force of the river and eons of time. The river was named in 1805 when Spaniard Gabriel Moraga and an exploratory force encamped by the river's foothill mouth. Since the day was Epiphany, he dubbed it *El Rio de los Santos Reyes* or "River of the Holy Kings" for the Christmas Magi.

The narrow road was built by convict labor in the 1930s. It turns away from the river and traverses steep ridges ragged with chaparral and broken by rocky crags. After a few switchbacks, the drive crosses Ten-Mile Creek, a tumbling stream locked in a shallow granite canyon. A mile after crossing the creek, the highway reaches Yucca Point and enters the inner gorge of South Fork Canyon. A thousand feet below this point lie the two great river forks. A 1-mile path descends rocky slopes to the river. The highway turns east and creeps shelflike across the steep canyon walls. The canyon slowly narrows, with the river rushing over boulders below.

Four miles from Yucca Point the road swings around Horseshoe Bend. A scenic pullout lies on the bend's apex. Soaring cliffs of metamorphosed ocean sediments tower overhead, while the Kings River, just a couple hundred feet below the overlook, roars and foams through boulder-choked rapids. This is a place of savage beauty, a marvelous page of geological history that is ever-changing yet somehow eternal. Be careful pulling off the highway, especially coming from the west, for the road curve is sharp and blind. After another mile the drive, now alongside the river, cuts through an abrupt gap called the Portals of the Kings, where more cliffs stairstep away from the road. Boyden's Cave, a private grotto, lies on the river's south bank in a tall gray cliff of marble. The cliff is composed of an ancient limestone that metamorphosed into marble by underground heat and pressure. Guided tours are offered daily from spring through fall.

The road snakes along the river's north bank as it runs eastward. The river is a strong, commanding presence. Its untamed waters, filled with spring runoff, are a raging, frothy torrent hemmed in by granite boulders. The canyon here is a classic V-shaped gorge excavated by millions of years of running water. The river's steep gradient coupled with prodigious amounts of water, especially in spring and while the Sierra's great glaciers melted, form a sharp tool that slowly deepens the canyon. Grizzly Creek Falls tumbles over granite bedrock partway up the canyon. A national forest picnic ground sits under nearby shade trees.

CEDAR GROVE AND ZUMWALT MEADOWS

The drive reenters Kings Canyon National Park several miles farther upstream. Just after the road enters the park, the topography changes abruptly. The V-shaped river gorge broadens and assumes the classic U-shape of a glacier-carved valley. Four gorgeous granite valleys grace the western slope of the Sierra Nevada—famed Yosemite Valley, dammed Hetch Hetchy, remote Tehipite on the Kings River's Middle Fork, and Kings Canyon. John Muir, the famed pioneer naturalist, called it "a rival to Yosemite," and wrote in 1891, "In the vast Sierra wilderness far to the southward of the famous Yosemite Valley, there is a yet grander valley of the same kind." Muir's century-old words still ring true. Kings Canyon is indeed grand, and unlike its famed northern counterpart, it is virtually pristine and almost unvisited.

As the road climbs, the valley broadens, and tall pines and incense cedars tower over river benches. Just up the highway at 4,600 feet sits **Cedar Grove.** The site, named for the shaggy cedars along the river flat, is the human focus of the canyon. Here sits the old Cedar Grove Ranger Station with maps, information, and displays about the park. Nearby, spread along the river, are four large campgrounds—Sheep Creek, Sentinel, Canyon View, and Moraine. Other visitor services include a small motel, diner, laundromat, showers, and service station. Several good trails begin here, including the Cedar Grove Overlook Trail, a 5-mile round-trip that climbs to a viewpoint on the valley's rocky north slope.

The Kings Canyon Highway traverses the valley floor for 6 miles more to the road's end at Copper Creek. A short trail climbs up from the drive to Roaring River Falls, a gushing waterfall that plunges down a cliff-locked granite canyon to an emerald pool. This tributary is an actual river that drains some of the park's most inaccessible backcountry. The 3-mile-long Motor Nature Trail begins just past the falls and parallels the river's north bank down to Cedar Grove along a dirt road. This is a good side trip on your return journey.

Zumwalt Meadows sits another mile up the drive. This spacious grassland is rimmed with tall pines and traversed by the meandering Kings River, with its deep, cold currents riffling over boulders. A 1.5-mile nature trail loops through the meadow, making a superb hike. The trail crosses the river on a bridge, threads through tall grass and silent forest before emerging on a broken talus slope. North Dome lifts its craggy 8,719-foot summit to the north, while the vertical cliffs of Grand Sentinel soar southward. The drive segment ends a mile past Zumwalt Meadows. Beyond lies the great wilderness of Kings Canyon, a wild, untrammeled region of peaks, meadows, canyons, and cirques that comprises over 90 percent of the park's total area. The wilderness, coupled with Sequoia's wilderness, composes California's largest wilderness area. Numerous trails fan out from here into the backcountry. A good day hike climbs 4 miles to Mist Falls, one of the park's largest waterfalls. Other trails roam up Bubbs Creek and Paradise Valley to the Pacific Crest Trail below the serpentine Sierra crest. Highway travelers must turn around at road's end and retrace the King's Highway back to Grant Grove and its intersection with the Generals Highway (CA 198).

GENERALS HIGHWAY

The Generals Highway scenic drive segment heads east from its intersection with the Kings Canyon Highway, edging along a ridgetop. Redwood Canyon Overlook is reached after 4 miles. This scenic view looks south into the 3,400-acre Redwood Mountain Grove, the largest remaining stand of sequoias in the world. More than

15,000 sequoias larger than a foot in diameter and many thousands more younger trees grow in moist Redwood Canyon and on Redwood Mountain.

Quail Flat lies just down the highway. A left turn on a forest road descends to Hume Lake in Sequoia National Forest, while a right turn leads 1.5 miles down a rough road to Redwood Saddle and the Redwood Canyon Trailhead. Sixteen miles of trail explore the ancient sequoia forest, passing Barton's Post Camp, an old logging camp, the Hart Tree, and the Fallen Goliath. A mile down the drive lies 7,100-foot **Kings Canyon Overlook** with marvelous views into the deep gorges of the Middle and South Forks of the Kings River. The next viewpoint is on the border of Kings Canyon National Park and Sequoia National Forest at **Big Baldy Saddle,** the high point on the Generals Highway at 7,600 feet. An excellent 4-mile, round-trip trail traverses Big Baldy Ridge to Big Baldy's 8,209-foot granite-domed summit. Sequoias stud Redwood Canyon to the west, their lacy canopies towering over surrounding trees. The drive meanders southeast from here, dipping in and out of shallow ravines to Stony Creek Resort, which offers groceries and lodging but no gas. The national forest's forty-nine-site Stony Creek Campground sits a half mile beyond on the wooded banks of trickling Stony Creek. The drive enters 403,023-acre Sequoia National Park a mile later.

SEQUOIA TREES

Sequoia National Park is the cradle of the giant sequoia. Here, on high rounded ridges that catch Pacific moisture, the sequoia still flourishes in immense groves. This is a place that startles the imagination and forces the visitor to step back and contemplate important questions like time and space. Mature sequoias are so massive and so old that it confounds the senses. To stand in the shadow of these forest giants is to stand in a shadow that fell when Sir Francis Drake, the first European to see California, sailed the *Golden Hinde* up the coast in 1579. These forest sentinels have stood for than ninety human generations, taking the dictionary's definition of a human generation as thirty years. Sequoias, next to the venerable bristlecone pine, are the world's second-oldest living trees.

Sequoias grow from tiny seeds the size and weight of oat flakes bundled in egg-size cones that hang as long as twenty years on the tree's upper branches. Soil and moisture conditions must be just right for the seeds to germinate. The trees have few enemies besides the saw. The tree's thick, cinnamon-red bark is resistant to fire and insect damage. The trees continue growing until death, which usually comes during severe windstorms that topple them. Sequoias have shallow, spreading root systems with no main taproot to anchor them. The trees grow in excess of 300 feet, live to 3,200 years, weigh as much as 1.4 million pounds, and boast base diameters as thick as 40 feet.

Sequoias once spread across North America, but over the last ten million years climatic changes isolated the species to the western slopes of the Sierra Nevadas. Today, they grow only in seventy-five groves scattered across a 260-mile range

Fire-scarred sequoia trees dominate the forest in the General Grant Grove at Kings Canyon National Park along the Kings Canyon Highway.

between 5,000 and 7,000 feet. Thirty of the groves lie in Kings Canyon and Sequoia National Parks. Their close relatives are the coast redwood in California and the rare dawn redwood in a remote Chinese valley. Sequoias were named by an Austrian botanist for Sequoyah, the Cherokee who devised an alphabet for his people's language.

LOST GROVE TO LODGEPOLE

The drive, after entering the park, swings through fifty-acre Lost Grove, a stand of 200 mature sequoias. A couple of short trails explore the grove. The road crosses Dorst Creek, named for the park's first superintendent, Army Captain Joseph Dorst. Dorst Campground, with 204 sites, nestles in a thick forest of white and red firs. **Muir Grove** is an almost pure stand of more than 1,000 mature sequoias and lies at the end of a 2-mile path that begins here. The highway climbs to 7,335-foot Little Baldy Saddle and then drops south and east 7 miles around Little Baldy, an 8,044-foot granite dome. Then the drive continues on to Lodgepole on the Marble Fork of the Kaweah River. En route the road passes Halstead Meadow and runs through a mixed conifer forest of pine, fir, incense cedar, and occasional western juniper.

Lodgepole, the logistic center of Sequoia National Park, tucks into a steep glacier-carved valley below the tall, craggy peaks of the Silliman Crest. A large visitor center details the park's unique natural history, geology, and history, as well as dispenses essential information on camping, hiking, and backcountry exploring.

Nearby is 214-site Lodgepole Campground and nearby showers, food service, and gas; campground reservations are necessary in summer. A trail climbs almost 2 miles up the river to gushing Tokopah Falls.

THE GIANT FOREST

The highway bends away from Lodgepole and traverses a rounded ridge blanketed with sequoias—the Giant Forest. The forest was named by John Muir and offers an unforgettable look at several pristine sequoia groves. The grove was first seen by Anglo-Americans when Yokuts guided farmer Hale Tharp to the forest in 1858.

Almost 3 miles from Lodgepole, the road reaches the **General Sherman Tree,** the world's largest living organism. This huge patriarch is a marvel, dwarfing even the surrounding sequoias. The 2,700-year-old tree towers 274.9 feet above its 36.5-foot-thick trunk and boasts a volume of 52,500 cubic feet of wood. All the events and inventions that made western civilization possible have occurred during this giant's lifetime—from the Greek philosophers and the birth of Christ to the automobile and the invention of printing and paper. The excellent **Congress Trail** begins here and loops through the sequoia woods for 2 miles, passing numerous other tall trees, including the President, McKinley, and Chief Sequoyah Trees, and the House and Senate tree groups.

The Giant Forest is lined with sequoias. The only way to really begin to fathom the sequoia's sheer size and regal beauty is by parking the car and walking into the cathedral groves. An age-old hush envelops the towering trees, with only an occasional call from a woodpecker or Steller's jay and a whisper of wind in the high branches breaking the silence. Ponderosa pine, sugar pine, and white fir mingle with the sequoias, but even these trees, giants of their own species, are dwarfed by the mighty cinnamon-barked sequoias. Under the giants, Pacific dogwood, western azalea, and California hazelnut scatter about the forest floor. Occasional meadows, resplendent with summer wildflowers, break the forest shade.

More than 40 miles of trail lace the Giant Forest. Many begin at the Giant Forest Village a few miles south of the General Sherman Tree, including the Big Trees Trail around Round Meadow and the mile-long loop of Hazelwood Nature Trail, which is wheelchair accessible. Several visitor facilities cluster here—a visitor information kiosk as well as the Giant Forest Lodge. The 3-mile Crescent Meadow Road begins at the village and winds out to Moro Rock and Crescent Meadow. This spectacular road explores some of Sequoia's best roadside scenery.

Moro Rock, 2 miles from the village, is an abrupt 6,725-foot granite precipice that overlooks the Kaweah River gorge and the sawtooth skyline of peaks along the Great Western Divide. The airy summit is reached by a short, quarter-mile trail and a 400-step staircase. Crescent Meadow is surrounded by sequoias and sits at the road's end. Several trails roam the meadow and woods including a 1-mile hike to Tharp's Log, a hollowed-out sequoia log used as a camp by early rancher Hale Tharp, and the 71-mile High Sierra Trail that ends atop Mount Whitney.

Past the Crescent Meadow turn-off, the drive begins losing elevation, and after a mile the highway passes the Four Guardsmen—four sequoias guarding the Giant Forest's western gates. At Commissary Curve a narrow, winding side road drops down 6.4 miles to Crystal Cave. A guided forty-five-minute tour in summer explores the cave, the only one open in the park. No trailers, RVs, or buses are allowed on the cave entrance road.

DOWN THE KAWEAH RIVER

The drive begins falling steeply past Crystal Cave Road, uncoiling like an asphalt serpent down steep slopes into the deep canyon of the Kaweah River's Middle Fork. In the next 8 miles, the road loses more than 3,000 feet in elevation, passing from the damp sequoia forest to dry oak woodlands to chaparral-studded foothills. The temperature rises as the road drops into the lowlands. **Amphitheater Point** is a great overlook a couple of miles downhill. Moro Rock looms overhead and snowy peaks punctuate the eastern horizon. Big Fern Springs makes a good stop on a hot day, with thick oak shade and huge chain ferns. These ferns are California's largest native ferns, with 6-foot-long fronds. Hospital Rock is on a bench above the Kaweah River and offers numerous Native American sites including pictographs and bedrock mortars for grinding seeds. Nearby at 2,820 feet lies twenty-nine-site Buckeye Campground.

The drive runs west down dry slopes above the river, passing forty-four-site Potwisha Campground. The site is named for a tribe of Monaches who often camped here. The Marble Fork joins the Middle Fork of the Kaweah River near the campground. The Kaweah River, with three other forks, drains most of Sequoia National Park. Its waters, fed by melting snow, gush into the San Joaquin Valley and feed lush fruit orchards and fields. The river is named for the Kaweah Indians. The road passes under Tunnel Rock farther down the canyon and reaches the park's **Foothills Visitor Center** and headquarters. Near the entrance station sits a massive hand-carved sign in the shape of a Native American head, which has welcomed visitors to the park since the 1930s.

Past the park boundary, the highway picks up the designation of CA 198 and continues west down the Kaweah River. As the road and river drop, the surrounding mountains lower into foothills and the canyon broadens into a valley. The road runs through Hammond and Three Rivers, passing the 25-mile Mineral King Road, which follows the Kaweah's East Fork to a pretty mountain-locked basin. Seven miles later the drive skirts the south shore of Lake Kaweah, a wide reservoir. Horse Creek Recreation Area, with an eighty-site campground, boat ramp, and picnic area, scatters along the lakeshore. Past the dam, the road drops into fertile orchards on the eastern edge of the San Joaquin Valley. The drive ends at Lemon Cove. Continue west on CA 198 through croplands to Visalia and California Highway 99.

18

Angeles Crest Scenic Byway

LA CANADA TO MOUNTAIN TOP JUNCTION

GENERAL DESCRIPTION: A 66-mile-long highway that climbs from La Canada to the lofty, forested crest of the San Gabriel Mountains north of Los Angeles.

SPECIAL ATTRACTIONS: Angeles National Forest, Mount Wilson Observatory, San Gabriel Wilderness Area, Sheep Mountain Wilderness Area, San Andreas Rift Zone, Mount Wilson Viewpoint, Devil's Canyon Overlook.

LOCATION: Southern California, north of Los Angeles and Pasadena.

DRIVE ROUTE NUMBER AND NAME: California Highway 2 (Angeles Crest Highway).

TRAVEL SEASON: May through October. The road closes after the first snow and reopens

when conditions permit, which can be as late as June. The road is open, however, to the ski areas along the route.

CAMPING: Several Angeles National Forest campgrounds are spread along the drive; many other forest campgrounds lie just off the main highway. Check a forest map for their locations.

SERVICES: No services are found along the drive. Services are at either end of the road at La Canada and Wrightwood.

NEARBY ATTRACTIONS: Rim of the World Scenic Byway, San Bernardino National Forest, Big Bear Lake, Los Angeles, Cucamonga Wilderness Area, Placerita Canyon State Park, Silverwood Lake State Recreation Area.

THE DRIVE

The 66-mile Angeles Crest Highway is simply breathtaking. It's one of southern California's best scenic drives. The two-lane, paved road ascends to the twisting crest of the San Gabriel Mountains north of the Los Angeles Basin. The spectacular road, far removed from the hustle, smog, and traffic of nearby cities, accesses startling landscapes that seem out of character with the usual conceptions of southern California.

A rare peace is found atop these mountains. The wind, sweeping off the ocean, whispers through ancient limber pines at timberline; long views of other snow-capped ranges, dusty desert basins, and distant city streets stretch out beyond abrupt ridges; and the elemental earth seems unchanging and almost unmarked by the passage of man. The mountains are chaotic, shaped and changed by faults, uplifts, and

earthquakes. Its ecosystems include dense chaparral-covered hillsides, windy boreal forests, and woody glades filled with wildflowers and ferns.

Like southern California's other mountain ranges, elevations and climates here vary dramatically from mountain base to summit. Elevations range from 1,200 feet at the drive's west end to 7,901 feet at Dawson Saddle. Annual precipitation changes with elevation. Pasadena, on the range's southern front, averages 20 inches of rain yearly, while Mount Wilson, only 6 miles north, is doused with 35 inches. Summer temperatures are usually in the nineties in the lowland valleys, but as the road climbs the temperature drops to daily highs in the seventies or low eighties. Occasional thunderstorms darken summer afternoons. Spring and fall are cooler. Winters atop the peaks are cold, with freezing temperatures and snow from November through March. The highway is closed and unplowed from Islip Saddle to Big Pines, providing a good cross-country ski track. It closes with the first snow and opens when the last snow melts. In 1992 the road was closed until June 12. Be prepared in winter for icy roads, particularly on shaded corners, by using snow tires or chains.

LA CANADA TO MOUNT WILSON

The drive begins at the intersection of CA 2 with Interstate 210 in La Canada just northwest of Pasadena. Turn north on CA 2. The road leaves the city suburbs behind after 2 miles and at 2.6 miles enters Angeles National Forest. The drive, a national forest scenic byway, edges onto the precipitous western slope of Arroyo Seco. Angeles National Forest covers 694,187 acres that include the San Gabriel Mountains north of Los Angeles. The forest boasts a wide range of plant communities from chaparral to pine and fir forests, offers more than one hundred campgrounds and picnic areas, and is threaded by more than 550 miles of hiking trails, including 176 miles of the Pacific Crest Trail. Mount San Antonio, known locally as "Old Baldy," is the 10,064-foot high point in both the national forest and the San Gabriel Mountains. Angeles National Forest, originally called the San Gabriel Forest Reserve, was created in 1892.

The twisting road steadily climbs above the canyon, and after 8 miles passes **Clear Creek Vista.** Another mile up the highway on the south slope of 5,557-foot Josephine Peak is Clear Creek Information Center. Nearby is Switzer Picnic Area with twenty-two tables. This site was an 1880s public camp, accessible by pack train and run by Commodore Perry Switzer. The highway also intersects the Angeles Forest Highway (Forest Road FH59) just west of the picnic area, providing access to the western section of the San Gabriels.

The warm south-facing mountain slopes above the drive here are densely covered with chaparral, including sagebrush, manzanita, whitethorn, and chamise. Chaparral climbs to elevations of 5,000 feet and covers 65 percent of Angeles National Forest. The moist, cool, north-facing slopes are blanketed by forests of pine, fir, and oak. As the highway ascends eastward, the chaparral fades out and coniferous forests dominate.

By 12 miles the highway rises to 4,000 feet, and 2 miles later reaches Red Box Gap and the Mount Wilson Road. This 5-mile-long road makes a good side trip to the top of 5,710-foot **Mount Wilson,** a local landmark, and the famed Mount Wilson Observatory with its 100-inch telescope. A picnic area, scenic overlook, small museum, and weekend tours of the observatory are found atop the mountain. The peak is named for pioneer settler Benjamin D. Wilson, who, with Mexican and Indian labor, built a trail to the summit in 1864 to bring needed lumber to the valley below. The mountain's clear air led Harvard professor W. H. Pickering to build a telescope on the summit in 1889. Shortly afterward the Pasadena and Mount Wilson Toll Road Company built a 10-foot-wide road up the peak.

Past the Mount Wilson turn, the road runs east above the thickly wooded canyon of the West Fork of the San Gabriel River. Past Shortcut Picnic Area and Shortcut Saddle, it turns away from the canyon and follows a high ridge crest east and then north through pine forests. The road swings around 5,908-foot Vetter Mountain. A good 1.5-mile-long hike begins at Charlton Flat Picnic Area and climbs up a shallow valley to the fire lookout atop the peak. Another easy hike starts at the picnic ground and climbs east to Mount Mooney and Devil's Peak. Both offer great views into the 36,137-acre San Gabriel Wilderness Area, a rugged land of peaks and canyons bounded on the south by the San Gabriel River and on the north by the Angeles Crest Highway. The region, one of the nation's first established wilderness areas, was protected as a primitive area in 1932.

DEVILS CANYON AND CHILAO VISITOR CENTER

Devils Canyon Overlook, the next road stop, sits on the edge of the San Gabriel Wilderness Area and deep Devils Canyon. The high crest of the San Gabriel Mountains runs east from here, forming an open, south-facing horseshoe. The San Gabriels are one of California's Transverse Ranges. These sierras trend east-west, instead of the north-south orientation of other California ranges. The Transverse Ranges, along with the Uinta Mountains in Utah, are the only east-west ranges in the continental United States. The ranges run from Santa Barbara on the coast to San Gorgonio Pass and have long separated northern California from southern California.

The looming San Gabriels are young mountains, composed primarily of granites and ancient metamorphic rocks, which, says geologist H. C. Storey, have "... been as intensively faulted and fractured as probably any other region in the world." The range is laced with faults, including the San Gabriel Fault and the famed San Andreas Fault, which runs through Swarthout Valley on the east end of the highway and below the range's northern escarpment. The mountains are still growing, as much as 5 inches each century.

The drive reaches **Chilao Visitor Center** and campground just beyond the overlook. The visitor center offers displays on the forest's history, natural history, and geology, as well as books and hiking information. Ranger-led nature hikes and self-

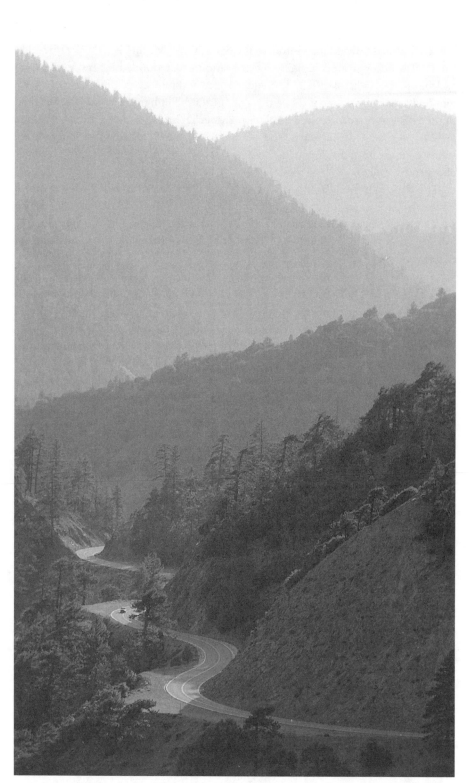

The Angeles Crest Highway climbs serpentine fashion out of narrow canyons of the San Gabriel Mountains.

guided trails help introduce visitors to the San Gabriel Mountains. The nearby 111-site Chilao Campground, at 5,300 feet elevation, is surrounded by grassy meadows and an open woodland of Jeffrey, Coulter, sugar, and ponderosa pine. Several excellent trails roam the country above the campground. Timbered Chilao Flat was used in the 1870s to pasture livestock stolen by rustler Tiburcio Vasquez. An unconfirmed local legend says Jose Gonzales, one of Vasquez's herders, killed a bear here with a knife, earning him the nickname "Chillia" or Hot Stuff. The spelling was later changed to Chilao.

The drive climbs away from Chilao and 7 miles later reaches **Three Points.** This lofty pass is a major trailhead for the Pacific Crest Trail, a 2,500-mile path that runs from Mexico to Canada. The trail parallels the highway from here east to Wrightwood and offers many excellent day hikes and short backpacking trips in Angeles National Forest.

CLOUDBURST SUMMIT TO INSIPIRATION POINT

The highway swings onto the north side of the range crest at 7,018-foot Cloudburst Summit and drops down through a pine forest on the north slope of 8,038-foot Waterman Mountain and the Kratka Ridge. Two ski areas—Mount Waterman and Snowcrest Ski Area—are found along this road stretch. Buckhorn Campground, with thirty-eight sites, also nestles in a shallow canyon just north of the drive. This beautiful spot amid incense cedars and evergreens lies along fern-lined Little Rock Creek. Three picnic areas sit alongside the road, offering spectacular views northward to the Mojave Desert. **Jarvi Memorial Vista,** a lookout at the head of Bear Creek named for a former forest supervisor, gives a spectacular view down-canyon. Short Sierra Alta Trail loops down from the overlook.

Endangered Nelson's bighorn sheep are sometimes spotted on the steep mountain slopes above the highway. More than 700 bighorns thrive in Angeles National Forest. Other wildlife in the range includes black bear, mule deer, bobcat, mountain lion, gray fox, Pacific rattlesnake, Mojave green rattlesnake, pinyon mouse, and kangaroo rat. A great variety of birds frequent the forests—including crows, quail, woodpeckers, and jays.

Past Jarvi Vista the highway crosses Windy Gap, sweeps around the north side of Mount Islip, and winds northeast to 7,901-foot Dawson Saddle. The road edges around more high peaks and reaches Vincent Gap, where the Pacific Crest Trail crosses the drive. A popular 4-mile-long hike climbs from here to the summit of rocky 9,399-foot Mount Baden-Powell, a sharp peak named for the founder of the Boy Scouts. Near the summit, the trail winds through 2,000-year-old, wind-stunted limber pines.

The Pacific Crest Trail skirts the road from Vincent Gap. **Inspiration Point** lies 3 miles east of Vincent Gap atop the ridge crest at 7,386 feet. Marvelous views spread out below this lofty overlook. On clear days the Catalina Islands are visible offshore. The rugged 44,000-acre Sheep Mountain Wilderness Area, cleaved by deep canyons and lorded over by abrupt peaks, stretches southward above the head-waters of the San Gabriel River. To the southeast towers the range high point, snowcapped 10,064-foot Mount San Antonio, also known as Old Baldy. The peak's alpine summit can be reached from Blue Ridge via a 10-mile-long trail.

BIG PINES TO MOUNTAIN TOP JUNCTION

The highway begins dropping at Inspiration Point, spiraling down the north slope of Blue Ridge. Two miles from Inspiration Point the drive reaches **Grassy Hollow Visitor Center** on the San Andreas Fault. Displays here explain the fault, and a self-guided auto tour explores the surrounding earthquake features. Other summer interpretive programs and short nature trails detail the area's natural history and geology. The San Andreas Rift Zone runs southeast to northwest through the pine-covered valley here. Note the differing rock types on either side of the valley, evidence of the fault's lateral movement.

Two downhill ski areas—Mountain High East Ski Resort and Ski Sunrise—are found above Big Pines. Several national forest campgrounds, including 115-site Table Mountain Campground, are popular summer getaways from the heat of surrounding lowland valleys. Just north of the drive on Big Pines Highway is Jackson Lake, one of the forest's few trout fishing lakes. Farther north lies stunning **Devil's Punchbowl County Park,** a jumble of upturned, tilted sandstone slabs eroded into bizarre shapes.

The scenic drive turns southeast from Big Pines and drops down Swarthout Valley along the San Andreas Fault to the mountain community of Wrightwood. Past the town, the road dips steeply on 6 percent grades and rapidly drops away from the ponderosa pine forest into a strange woodland of sagebrush, western juniper, and Joshua trees. A mile after leaving Angeles National Forest, the drive ends at Mountain Top Junction, the intersection of CA 2 and California Highway 138. A right turn heads 9 miles down Cajon Canyon to Interstate 15 northwest of San Bernardino.

CALIFORNIA

N

Kilometers
0   6
Miles
0   6

SAN
GORGONIO
WILDERNESS

Onyx Peak
9,114 ft.

Pacific Crest Trail

38

Onyx
Summit

Cienega
Seca

Heart Bar
Campground

Baldwin
Lake

18

San Gorgonio
Campground

Aspen
Grove

San Gorgonio
Mountain
11,499 ft.

Bear
Mountain
Ski Resort

Sugarloaf
Mountain
9,952 ft.

Big Bear City

South Fork
Campground

Snow
Summit
Ski Area

Serrano
Campground

Big Bear Lake

Big Bear
Lake

Barton Flats
Campground

Barton Flats
Visitor Station

San Bernardino
Peak
10,659 ft.

Vivian Falls

To Lucerne Valley

Santa Ana River

Mill Creek
Canyon

Lake View
Point

Thurman Flats
Picnic Area

Mill Creek
Ranger Station

Snow Valley
Ski Area

Keller Peak
7,882 ft.

Children's
Forest

SAN BERNARDINO
NATIONAL
FOREST

Green Valley
Ski Area

Running
Springs

18

Heaps Peak
6,421 ft.

38

Arboretum

Pacific Crest Trail

Skyforest

330

Redlands

Lake
Arrowhead

Rimforest

Lake Arrowhead

173

SAN ANDREAS RIFT ZONE

To Hesperin

Crestline

Baylis Park
Picnic Area

Arrowhead
Peak
4,237 ft.

18

San Bernardino

10

Silverwood
Lake

138

Panorama
Point

Waterman
Canyon

215

215

To
Cajon Pass

To
Victorville

To
Los Angeles

Rim of the World Scenic Byway

SAN BERNARDINO TO REDLANDS

GENERAL DESCRIPTION: An 87-mile-long, open-loop drive that climbs from San Bernardino to the forested crest of the San Bernardino Mountains, winds along the mountain rim to the resort town of Big Bear Lake, and drops down through thick forests and deep canyons to Redlands.

SPECIAL ATTRACTIONS: San Bernardino National Forest, Lake Arrowhead, Big Bear Lake, San Gorgonio Wilderness Area, hiking, fishing, boating, skiing.

LOCATION: Southern California, east of Los Angeles.

DRIVE ROUTE NUMBERS AND NAME: California Highway 18 and 38 (Rim of the World Scenic Byway).

TRAVEL SEASON: Year-round. Temperatures in the higher elevations are cooler than in the surrounding basins. Snow falls in the winter. Expect icy road conditions and use chains or adequate snow tires.

CAMPING: Six San Bernardino National Forest campgrounds scatter along the drive. Many other forest campgrounds, including group sites, lie close to the scenic byway route. Most open in May and close in October.

SERVICES: Services are available along the drive in the many resort communites. All services are found in San Bernardino and Redlands.

NEARBY ATTRACTIONS: Angeles Crest Scenic Byway, Angeles National Forest, Cucamonga Wilderness Area, Silverwood Lake State Recreation Area, Joshua Tree National Park, San Jacinto Mountains, Los Angeles.

THE DRIVE

The Rim of the World Scenic Byway, composed of CA 18 and CA 38, travels 87 miles from San Bernardino to the Mill Creek Ranger Station on the east side of Redlands. The road traverses the forested crest of the San Bernardino Mountains, southern California's highest mountain range, and offers spectacular views of surrounding ranges and the Los Angeles Basin below. The drive passes several resort communities, notably Big Bear Lake, four ski areas, and 58,669-acre San Gorgonio Wilderness Area with 11,499-foot San Gorgonio Mountain, southern California's tallest peak.

Elevations along the drive vary from just over 1,000 feet at San Bernardino to over 8,000 feet, offering a diverse range of temperatures and climates. Summer temperatures can be in the nineties at the drive's start and in the cool seventies atop the mountains. Expect night temperatures as low as fifty degrees. Afternoon thunderstorms are frequent in late summer. Spring and fall offer brisk, but mild weather, while winters are cold and snowy from November to March. Snowfall totals reach 45 to 50 inches each winter. Be prepared for icy roads during or after winter storms by using snow tires or carrying chains.

UP WATERMAN CANYON

The drive begins at the national forest boundary on the north side of San Bernardino. Travel north on Waterman Avenue (CA 18) from Interstate 10 to the forest boundary. Waterman Avenue is a north–south street and also can be reached by driving east from Interstate 215. The highway, as it enters the national forest, crosses the famed San Andreas Fault at the base of the San Bernardino Mountains.

The San Andreas Fault or Rift Zone stretches some 650 miles from the Mexican border to Cape Mendocino north of San Francisco and is one of the world's longest and most active faults. The fault zone, varying from 100 yards to a mile wide, separates the enormous Pacific and North American crustal plates. The two plates have been creeping past each other for the last thirty million years at a rate of about 2 inches annually. Geologists call the slippage along the horizontal fault a strike-slip fault. It creates frequent earthquakes, but tremors, occurring almost daily, are generally unnoticed. Most movement along the fault occurs in large, sudden jumps. The plates become locked against each other, and strain builds until a quick release creates an earthquake. The greatest movement recorded in historic times was the 21 feet the fault slipped at Point Reyes in the 1906 San Francisco earthquake. Big Bear Lake was the epicenter of a June 1992 quake along a branch fault of the San Andreas. The San Andreas Fault runs through San Gorgonio Pass between the San Bernardino and San Jacinto Mountains along the southern base of the San Bernardinos, then heads northwest through Cajon Pass and along the northern edge of the San Gabriel Mountains.

After entering the national forest, the drive begins climbing steeply up the western, chaparral-covered slopes of Waterman Canyon. The four-lane road rapidly gains elevation, reaching 4,000 feet after only 8 miles. Two overlooks, **Inspiration and Panorama Points,** provide excellent views. After 9 miles, the highway narrows to two lanes and joins California Highway 138 and the national forest Rim of the World Scenic Byway. By 12 miles the road levels out and begins winding east along the mountain crest.

Baylis Park Picnic Area sits along the granite rim surrounded by a shady forest of pine, oak, and cedar. Marvelous views of San Bernardino and the lofty San Jacinto Mountains lie to the south. The area is named for John Baylis, who was instrumental in having the drive built in the early 1900s.

At nearby Rimforest a 2-mile drive up Bear Springs Road leads to 6,153-foot-high Strawberry Peak Lookout. Built in 1933, it is staffed during the fire season from May to November and offers great views of the surrounding forest, including Lake Arrowhead. Dogwood Campground, with eighty-two sites, lies north off the highway.

HEAPS PEAK TO LAKE VIEW POINT

The drive runs east along the mountain rim and passes California Highway 173, a short highway running north 2 miles to Lake Arrowhead, an attractive lake lined with summer cabins. Unfortunately for recreationists, most of the lake's shoreline is private property, and only landowners can launch boats. Get information and maps of San Bernardino National Forest at the Arrowhead Ranger District office, which is just before Skyforest and past the turn to Lake Arrowhead. The 737,280-acre forest, including both the San Bernardino and San Jacinto ranges, is America's most used national forest. Lying within two hours of some ten million people, the forest records more than six million visitor-use days annually. Parts of the forest along the drive were severely burned in the great fires of 2003. Switzer Park Picnic Area is near the ranger station.

Heaps Peak Arboretum, at 5,996 feet, offers a good, short nature hike that introduces visitors to the area's plant life. This site was devastated by a 1922 forest fire. Trees were replanted from 1928 until World War II. In 1982 the Rim of the World Interpretive Association, in cooperation with the U.S. Forest Service, began to develop the area into an arboretum. The easy 0.7-mile-long trail loops through the forest, passing a variety of native trees including Coulter, ponderosa, Jeffrey, and sugar pines, California black oak, incense cedar, white fir, Pacific willow, and Pacific dogwood. A small grove of giant sequoias, planted in 1930, already lift their stately crowns high above the forest floor. When they mature in another thousand years or so, they will take their place as some of the world's largest living things.

Past Heaps Peak the drive turns away from the rim and passes through Running Springs and Arrowbear Lake, both small resort towns with food and lodging. A good side trip turns east on Forest Road 1N96 at Deer Lick Ranger Station, just past Running Springs. Three miles up the road is the national Children's Forest, which was started after a fire burned the original forest in 1970. Contributions by concerned schoolchildren helped replant the area in 1971. A wheelchair-accessible trail, with interpretive signs in Braille, meanders through the forest. The forest road continues to 7,882-foot Keller Peak Lookout.

The drive runs east up shallow Snow Valley, past Snow Valley ski area; Ski Green Valley, an alpine ski and snowboard resort; and Rim Nordic cross-country ski area. This high area is studded with granite boulders and coated with an open forest of oaks and pines. It is popular with cross-country skiers in winter. The established ski areas here and at Big Bear Lake pile up lots of man-made snow and offer skiing until late March.

Past Snow Valley the road climbs to a divide that separates the Pacific and Great Basin drainages. An overlook here, **Lake View Point,** offers glimpses of azure Big Bear Lake and beyond to the rugged snowcapped peaks in the San Gorgonio Wilderness Area. The drive twists east under the windy, fir-clad summits of Crafts and Butler Peaks to Big Bear Lake. CA 18 and CA 38 join here at the stone dam.

A Swainson's hawk perches on a fence post along the Rim of the World Scenic Byway.

Go north or left on CA 38 around the lake's north shore. The south side of the lake, including the town of Big Bear Lake, is a residential and business area.

BIG BEAR LAKE

Seven-mile-long, 3,000-acre Big Bear Lake was formed by an arch dam completed in 1911. This and an earlier dam built in 1884 provide cities in the San Bernardino

Valley with water. This dam on the Bear Creek branch of the Santa Ana River often released most of the lake's water for downstream irrigation until the 1970s, when agreements between landowners and water users stabilized the lake level. The small, original lake here was given its name in 1845 when a posse of ranchers searching for Indian cattle rustlers shot twenty-two bears in the area.

The placid lake is now lined with resort facilities and the towns of Big Bear Lake and Big Bear City, offering a wide range of outdoor recreation. Campers use thirty-six-site Coldbrook and fifty-two-site Pineknot Campgrounds on the south shore near Snow Summit ski area, and 101-site Serrano Campground on the north shore. Fishermen angle for trophy-size rainbow and brown trout, large channel catfish, both large- and small-mouthed bass, panfish, and crappie. Two ski areas—Snow Summit and Bear Mountain—adorn the wooded slopes south of the lake with seventy-five trails, twenty lifts, and seven snowboard parks.

The drive skirts the lake's north shoreline, winding through pine woodlands and open meadows. Grout Bay Picnic Area, on a spit of land south of the town of Fawnskin, is a good spot to see bald eagles in winter. The Big Bear area protects as many as thirty bald eagles, the largest winter population in southern California. Farther down the lake past Serrano Campground is Meadow's Edge Picnic Area, a boat ramp, and Big Bear Ranger Station and Discovery Center. A pamphlet is available here for the self-guided auto tour on the **Gold Fever Trail.** The tour meanders on gravel roads through Holcomb Valley north of the lake, past the remnants of an 1860s gold rush that include abandoned mines, cabins, arrastres, and a solitary grave. Two-mile-long Cougar Crest Trail begins a half mile west of the ranger station at a parking area off the drive. The trail climbs north through a mixed conifer forest to the Pacific Crest National Scenic Trail, which offers easy day and overnight hikes in the Big Bear Lake region.

ONYX SUMMIT TO BARTON FLATS

East of the lake, about 3 miles from the ranger station, CA 38 rejoins CA 18. Turn south on CA 38 and continue through Big Bear City and across the wooded Bear Valley. After a few miles the drive leaves the summer cabins behind and rolls past shallow canyons filled with open areas of sagebrush and rabbitbrush and scattered woodlands of western juniper and Jeffrey pine. The road climbs onto the broad, east shoulder of Sugarloaf Mountain, thick with juniper and mountain mahogany, and then crests 8,443-foot Onyx Summit, the drive's high point.

Past the summit, the road drops south, swings west along Cienaga Seca Creek, and 6 miles later reaches ninety-five-site Heart Bar Campground. A rough forest road heads south from the campground's west end and climbs up to the Aspen Grove Trailhead on the edge of 59,969-acre San Gorgonio Wilderness Area. A short walk up Fish Creek leads to one of two known groves of quaking aspen in California's southern mountains. The other grove lies in a steep gully southeast of Big Bear Lake. Aspens, one of North America's most widely distributed trees, are commonly found in the Rockies, Canada, northeastern United States, as well as in handsome groves alongside high Sierra meadows. The farthest south that aspens grow is atop the San Pedro Martir Mountains in Baja California. The wilderness area also harbors limber pines as old as 2,000 years, endangered Nelson bighorn sheep, mountain lions, coyotes, eagles, bobcats, raccoons, mule deer, and black bears.

The drive runs west, first along the Santa Ana River and then edging the forested slopes south of the river. Three more excellent campgrounds—twenty-four-site South Fork, fifty-four-site San Gorgonio, and fifty-two-site Barton Flats—lie along this road section. These make wonderful overnight stops, with grassy meadows and towering Jeffrey and sugar pines. Jenks Lake near Barton Flats and the Santa Ana River both offer good trout fishing. These campgrounds also serve as jumping-off points for backpackers heading into the San Gorgonio Wilderness. South Fork Trailhead is popular. The glacier-sculpted summit of 11,499-foot San Gorgonio Mountain looms in the south almost 9 miles away. More than 96 miles of trails lace the wilderness area leading to deep canyons, meadows sprinkled with iris, lupine, and shooting star, and magnificent views of the surrounding deserts.

Barton Flats Visitor Center dispenses information on the San Bernardino National Forest and the San Gorgonio Wilderness Area, including maps, books, and free wilderness permits. Permits are required to enter the wilderness, protecting its delicate ecosystems from overuse. Daily quotas limit the number of backcountry travelers departing from trailheads and ensure a quality wilderness experience. Several good nature trails thread through the forest near the ranger station. The easy Ponderosa Vista Nature Trail interprets the area's plant communities and wildlife, while the Whispering Pines Nature Trail uses Braille signs to introduce physically challenged visitors to the forest.

DOWN MILL CREEK CANYON

Past the visitor center, the drive winds west and then south for 11 miles around the densely forested flank of San Bernardino Peak. On the mountain's south side, the road quickly loses elevation, passing from the conifer forest into brushy chaparral. At the bottom of Mill Creek Canyon, a broad valley paved with rocky cobbles and boulders, the highway sharply swings west. A good side trip heads east here up Forest Home Road. At the road's end, a short trail crosses Mill Creek and climbs to the national forest's tallest waterfall on Vivian Creek. Monkeyface and Forest Falls are farther west down the canyon. All the falls are best seen in early spring, when melting snow swells the otherwise trickling streams.

The highway drops west down Mill Creek Canyon, passing Thurman Flats Picnic Area. A mile later the scenic drive leaves the national forest and recrosses the San Andreas Fault. The drive ends a couple of miles later at Mill Creek Ranger Station. Forest information, maps, and wilderness permits are available here. CA 38 continues west into Redlands and joins I-10.

20

Palms to Pines
Scenic Drive

BANNING TO PALM DESERT

GENERAL DESCRIPTION: A 66-mile-long, two-lane highway that climbs from Banning over the scenic San Jacinto Mountains and down into Palm Desert in the Coachella Valley.

SPECIAL ATTRACTIONS: Mount San Jacinto State Park, San Jacinto Wilderness Area, Idyllwild, Santa Rosa Wilderness Area, Palm Springs Aerial Tramway, hiking, rock climbing.

LOCATION: Southern California from Banning to Palm Desert.

DRIVE ROUTE NUMBERS AND NAME: California Highways 243 and 74 (Palms to Pines Highway).

TRAVEL SEASON: Year-round. The upper reaches of the drive receive snow in the winter. Temperatures in the lower valleys,

however, are mild with highs in the sixties and seventies. Expect hot weather in summer, particularly near Palm Desert, with highs in the hundreds. Mountain weather is pleasant. Summer weekends can be very busy.

CAMPING: Nine San Bernardino National Forest campgrounds and two state park campgrounds. Most are closed in the winter.

SERVICES: All services are found in Banning, Idyllwild, and Palm Desert.

NEARBY ATTRACTIONS: Rim of the World Scenic Byway, Palm Springs, Palm Springs Desert Museum, Living Desert Wildlife and Botanical Park, Joshua Tree National Park, Anza-Borrego State Park, Cleveland National Forest, Salton Sea, Mecca Hills County Park, Los Angeles.

THE DRIVE

The Palms to Pines Highway, following CA 243 and CA 74, is exactly that—a sinuous 66-mile-long highway that climbs from the palm-studded lowlands of the Coachella Valley and Palm Springs to lofty pine forests that cling to the steep, rocky slopes of the San Jacinto Mountains. The San Jacintos are the northernmost sierra in the Peninsular Range, a long chain of mountains that extends southward to the tip of Mexico's Baja California. They present an immense front to the east, forming one of North America's tallest mountain escarpments—over 10,000 vertical feet lies between 458-foot-high Palm Springs and the windswept summit of 10,804-foot San Jacinto Peak. This huge difference in elevation makes a drive into the San Jacintos a telescoped journey from Mexico's Sonoran Desert ecosystems to the subalpine forests and Arctic tundra of northern Canada perched along the range crest.

157

The differences in elevation make a marked difference in climate and temperature along the drive. While summer temperatures in Palm Desert regularly register above 110 degrees, the temperatures in Idyllwild rarely climb out of the eighties. Summer days are generally clear and calm, with occasional afternoon thunderstorms atop the mountains. Winters are very pleasant in the Coachella Valley, with highs in the sixties and seventies. The weather is more unpredictable in the mountains, with snow falling along the drive's upper elevations. Spring brings strong winds to San Gorgonio Pass on the drive's north end. The pass funnels powerful Pacific air currents down the Coachella Valley and sweeps clouds of dust and sand toward the Salton Sea. Annual precipitation ranges from 6 inches in Palm Springs to more than 36 inches in the mountains.

BANNING TO INDIAN VISTA

The scenic drive begins at the 8th Street Exit on Interstate 10 in Banning east of Los Angeles. Turn south from the interstate and follow CA 243. Banning, platted by stagecoach operator Phineas Banning in 1883, sits on broad San Gorgonio Pass. The pass separates the San Jacintos from the San Bernardino Mountains, part of the Transverse Ranges that run west to the Pacific Ocean. The heralded San Andreas Fault, a huge rift zone that marks the boundary between the North American and Pacific crustal plates, passes along the eastern margin of the San Jacinto Mountains and runs northwest through the 2,500-foot-high pass. The pass has long been a pathway between California's interior desert and the Los Angeles basin. Early Indian trails passed through it; later it was a stage route followed by the Southern Pacific Railroad and I–10.

The road winds sharply up steep mountain slopes south of Banning, crossing arid hillsides strewn with rounded granite boulders. After 3 miles the road reaches 3,000 feet and enters a chaparral ecosystem. Chaparral dominates much of southern California, cloaking the region's hot, dry land with dense shrubbery up to 15 feet high. The chaparral plants—including chamise, coffeeberry, bear brush, quinine bush, scrub oak, and manzanita—survive with thick, woody trunks and small, leathery leaves that conserve precious moisture. Chaparral generally claims the middle range of mountain slopes, forming a transition zone between desert plants and mountain forests on warm, south-facing hillsides.

After twisting upward for 7 miles, the grade levels out on McMullen Flat and enters thick stands of oak and the San Bernardino National Forest. The 650,000-acre forest is America's most used national forest. It encompasses both the San Jacinto and San Bernardino Mountains. By 11 miles the drive reaches 5,000 feet and pines scatter among the oak woodland. The drive runs along the western edge of Black Mountain Scenic Area and passes two-acre **Lake Fulmor,** which offers good trout fishing in spring, summer, and fall. A short nature trail threads through the surrounding Kellogg oak, pine, and manzanita forest.

Past the lake, the highway climbs onto a ridge and stops at **Indian Vista Point.**

California Highway 243 climbs into the San Jacinto Mountains.

This overlook offers marvelous views to the west. The San Jacinto Valley, sprinkled with green farms and orderly towns, spreads out below. Farther west towers the long ridge of the Santa Ana Mountains topped by 5,687-foot Santiago Peak above the glint of Lake Elsinore. The snowcapped crowns of the San Gabriel and San Bernardino Mountains loom to the northwest, while Palomar Observatory's white dome atop forested Palomar Mountain rises in the southwest. Closer at hand lies chaparral-covered 5,790-foot Indian Mountain.

INTO THE SAN JACINTO MOUNTAINS

The drive winds east and then south into the heart of the San Jacinto Mountains. A mixture of black oak, sugar, Coulter, ponderosa, and Jeffrey pine woodland lines the highway, with a thick undergrowth of ferns and flowers in lush, well-watered side canyons. Two forest roads leave the main highway and explore the mountains. Black Mountain Road (Forest Road 4S01) climbs 5 miles to thirty-four-site Boulder Basin Campground, a great overnight spot shaded by pines, firs, and tall manzanitas. The road continues on to **Fairview Point** overlooking San Gorgonio Pass. Farther down the drive, Forest Road 4S02 provides access to Fern Basin, Marion Mountain, and Dark Canyon forest campgrounds. Trout fishing is good in nearby streams. Fuller Mill Creek Picnic Ground sits alongside the highway just past the Boulder Basin turnoff.

Just past the forest road turnoffs, the highway skirts the edge of 13,521-acre **Mount San Jacinto State Wilderness and Park,** a mostly wild parkland that adjoins the national forest's 20,864-acre San Jacinto Wilderness Area. The park, traversed by the Pacific Crest Trail, boasts 54 miles of trail and four peaks more than 10,000 feet, including 10,804-foot San Jacinto Peak, southern California's second-highest summit. The peak is best climbed by ascending the strenuous 5.6-mile-long Marion Mountain and Seven Pines Trails, which switchback 4,600 feet up through thick forest to the bald, windswept mountaintop. The **Palm Springs Aerial Tramway** ascends the east flank of the park, climbing 5,873 feet from Chino Canyon near Palm Springs to a lofty vantage point at Mountain Station. The state park operates two campgrounds. Stone Creek Campground, off Forest Road 4S02, offers fifty sites; and Idyllwild Campground, next to park headquarters in Idyllwild, has thirty.

The drive meanders through the town of Pine Cove and drops down into **Idyllwild,** a picturesque resort community nestled in Strawberry Valley. The town was originally called Raynetta by George Hannah, its first postmaster, after his two children Raymond and Henrietta. Laura Rutledge, who managed a tuberculosis sanitarium here, called a second post office in a local hotel Idyllwild and residents began using that name.

The town offers lodging and dining and is surrounded by mountains. To the east towers 8,823-foot **Tahquitz Peak.** The Cahuillas said the summit was the fearful home of a powerful medicine man who stalked through the canyons at night and made bad weather. Tahquitz and neighboring Suicide Rock are acclaimed rock climbing areas with hundreds of routes ascending their white granite slabs and buttresses. Idyllwild also makes a good base for hikers. Numerous trails roam the forests, canyons, and peaks above town. Good hikes include the Ernie Maxwell Scenic Trail, Devils Slide Trail, and Deer Springs Trail to the domed summit of Suicide Rock.

LAKE HEMET AND GARNER VALLEY

The road runs south from Idyllwild, descending gradually through a mixed pine and oak forest for a few miles to the junction of CA 243 and CA 74. The drive turns east on CA 74. Palm Desert lies 37 miles ahead. The drive quickly ascends to Keen Camp Summit between Keen Ridge on the east and Baldy Mountain on the west and then drops down into broad Garner Valley. The turn to Lake Hemet and Lake Hemet Picnic Area is almost 2 miles below the pass summit. The reservoir, tucked between forested ridges, offers good fishing for largemouth bass, channel catfish, bluegill, and rainbow trout. Boating is permitted at Lake Hemet, the largest body of water in the San Jacintos. No swimming is allowed. Hurkey Creek Campground, with one hundred campsites, lies east of the highway at the lake turn.

The highway runs southeast through the wide Garner Valley. The trickling South Fork of the San Jacinto River meanders across the valley, passing sagebrush, open pine forests, and grazing cattle. The high ridge of Thomas Mountain dominates the western skyline, while the ragged crest of the southern San Jacinto Mountains marches across the eastern horizon. The Pacific Crest Trail traverses these peaks, which include 7,565-foot Apache Peak, Palm View Peak, and Lion Peak. The

Butterfield Overland Mail Company route ran through this valley on its way to Los Angeles and San Francisco. Beginning in 1858, the Butterfield stages carried both mail and passengers. A stage station, now part of a private campground, once sat in Garner Valley.

The road slowly rises past vacation homes in Pine Meadow to the intersection with California Highway 371 and the Pacific Crest Trail. The highway swings east and crosses Santa Rosa Summit. This low pass separates the San Jacinto Mountains from the Santa Rosa Mountains, which are a steep, rugged range seamed by deep canyons with brush- and boulder-covered slopes that reach south to Anza-Borrego Desert State Park.

DOWN TO PALM DESERT

Past the summit, the highway begins dropping toward the Coachella Valley. Pinyon Flats Campground sits 7 miles east of the summit. This pretty eighteen-site campground, open year-round, is surrounded by pinyon pines, junipers, yucca, and sagebrush. The southern trailhead for scenic Palm Canyon is 3 miles west of the campground. The trail twists 14 miles down the canyon to Palm Springs. The canyon's lower reaches, on the Agua Caliente Indian Reservation, harbor more than 3,000 California fan palms along its year-round stream.

Steep grades begin a mile past the campground as the highway bends around the south flank of conical 4,775-foot Sugarloaf Mountain. **Cahuilla Tewanet Vista Point** is an excellent overlook just off the highway here. The view is riveting, with the ragged, barren slopes of Deep Canyon falling away below. Southward stretches the Santa Rosa range, its forested peaks spotted with granite outcrops. Much of this land lies within the Santa Rosa Wilderness Area.

After the overlook, the drive leaves the national forest and enters the twenty-five-million-acre **California Desert Conservation Area** administered by the BLM and National Park Service. A viewpoint atop Seven-Level Hill provides a raven's-eye view of Palm Desert, the Coachella Valley, and beyond to the Little San Bernardino Mountains in Joshua Tree National Monument. The steep, dry mountainside below the vista is dotted with widely spaced creosote bushes, yellow-flowered brittlebushes, fleshy agaves topped with slender stalks, crimson-tipped ocotillos, and teddy-bear cholla cacti.

The highway spirals down precipitous slopes below the overlook and in 4 miles reaches the mountain base. The BLM runs a visitor center on CA 74 just outside Palm Desert. Stop by for exhibits, information, books, trail guides, and area maps. The road passes barren hills and then runs straight into Palm Desert and CA 111. Palm Springs lies to the west, while Indio and I-10 are immediately eastward. Besides its salubrious climate, Palm Springs offers several excellent attractions—the Palm Springs Desert Museum with exhibits on the California desert and the Living Desert, a unique reserve that displays native plants, animals, and birds in six desert habitats.

Mexican Border Scenic Drive

EL CAJON TO BOULEVARD

GENERAL DESCRIPTION: A 49-mile drive that parallels the United States and Mexico border between El Cajon near San Diego and Boulevard on Interstate 10. The drive runs over rolling chaparral-covered mountains and broad valleys.

SPECIAL ATTRACTIONS: Tecate (Mexico), Potrero County Park, San Diego Railroad Museum, hiking, bicycling.

LOCATION: Far southern California.

DRIVE ROUTE NUMBER AND NAME: California Highway 94 (Campo Road).

TRAVEL SEASON: Year-round.

CAMPING: Camping is available at Potrero and Lake Morena San Diego County parks as well as in adjoining Cleveland National Forest.

SERVICES: All services in San Diego and El Cajon; limited services in Tecate, Campo, and Boulevard.

NEARBY ATTRACTIONS: San Diego, Cabrillo National Monument, Tijuana, Hauser Wilderness Area, Pine Creek Wilderness Area, Cleveland National Forest, Laguna Recreation Area, Cuyamaca Rancho State Park, Anza-Borrego State Park.

THE DRIVE

This 49-mile-long highway traverses rolling chaparral-covered hills and broad valleys in the southern Peninsular Ranges east of San Diego. The drive follows CA 94 along the United States and Mexico border between El Cajon and Boulevard and offers an excellent back road adventure on a seldom traveled scenic route. The mountains separate the hilly country around San Diego from the hot, arid Colorado Desert that spreads eastward from the range base to the Imperial Valley and the Colorado River. The paved, two-lane highway has numerous pull-offs and side roads that explore the surrounding mountains. Traffic, generally local, is light to moderate.

The climate in San Diego and environs is just about perfect. Expect warm summer temperatures between seventy and ninety, with hotter weather in the lower valleys. Both spring and fall temperatures range from sixty to eighty with cool nights, occasional clouds, and light rain showers. The fierce Santa Ana winds that blow across the desert to the northwest can rage through the mountains in autumn. Winters are mild and pleasant. Expect highs in the fifties and sixties, with chilly

nights. Snow is a rarity, even on the higher peaks this far south, although heavy rains fall in February and March.

SPRING VALLEY TO TECATE

The drive starts at the intersection of Campo Road (CA 94) and Jamacha Road (CA 54) in Spring Valley just south of El Cajon. Jamacha Road runs south through El Cajon from Second Street and Interstate 8. CA 94 begins in downtown San Diego, off Interstate 5, and runs northeast to its junction with CA 54. Turn south on CA 94, also called the Campo Highway. The road crosses the usually dry Sweet-water River after a half mile and turns east up broad Steele Canyon. It climbs steadily up the brushy canyon, passing numerous residential areas including Indian Springs and Jamul. After 5 miles, the highway crosses a low divide and heads across a wide valley broken by hay fields, grazing horses, and small rancheros. Jamul Butte, a rounded cone, looms north of the drive and the low Jamul Mountains rise to the west. Oak and sycamore trees line shallow creeks that seam the undulating valley floor.

The drive descends through a thick oak forest and then follows Dulzura Creek to the small town of Dulzura at 1,240 feet. The road continues past the town along the tree-lined creek, passing small ranches with grassy meadows before reaching Dulzura Summit. White Mountain and Mother Grundy Peak tower to the north, their steep, rounded slopes littered with white granite boulders. The road then drops steeply down the summit's east slope and quickly reaches Cottonwood Creek, a placid stream that meanders through a broad valley. The road then winds up an abrupt, narrow canyon. A dense woodland of oak and sycamore lines Potrero Creek in the canyon alongside the highway. Brushy hillsides climb the steep slopes of 3,406-foot Potrero Peak to the north and Tecate Peak to the south.

Chaparral, which blankets most of the higher mountains along the drive, is a woodland of stunted scrubby trees adapted to the thin hillside soils and dry Mediterranean climate that prevails here. Chaparral plants typically have woody trunks and small, thick leaves that conserve precious winter and spring moisture for the hot, arid summer months. Chaparral covers about 7 percent of California and is the dominant plant community of the state's southwestern corner from San Luis Obispo to the Mexican border. It generally thrives on steep mountainsides, while oak woodlands and grasslands carpet the moister valley floors. Common chaparral species include scrub oak, chamise, and manzanita. One of California's rarest tree species—the Tecate cypress—grows in a few isolated stands on Otay Mountain and Tecate Peak southwest of the drive. The tree thrives on infertile soils that lessen competition from the surrounding chaparral. The trees are relict stands of more extensive cypress forests that flourished in wetter times. Two other endemic species also inhabit the mountains—Otay manzanita and Otay ceanothus, a member of the buckthorn family.

The road steadily climbs above Potrero Creek. White granite boulders, smooth

Tecate Peak straddles the United States–Mexico border along California Highway 94 east of Dan Diego.

and round from erosion, are scattered across the green mountain slopes. In the midst of the canyon, a side road (California Highway 188) turns south and runs 3 miles south to the border with Mexico and the quaint Mexican village of **Tecate,** famed for its Tecate *cerveza* or beer. Tecate, unlike Tijuana 30 miles to the west, is a relatively quiet border town. Tecate also is known for its quality, rugged bricks, which are shipped across the border to grace southern California homes and patios. The local brewery and a colorful town fair held late in summer are the popular visitor attractions.

POTRERO AND CAMPO

Past the Tecate turn, the drive swings around the southeast flank of brushy-shouldered Potrero Peak, leaving the meager creek and entering the small village of Potrero at an elevation of 2,323 feet. Potrero, a Spanish word that means "pasturing place," has been cattle country since the late nineteenth century.

The drive crosses a rolling basin, passing small ranches and open pastures fringed by oak glades before dropping into a broad forested canyon. It crosses Campo Creek at Canyon City and bends northeast along the stream. The canyon quickly opens into a broad, grassy valley floored with hay fields and flanked by low granite hills. The long-distance Pacific Crest Trail, running from Mexico to Canada, begins just south of here on the Mexican border.

Historic **Campo** lies at the west end of the pastoral Campo Valley. The valley and village received their name from Mexicans who camped here. Before the Mexicans, the local Indians, a Yuma tribe called the Diegueños, hunted game and gathered plants in the fertile valley. They called the area *Milquatay* or "Big Foot," which describes the valley's rough shape.

In the mid-nineteenth century American settlers put down roots here. By 1870 the valley had a population of 400, with so many Texans that the area was dubbed "New Texas." Throughout the late nineteenth century, the settlers and soldiers battled Mexican bandits who raided across the tenuous border to steal cattle and horses. Violence was a way of life, and captured bandits swung from Campo's big oak trees.

Campo quieted down by the turn of the twentieth century but became a railroad hub. In 1916 the San Diego and Arizona Railway reached Campo and then its terminus at El Centro in 1919. The train's final passenger run was in 1951, although freight trains passed through until the 1980s.

This colorful part of Campo's history is now preserved in the San Diego Railroad Museum, operated by the Pacific Southwest Railway Museum Association to preserve and interpret southwestern railroad history. The museum offers a fascinating collection with more than eighty major relics, including steam locomotives, passenger cars, freight cars, and cabooses. Walking tours with knowledgeable docents are available along with weekend excursions on vintage trains.

Past Campo the drive runs across the broad valley and climbs up a shallow canyon. A turn north leads to 3,250-acre Lake Morena County Park, a reservoir lying amid grasslands and a mixed woodland of chaparral and live oaks on the high eastern slope of the Laguna Mountains. The popular regional park, at an elevation of 3,000 feet, offers much for the outdoor enthusiast. The reservoir, occasionally drawn down for irrigation, yields some great fishing. The trout bite in winter, while the bass and panfish offer good fishing in the warmer months. The lake record for a largemouth bass is a hefty nineteen pounds three ounces. Boat rentals are available. The Pacific Crest Trail meanders through the park, allowing for hiking fun. The park also offers an oak-shaded eighty-six-site campground.

The last 9 miles of the drive from the east end of the Campo Valley to Boulevard runs through shallow canyons surrounded by rolling granite-studded hills, which are lightly coated with oaks and sagebrush. As the road runs east, the elevation drops, and the climate dries and warms. The drive ends in Boulevard. Turn north to I–8. CA 94 continues east, dropping down to the Mexican border and Jacumba. Eastward spread the hot Colorado Desert and rows of barren mountain ranges and valleys.

Joshua Tree National Park Scenic Drive

GENERAL DESCRIPTION: A 65-mile drive that crosses wide basins studded with creosote bushes and rough granite mountains in Joshua Tree National Park.

SPECIAL ATTRACTIONS: Lost Palms Oasis, Lost Horse Valley, Hidden Valley, Queen Valley, Joshua trees, Joshua Tree Wilderness Area, hiking, rock climbing.

LOCATION: South-central California east of Los Angeles.

DRIVE ROUTE NAMES: Pinto Basin Road, Park Boulevard, Keys View Road.

TRAVEL SEASON: Year-round.

CAMPING: The national park has eight campgrounds and one group campground.

Several have no running water. Check the Joshua Tree National Park official Web site for information on reservations and possible site closures.

SERVICES: All services available at Indio and Palms Springs to the southwest and Joshua Tree, Yucca Valley, and Twentynine Palms to the north.

NEARBY ATTRACTIONS: Palm Springs, Palm Springs Desert Museum, Living Desert Wildlife and Botanical Park, Anza-Borrego State Park, Salton Sea, East Mojave National Scenic Area, Palms to Pines scenic drive, Mount San Jacinto State Park, San Bernardino National Forest, Rim of the World Scenic Byway.

THE DRIVE

The Joshua Tree National Park scenic drive wends across 65 miles of spectacular desert scenery in southern California. The road slices across wide Pinto Basin flanked by rock-strewn mountains, crosses the ecological boundary between the Colorado Desert and the Mojave Desert, and climbs into valleys studded with bizarre Joshua trees and granite buttresses and boulders. The national park, established in 1936, now preserves 1,018,122 pristine acres of southern Calfornia's desert. Included here are extraordinary forests of Joshua trees, an odd yucca that is a member of the agave family. This windy, sunburnt landscape is a place of opposites—a place of parched water holes and palm-shrouded oases, a place of alluvial bajadas and stony mountains, a wild place full of sound and fury, yet a place of serenity and discovery.

The park offers excellent year-round weather. Winters are generally pleasant and dry, with high temperatures in the fifties and sixties. The lowland temperature around Twentynine Palms and Indio is as much as ten degrees warmer than the high desert in Queen Valley. Occasional snow falls in the upper elevations, and nights are chilly. Spring is warm and often windy. Summers can be very hot, although the park highlands are surprisingly cool compared with the inferno in the lower valleys. While Indio or Twentynine Palms roast under hundred degree weather, the park's upper reaches are in the eighties or low nineties. Nights at the higher elevations are also comfortably cool. Afternoon thunderstorms build up on occasional July and August afternoons, unleashing heavy downpours on the desert. The park receives 7.5 inches of rain annually, with 40 percent of that falling from July through September. Watch for flooding in canyons and washes after these periodic storms. Autumn brings warm days and clear skies. The fierce Santa Ana winds—strong winds that sweep out of the northeast—often blow across the park in fall. Many of the campgrounds are surrounded by cliffs and boulders, offering some shelter from the gale.

COTTONWOOD SPRING AND PINTO BASIN

The scenic drive begins on Interstate 10, 24 miles east of Indio. Exit the highway and turn north on Pinto Basin Road. The road climbs away from the interstate across a wide sloping "bajada" south of the Cottonwood Mountains, and enters Joshua Tree National Monument after 1 mile. A short distance farther the road winds up broad Cottonwood Canyon, its dry wash littered with flood-strewn cobbles. The canyon separates the Cottonwood Mountains on the west from the Eagle Mountains to the east. After 6 miles the drive climbs out of the canyon and onto a high bajada north of the mountains. Here, almost 7 miles north of the interstate, sits **Cottonwood Visitor Center.** This small outpost and entrance station dispenses camping and hiking information and answers questions about the park. East down a short spur road lies the sixty-two-site Cottonwood Campground.

An excellent 1-mile trail begins in the campground and threads across barren, rolling hills to lush **Cottonwood Spring,** an oasis of seeping water surrounded by towering cottonwoods and palms. The spring gushed as much as 3,000 gallons of precious water a day at the turn of the nineteenth century, but today it is reduced to a meager trickle. The palms were apparently planted around 1920. Cottonwood Spring, like Joshua Tree's other four oases, is formed by faults related to the famed San Andreas Fault that runs along the monument's southwestern border. The faults permit underground water to percolate up along the fault line to the earth's surface, where it flows out as a spring. Water in any desert spells relief. Shrubs and trees line the water here, providing both a home and a watering hole for thirsty birds and animals. The spring is a good place to observe birds.

The road runs northeast across a gently sloping bajada, crosses Smoke Tree Wash, bends northwest around rough, stony ridges on the eastern end of the Hexie Mountains, and runs across broad **Pinto Basin.** This huge, barren basin is surrounded by the Pinto Mountains on the north, Coxcomb Mountains on the east, Eagle Mountains on the south, and the Hexie Mountains on the west. The basin encompasses much of the park's central and eastern portions and is named for the "pinto" horse colors of 3,983-foot Pinto Mountain to the north. The area was not always so arid. Thousands of years ago during wet post–glacial periods the basin was forested and traversed by a meandering river. Ancient peoples found the environment hospitable, with plentiful game and plants. Evidence of their long occupation was found in the 1930s by amateur archaeologist Elizabeth Crozier Campbell in the basin's remote eastern reaches. Spear points, scrapers, and other hunting artifacts of "Pinto Man" have since been uncovered in other parts of the basin and southern California's deserts.

Miners also left their mark on Pinto Basin. Numerous abandoned mines worked between 1880 and 1940 scatter along the basin's edge. The Golden Bell, Eldorado, Golden Bee, and Silver Bell Mines lie just south of the drive on the basin's west end. In the 1920s the basin was the site of a land scam. The Lake County Development Syndicate acquired several parcels in Pinto Basin and proclaimed the sere valley "ready for an attempt at development." Their sales letter promised ". . . to drill for water. . . so that in time to come we may see Pinto Basin changed from desert to highly developed ranches and farms." The speculation fell flat when little water was discovered.

DESERT NATURAL HISTORY

Precipitation and temperature, coupled with elevation, determine the plant communities that inhabit a landscape. As one climbs in elevation, the temperature drops and precipitation increases. Nowhere is this eco-maxim more apparent than in deserts. Joshua Tree's highest mountains are fringed with forests of pinyon pine and juniper, plants representative of the Great Basin Desert in Utah and Nevada. The low valleys, like Pinto Basin, are populated by scrubby plants adapted to an extreme climate. Summer temperatures regularly reach 110 degrees and less than 4 inches of rain fall in a year. Creosote bush, the basin's dominant plant, scatters across the ground. This shrub, with green waxy leaves and yellow flowers in spring, is one of the desert's hardiest and oldest plants. The creosote, instead of growing in size as a single plant, sends out branches that root themselves as a clone of the original. Northwest of the park in Johnson Valley grows King Clone, a 70-foot-long, 25-foot-wide ellipse that has thrived for more than 11,700 years—the world's oldest-known living organism.

Joshua Tree National Park and Pinto Basin balance on the edge of two of North America's great deserts. The Colorado Desert subdivision of the vast, lowland Sonoran Desert lies to the south, while the higher Mojave Desert is to the north. The two deserts meet and mingle in the park. The transition zone where the two meet runs along the south and north sides of Pinto Basin. As the road heads west across the basin, it slowly climbs and leaves the Colorado Desert's characteristic plants—smoke tree, ocotillo, fan palm, palo verde, and cacti. A couple of interesting stops explore these plants.

OCOTILLO PATCH AND CHOLLA CACTUS

First, the road passes the Ocotillo Patch. The ocotillo is a strange plant with spindly arms studded with thorns. Rain brings a coat of leaves to the branches and bright crimson flowers on their tips. A mile and a half farther lies the Cholla Cactus Garden. A quarter-mile self-guiding trail explores a dense stand of Bigelow cholla. This cactus, nicknamed "teddy bear" and "jumping" cholla, is covered with a thick mat of long spines, each hooked with a microscopic barb. If the cactus is accidently brushed against, the spines attach onto the new host and the joint detaches itself from the cactus to be rerooted elsewhere. Many people who frequent the desert carry pliers to remove the painful joint when hiking in cactus country. Other plants seen along the trail include buckhorn and pencil cholla, calico cactus, climbing milkweed, and jojoba.

After the cholla garden, the drive ascends the western slope of the basin and after 3 miles enters a broad canyon. A few miles later the road empties onto a high, rolling plain broken by rounded granite outcrops. Two campgrounds sit just east of the drive—eighteen-site White Tank and eighteen-site Belle. Both are peaceful overnight spots surrounded by eroded rocks. The 0.3-mile Arch Rock Trail explores the rock maze east of White Tank Campground, passing a unique granite arch. A short scramble south from the arch leads through a narrow, cliff-lined passage to the remains of White Tank, a small catchment built by early cattlemen to provide water for their stock. Farther east a couple of miles hides Grand Tank, another stock dam with water up to 20 feet deep during wet seasons. A rough 1.25-mile path heads cross-country to this large water hole.

PARK BOULEVARD

Several miles past Belle Campground or 37 miles from I–10, the drive intersects Park Boulevard. Turn west on this road; it turns right and drops 8 miles down Utah Trail to Twentynine Palms and the park headquarters and visitor center. The drive runs southwest and after 2 miles passes Live Oak and Split Rock picnic areas. A narrow dirt road twists south to Live Oak Tank, a small dam built by early cowboys. The large oak that gave the site its name towers against a rocky outcrop called Pope's Head. The unusual oak is a hybrid, a cross between the valley oak and the turbinella oak. Jumbo Rocks Campground, with 124 campsites, lies a mile and a half farther up the drive. This spacious campground nestles in a maze of jumbled granite—Jumbo Rocks—with each site well spaced and private. Excellent 1.7-mile Skull Rock Trail begins at the campground's amphitheater near Loop E and winds through boulder piles to rounded Skull Rock. Signs along the trail explain desert plants and geology. Past the rock the trail crosses the road and slices through bedrock canyon before looping back to the campground entrance.

JOSHUA TREES

After Jumbo Rocks, the drive enters **Queen Valley** and the heart of Joshua Tree National Park. This huge valley, bounded on the north by Queen Mountain, spreads its broad floor southward to a low divide separating it from Pleasant Valley. The road runs across the valley through a ragged forest of Joshua trees, a fanciful plant that resembles trees found in Dr. Seuss books. The Joshua tree, one of California's most striking plants, has elicited strong reaction from travelers. Explorer John C. Fremont called them in 1844 "the most repulsive tree in the vegetable kingdom." J. Smeaton Chase wrote in 1919, "A landscape filled with Joshua trees has a nightmare effect even in broad daylight; at the witching hour it can be almost infernal." Forty-niner William Manly said they were "a brave little tree to live in such a barren land." While early pioneers called them "dagger trees," it was Mormon colonists en route to southern California who saw them as the biblical prophet Joshua lifting spiked arms heavenward in supplication and prayer.

The Joshua tree, *Yucca brevifolia*, is the Mojave Desert's symbolic plant. The plant's range from southeastern California to southern Nevada and northwestern Arizona closely follows the desert's boundaries, occurring generally above 3,500 feet. Here in the park, the tree's southernmost limit, the Joshua tree grows in the higher, moister valleys in the monument's northern reaches. The tree grows as tall as 40 feet with a diameter of 4 feet. It's difficult to ascertain the age of the monument's biggest Joshua trees, but with an annual growth rate of 1.5 centimeters, the oldest are at least 800 years old.

The Joshua tree forests harbor a wide array of animals that rely upon the tree for shelter and food. More than twenty-five bird species nest in the branches and feed on insects in the tree. Wood rats build nests using the tree's spiked leaves. Termites, night lizards, and snakes use fallen trees for shelter. But the most amazing relationship is between the Joshua tree and the pronuba yucca moth. It appears that the moth, in exchange for pollinating the yucca flowers, is allowed to lay its eggs in the tree's developing fruit. The moth larvae eat some of the yucca seeds before boring out of the fruit wall and starting the process over again. The yucca was also the tree of life to the Serranos and Chemehuevis, who ate the seeds and fruit and used the fibers for sandals and baskets and the roots for a laxative and shampoo.

Just after the drive enters Queen Valley, the dirt Geology Tour Road heads south. This self-guiding nature road is an 18-mile round-trip that runs across Queen Valley. It then passes over a low divide and drops down to Pleasant Valley between the Hexie and Little San Bernardino Mountains. The road is not always passable in a two-wheel-drive vehicle; ask at the visitor center for road conditions. A road guide keyed to numbered posts is available at the road start and at the park visitor center.

LOST HORSE VALLEY AND KEYS VIEW

The drive passes through Joshua tree forests in Queen Valley before crossing Sheep Pass and entering Lost Horse Valley. This spectacular valley is studded with bulging granite rock piles that scatter across the valley like an archipelago of islands. Much of the park's granite is one-hundred-million-year-old monzogranite exposed on the earth's surface as the overlying gneiss eroded away. The dark gneiss still caps the

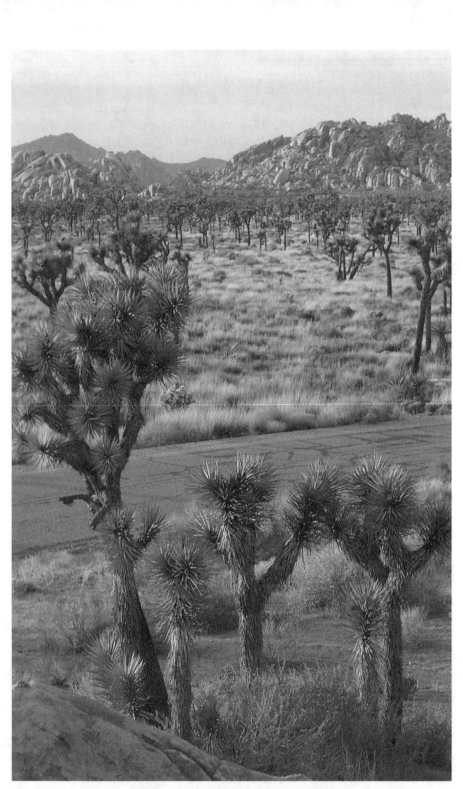

Joshua trees border the drive in Lost Horse Valley.

park's high peaks, but the pink and white granite dominates the northern valleys. Groundwater etched out cracks in the granite along weak joints, and water erosion attacked the rock forming the jumbled rock piles.

A good trail that overlooks Queen and Lost Horse Valleys begins a half mile west of Sheep Pass Group Campground. The 3-mile round-trip Ryan Mountain Trail climbs 800 feet to the 5,461-foot summit of Ryan Mountain. **Indian Cave,** a rock shelter used by ancient Indians, lies just west of the trail parking area. Down the road is thirty-one-site Ryan Campground and the location of the abandoned Ryan Ranch. Brothers Thomas and Jep Ryan had a small ranch here to provide water for their Lost Horse Mine. The ranch house burned in 1978. Nearby are eight graves, each ringed by boulders.

Beyond Ryan Campground, the drive turns sharply north at Cap Rock. An excellent side trip begins here and heads south 6 miles to Keys View, one of Joshua Tree's most spectacular views. The road traverses southern Lost Horse Valley, passing a thick stand of Joshua trees. The Lost Horse Loop Trail Press runs 2 miles from Keys View Road to Lost Horse Mine. The complete loop trail goes 8.4 miles past Lost Horse Mountain to a remote scenic valley. This hike explores the park's gold mining legacy. The mine eked out $350,000 between 1896 to 1900. The mine closed after the rich lode met a fault and disappeared. Today, all that remains are building foundations, cyanide settling ponds, and a stamp mill that crushed and processed the gold ore. Be cautious when walking around the mine site; dangerous pits and tunnels remain.

Turning away from the valley, the road climbs into the Little San Bernardino Mountains and ends at 5,185-foot Keys View. The overlook takes in one of California's grandest scenes: to the south glimmers the Salton Sea, to the southwest spreads the Coachella Valley floor, adorned with Palm Springs and Indio; the huge escarpment of the San Jacinto Mountains towers almost 10,000 feet above the valley, the high ridges and basins coated with snow; and west lies San Gorgonio Pass, gateway to Los Angeles, Mount San Gorgonio, southern California's highest peak, and the forested San Bernardino Mountains. The viewpoint is named for pioneer rancher and miner Bill Keys, who lived here from the early 1900s to his death in 1969 at age eighty-nine. Keys' Desert Queen Ranch, in the park's northern part, preserves a slice of the Old West. Ranger-led tours are given regularly from fall through spring; ask at a visitor center for a schedule.

HIDDEN VALLEY

The drive runs north from Cap Rock to thirty-nine-site Hidden Valley Campground. This area of rough granite domes and jumbled boulders is center stage for Joshua Tree National Park's rock climbers. More than 4,000 established climbing routes adorn the park's rocks. The mild winter and spring weather, coupled with diverse climbing challenges from easy beginner slabs to extreme bolted sport routes and vertical cracks, attract climbers from around the world. Some of the park's best and most accessible routes lie a stone's throw from Hidden Valley Campground. Intersection Rock at the campground entrance, the Old Woman and the Blob on the west side, and the Wall and Chimney Rock on the east all offer a plethora of excellent free climbs. Farther afield lies the vast Wonderland of Rocks, Real Hidden Valley, Saddle Rock, and the classic Headstone Rock at Ryan Campground. Several excellent climbing guides are available.

Hidden Valley, west of the campground, is a good place to explore on foot. The excellent 1-mile Hidden Valley Trail begins at the Hidden Valley Picnic Area and winds back to a rock-rimmed valley reportedly once used by cattle and horse rustlers to hide their stolen stock.

The drive, following Quail Springs Road, runs northwest from Hidden Valley and passes valleys flanked by granite ridges and domes and covered with Joshua trees and creosote bushes. After a few miles the road begins to descend. The road crosses the park boundary almost 9 miles from Hidden Valley. An entrance station here offers displays and visitor information. The drive drops down along Quail Wash, passing scattered homes and ends on CA 62 in the town of Joshua Tree. A turn west leads down the Twentynine Palms Highway to Yucca Valley and I–10. A turn east leads 15 miles to Twentynine Palms and the park's main visitor center. Two side roads along this stretch lead to 101-site Indian Cove Campground and lush Forty-nine Palm Oasis, where an excellent 4-mile, round-trip hike climbs to a palm-lined water hole.

Anza-Borrego Desert Scenic Drive

23

GENERAL DESCRIPTION: A 92-mile drive that runs through Anza-Borrego Desert State Park, passing remote canyons, eroded badlands, and sharp desert peaks.

SPECIAL ATTRACTIONS: Anza-Borrego Desert State Park, Southern Emigrant Trail, Box Canyon, California fan palm groves, Carrizo Badlands, hiking, four-wheel roads.

LOCATION: Far southern California.

DRIVE ROUTE NUMBERS AND NAMES: Imperial County S–2 (Imperial Highway), San Diego County S–2 (Great South Overland Stage Route), California Highway 78, San Diego County S–3 (Yaqui Pass Road), San Diego County S–22 (Montezuma Valley Road and San Felipe Road).

TRAVEL SEASON: Year-round. Expect hot temperatures in the summer; every day is usually over one hundred degrees. Be prepared by carrying adequate water and supplies. Best travel season is October through May.

CAMPING: Two excellent developed campgrounds in the state park; reservations needed between October and May. See the park's Web site. Also several backcountry camping areas with primitive, dry sites. Additional camping at Agua Caliente and Vallecito Regional Parks.

SERVICES: All services at Borrego Springs; limited services at Ocotillo.

NEARBY ATTRACTIONS: Salton Sea (245 feet below sea level), Cuyamaca Rancho State Park, Julian, Cleveland National Forest, Sunrise Scenic Byway, Palomar Mountain State Park, Palomar Observatory.

THE DRIVE

Anza-Borrego Desert State Park is a place of superlatives. California's largest state park stretches across a 600,000-acre wonderland of barren bajadas and alkali playas, broken badlands, abrupt canyons filled with graceful palms, and rock-rimmed mountain ranges. The park's diverse terrain, ranging from a high point of 6,193 feet on its western border to lowlands just above sea level near the Salton Sea, harbors an incredible diversity of wildlife habitats, plant communities, and climates. The park also boasts a colorful history that includes the 1774 route of Spanish explorer Juan Bautista de Anza, the 1849 Southern Emigrant Trail, and the famous Butterfield Overland Stage line of 1858. The park's name reflects its unique history and natural history—Anza honors its human exploration and Borrego, a Spanish term for bighorn sheep, symbolizes its wild desert heart. This 91-mile-long scenic drive

CALIFORNIA

To
I-15

Pacific Crest
Trail

86

79

Warner Springs

S22

Park
Visitor
Center

Borrego Palm
Canyon
Campground

Borrego
Springs

S3

VOLCAN MOUNTAINS

S22

S2

Pinyon
Ridge

Tamarisk
Grove
Campground

Yaqui
Pass

Kenyon
Overlook

78

Julian

78

Yaqui
Well

Scissors
Crossing

Earthquake Valley

ANZA-
BORREGO
STATE PARK

Whale Peak
5,320 ft.

Granite
Mountain
5,633 ft.

Blair Valley
Campground

VALLECITO MOUNTAINS

Box Canyon
Overlook

79

Vallecito Regional
Park and
Campgound

Agua Caliente
Regional Park
and Campgound

Carrizo Valley

Palm
Spring

Carrizo
Badlands

LAGUNA MOUNTAINS

CLEVELAND
NATIONAL
FOREST

Mountain
Palm Springs
Campground

Sombrero Peak
4,229 ft.

Sweeney
Pass

Overlook

COYOTE MOUNTAINS

To
San Diego

8

Bow Willow
Campground

JACUMBA MOUNTAINS

S2

Fossil
Canyon

Ocotillo

PINE CREEK
WILDERNESS

Pacific Crest Trail

To
El Centro

8

N

Tecate

UNITED STATES
MEXICO

2

0   Kilometers   10

0   Miles   10

travels over four different paved roads, explores the park's wonders, offers spectacular scenery, excellent camping, numerous historic sites, and great hiking trails.

Anza-Borrego Desert State Park is best considered a three-season parkland. Summers can be prohibitively hot. Expect daily high temperatures to be well above 100 degrees. Daytime temperatures in July, the warmest month, average 107 with nighttime lows dropping to seventy-five degrees. August's average highs are 106 degrees. When traveling here in summer, make sure your vehicle is in good operating condition and carry lots of water. Five gallons is not too much for a morning drive. Be sure to carry water and wear a hat when hiking in summer. Cooler temperatures are found west of the park atop the coastal ranges. Fall, winter, and spring days are pleasant, with highs ranging between sixty and ninety degrees. Winter nights can be chilly. Annual precipitation at park headquarters is 6.7 inches. January is the wet month, receiving only 1.2 inches of precipitation; while June is the driest, receiving no precipitation.

FOSSIL CANYON TO CARRIZO BADLANDS

The drive begins 90 miles east of San Diego at the I–8 interchange at Ocotillo. Head north into Ocotillo on Imperial County Road S–2. After 2 miles, the road heads northwest and leaves Ocotillo behind as it runs across a dry bajada. Cholla cacti and ocotillo scatter across the wide plain. Shell Canyon Road, offering an interesting side trip, begins on Ocotillo's outskirts. This road heads north into Fossil Canyon in the Coyote Mountains. The canyon boasts numerous 50-million-year-old marine fossils, including coral and oysters in its rocks. This area is part of the Yuha Desert Recreation Area administered by the Bureau of Land Management.

After about 8 miles the road enters San Diego County and Anza-Borrego Desert State Park. The road follows a broad valley filled with detritus and flanked by the barren Coyote Mountains on the north and the Jacumba Mountains on the south. These ranges, a jumbled mass of uplifted granite and sedimentary layers, form intermediate steps between the below-sea-level Salton Trough to the east and the 6,000-foot coastal ranges to the west.

After a few miles of slow climbing, the road passes **Carrizo Badlands Overlook.** This vista offers spectacular views into a badlands dissected by Carrizo Creek and its dry tributaries. A rainbow of colors—jade, yellow, white, rose, and cobalt—shade the twisted rock layers below. The sediments here have yielded a wealth of fossils—including saber tooth, mastodon, zebra, giant sloth, bison, llama, and camel—that inhabited a fertile savanna over two million years ago. More than 170 species of marine shellfish have also been identified here in lake and sea deposits. The park is considered one of North America's greatest repositories of Pliocene and Pleistocene fossils. A jeep road winds down Canyon Sin Nombre just north of the overlook into the heart of the badlands.

Just past the viewpoint, the road crosses 1,065-foot Sweeney Pass and drops down Sweeney Canyon to Carrizo Creek. Three miles from the overlook, a dirt

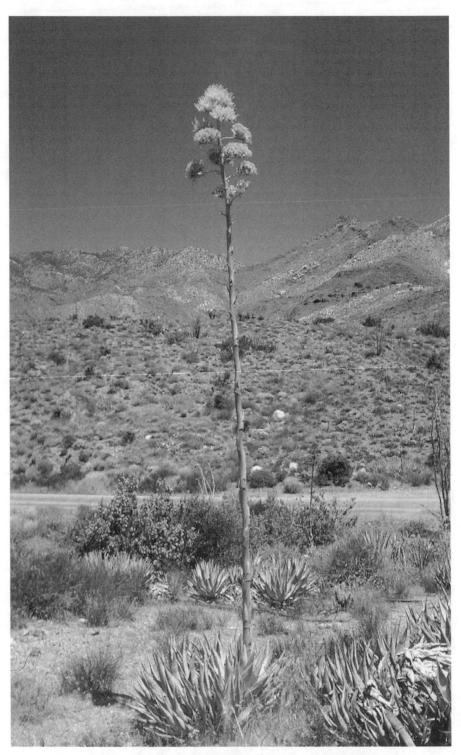

An agave blooms along Road S–2 in the heat of Anza-Borrego Desert State Park.

road runs south to Bow Willow Campground and the entrance to Bow Willow Canyon. The primitive campground offers sixteen sites. A good hike meanders up the canyon, passing desert willows and California fan palms.

MOUNTAIN PALM SPRINGS

Just up the road lies Mountain Palm Springs, an interesting oasis tucked into the dry granitic Tierra Blanca Mountains west of the road. Groundwater seeps along fault lines and waters six palm groves scattered along rock canyon floors. A moderate 2.5-mile round-trip hike on North Fork Trail leads up the north arm of Mountain Palm Springs Canyon to North Grove and Mary's Bowl Grove. Rare elephant trees are also found here. Another great 3-mile round-trip hike follows South Fork Trail up the south canyon branch to Pygmy Grove, with fifty palms, and farther on lies the Southwest Grove. A free, waterless, primitive campground sits at the canyon mouth.

The California fan palm, *Washingtonia filifera,* grows in scattered isolated colonies in Baja California, southwestern Arizona, and southeastern California. The trees thrive around springs in mountain canyons, forming lush oases that attract birds and animals. The park boasts twenty-five palm groves hidden in canyons. The palms reach heights of 50 feet with a trunk diameter of 3 feet. Dead leaves hang down from the palm's crown, forming a heavy skirt. The trees, unlike other desert plants that wait patiently for rain, need a plentiful and constant supply of water. Here in the park the palms are generally associated with the San Jacinto and Elsinore Faults, two main splinters of the San Andreas Fault, where groundwater is forced upward along fault lines. The Cahuillas, Shoshonean speakers in the park's north section, and the Kumeyaays, Yuman speakers in the south, long relied on the palm oases for food, water, and shelter. Numerous archeological sites, including bedrock mortars, potsherds, and rock art, recall their life in this austere land.

SOUTHERN EMIGRANT TRAIL

A few miles up the drive, a side road bumps east to **Palm Spring,** a state historical landmark. From Ocotillo to Scissors Crossing, the drive follows the route of the old Southern Emigrant Trail and the Butterfield Stage Line. Palm Spring, with its water and shade, made an ideal stage stop between the Carrizo Station to the east and the Vallecito Station to the west. The twenty-four-day stagecoach journey began in Missouri and ran more than 2,000 miles to San Francisco. Travelers complained bitterly of bad food, searing temperatures, and motion sickness. The Southern Emigrant Trail was a popular winter route to California and its gold fields in the 1850s. Most pioneers rejoiced when they reached the cool, shaded springs of Anza-Borrego after crossing the hot, arid trail from Yuma called *Jornada del Muerto* (Journey of Death).

Juan Bautista de Anza used a historic trail corridor east of here in 1774 in search of a good land route from Sonora, Mexico, to the California settlements. At the time, the Spanish sought to reinforce their northern California outposts to stave off a growing Russian presence. Captain de Anza and his scouting party marched northward through today's park, up Coyote Canyon between the San Ysidro and Santa Rosa Mountains, and into California's interior. A year later he returned with settlers, including 125 children, bound for Monterey. In upper Coyote Canyon north of Borrego Springs in the park's north section, the Anza Expedition Monument marks the spot where Salvador Ygnacio Linares was born on December 24, 1775, one of California's first nonnatives.

AGUA CALIENTE TO BOX CANYON

The scenic drive travels northwest up broad Carrizo Valley and reaches Agua Caliente Regional Park 9 miles from Palm Spring. This San Diego County parkland surrounds a number of warm mineral springs that gush up along the Elsinore Fault. The park offers a shady 140-site campground and a store. A pleasant 1.5-mile hike climbs up Moonlight Canyon south of the campground to a low saddle.

The drive runs 4 miles up a narrowing canyon carved by Vallecito Creek on the north flank of the Tierra Blanca Mountains to **Vallecito Regional Park.** This interesting park is another California historical landmark. It protects a reconstruction of this famous stage stop on the Butterfield Overland Mail route. The green marshes or cienegas along Vallecito Creek here were a welcome sight to parched travelers on the emigrant trail. This shaded spot in the broad Vallecito Valley lies beneath the green forested Laguna Mountains. A sod house was first built here in 1851 to protect pioneers from marauding Indians. It was expanded a few years later to a stage station. Butterfield Stage passenger Waterman Ormsby described the area in 1858, "Vallecito, or Little Valley, is a beautiful green spot—a perfect oasis in the desert . . . the green bushes and grass are a most refreshing relief from the sandy sameness of the desert." The park also has a forty-four-site campground and picnic area.

Past the county park, the road runs across broad Vallecito Valley. After 3 more miles, the road climbs steeply north over low mountains onto Mason Valley, a high, dry plain. The wagon-wheel ruts of the **Southern Emigrant Trail** are visible to the southeast as the road climbs out of Vallecito Valley. The drive swings east into abrupt Box Canyon on the valley's east side. Rough 5,633-foot Granite Mountain looms to the north. **Box Canyon Monument,** a mile up the draw, offers interpretations of the history of the pioneer trails that traversed the park. Box Canyon is a significant historical site. The Mormon Battalion under the command of Lt. Colonel Philip St. George Cooke hacked a wagon trail through the rocky canyon just south of today's roadway, using only hand tools. This opened the first wagon road into southern California. Traces of two old roads can be seen from the roadside overlook—the Mormon Battalion Trail above and the later Emigrant and Butterfield Mail Routes below.

The drive turns north from Box Canyon and traverses the eastern slope of Granite Mountain. A turnoff leads south for a half mile to a historic marker on the

Butterfield Mail Route in Blair Valley. A short hike leads from the marker up the well-preserved ruts of the old trail to Foot and Walker Pass on a rough divide that separates Blair and Earthquake Valleys. Passengers on the stage line and forty-niners on the Emigrant Trail often had to walk and push their wagons over this steep pass. Nearby is the free but primitive Blair Valley Campground.

EARTHQUAKE VALLEY TO YAQUI WELL

County Road S–2 runs northwest up Earthquake Valley another 6 miles to its intersection with CA 78 at Scissors Crossing. The valley is named for the regular tremors that occur along the Elsinore Fault, a major branch of the San Andreas Fault, that runs west of the valley. Scissors Crossing, named for the scissors-shaped convergence of roads here, was long the site of Indian villages and later the San Felipe Stage Station in the 1870s. Grassy cienegas or marshes watered by the peren-nial flow of San Felipe Creek made the area an attractive site.

Turn east from CR S–2 onto CA 78. The highway runs east past Sentenac Cienega, a lush marshland alive with birds and green plants that look out of place in this otherwise dry country. After a mile the drive winds down narrow Sentenac Canyon. A tangle of tamarisk, willows, and cottonwoods lines the twisting creek, while rocky hillsides above are studded with agaves and cacti. After a few more miles, the canyon opens into a broad, barren valley filled with alluvium. The drive follows the creek down the valley and reaches its next intersection with CR S–3 (Yaqui Pass Road) after 7 miles. Turn northeast on CR S–3.

Tamarisk Grove Campground, with twenty-seven sites shaded by towering tamarisk trees, lies a quarter mile up S–3. This developed campground has showers, running water, and restrooms; it usually requires reservations on weekends in the busy winter and spring seasons. Two short trails loop into the desert near the camp-ground. The mile-long Cactus Loop Trail winds across the rocky desert and offers a great introduction to the area's diverse desert plants. The Yaqui Well Trail travels 0.8-mile (1.6 round-trip) to a desert water hole that harbors an excellent selection of birds, including long-eared owl, Gambel's quail, ladder-backed woodpecker, canyon wren, western meadowlark, and house finch. More than 260 bird species have been identified at Anza-Borrego.

Yaqui Well, as well as other spring-fed oases, are also excellent places to spot the park's thirsty wildlife. Almost sixty mammal species, including twenty bat species and three types of kangaroo rats, inhabit the park's diverse landscape. Park mammals commonly seen are black-tailed hare, Audubon cottontail, antelope ground squirrel, skunk, raccoon, southern mule deer, and coyotes. Rarer animals are the mountain lion, bobcat, kit fox, ringtail, and the elusive Peninsular bighorn sheep. The bighorn or "borrego" ranges across the park's lofty peaks and rocky canyons. The park pro-tects about 300 of the nation's 400 sheep. Three populations scatter across the park in the Santa Rosa Mountains, Vallecito Mountains, and Carrizo Gorge. The bighorns are often seen in fall and early winter along the park roads.

The drive climbs steeply northeast up the flank of Pinyon Ridge. After 1.5 miles **Kenyon Overlook** is reached. This pull-off offers great views south to the ragged Pinyon and Vallecito Mountains and east to the glimmering blue Salton Sea. Past the overlook, the road climbs over 1,750-foot Yaqui Pass and drops north down a broad bajada to Borrego Valley. Yaqui Pass primitive campground lies just east of the drive.

THROUGH BORREGO SPRINGS

The drive meets Borrego Springs Road 5.5 miles north of the pass and bends left. Six miles later CR S–3 intersects San Diego County Road S–22 in the town of Borrego Springs. Head west on CR S–22. Borrego Valley was originally settled by ranchers including John McCain and the Clark Brothers. Later homesteaders planted alfalfa fields and citrus groves. Borrego Springs today is famed for its pink grapefruit and offers all services to travelers, including gas, groceries, lodging, and four golf courses.

The Anza-Borrego park headquarters and visitor center lies just west of town. The earth-bermed visitor center offers excellent displays on the park's natural history, geology, and history as well as naturalist-led programs. North of the visitor center is 117-site Borrego Palm Canyon Campground and an excellent hike up Borrego Palm Canyon to a shady palm grove. Palm Canyon Creek, which occasionally dries up in summer, shelters a lush riparian oasis. The hike is the park's most popular trail. It is filled with sound—the descending scale of a canyon wren, the rustle of palm-thatching in the wind, and the sweet song of running water

The drive, following CR S–22, climbs steeply south from the visitor center up rocky mountainsides. Winding in and out of dry canyons, the road quickly gains elevation. As it ascends, the roadside vegetation begins changing from desert plants to thick chaparral that covers rounded granite hills. Great viewpoints along the road offer vistas of Borrego Valley and the Salton Sea. Eleven miles from the visitor center, the drive crosses a lofty ridge crest and drops west into a broad grassy valley interrupted by dense oak groves and occasional pine trees. After the road crosses the Pacific Crest Trail, it ends at its junction with CR S–3. Continue west on S–2, San Felipe Road, down the broad valley alongside Buena Vista Creek for 5 miles to the drive's end at California Highway 79.

Mojave Desert Scenic Drive

GENERAL DESCRIPTION: This 59-mile-long scenic drive, following two desert back roads, traverses a spectacular slice of the 1.6-million-acre Mojave National Preserve past granite mountains, sand dunes, broad basins, and Joshua tree forests.

SPECIAL ATTRACTIONS: Cima Dome, Kelso Depot, Kelso Sand Dunes, Granite Mountains, Joshua trees.

LOCATION: Southeastern California in the Mojave National Preserve.

DRIVE ROUTE NAMES: Kelbaker Road, Kelso-Cima Road, Cima Road.

TRAVEL SEASON: Year-round. Expect hot summers with temperatures regularly over one hundred degrees. It is ten to twenty degrees cooler in the surrounding mountain ranges.

CAMPING: Two established campgrounds in the Preserve, as well as roadside camping areas. Other area camping at Providence Mountain State Recreation Area, a BLM campground at Afton Canyon, and several commercial campgrounds.

SERVICES: No regular services are found along the drive. Be sure your gas tank is full before leaving on the drive. Complete services are found in Barstow, Needles, Baker, and Las Vegas, Nevada.

NEARBY ATTRACTIONS: Mitchell Caverns, Providence Mountains State Recreation Area, Wild Horse Canyon Back Country Byway, Lake Mead National Recreation Area, Joshua Tree National Park, Amboy Crater National Natural Landmark, New York Mountains, Cinder Cones National Area, Turtle Mountain Natural Area, Calico Early Man Site, Lake Havasu, Las Vegas.

THE DRIVE

This scenic drive, following Kelbaker Road, Kelso–Cima Road, and Cima Road, crosses 59 miles of austere desert landscapes in the 1.6-million-acre Mojave National Preserve. This sprawling land is studded with sharp mountain ranges that tower above broad alluvium-filled valleys, a timeless place of distant horizons. At first glance, the desert here appears lifeless and inhospitable. But closer inspection reveals details of life—tree-lined springs that echo with bird songs; the showy colors of spring wildflowers draped across dry arroyos; and the sinuous track of a nocturnal sidewinder etched on a sand dune.

The Mojave National Preserve, administered by the National Park Service, is the pristine heart of the Mojave Desert, one of North America's five great deserts. The Mojave Desert reaches from the San Gabriel and San Bernardino Mountains

CALIFORNIA

To
Las Vegas

Mountain
Pass

Mescal Range

15

▲ Kokoweef Peak
6,036 ft.

Cima Road

Shadow Valley

Ivanpah
Mountains

To
Nipton

To Barstow

Teutonia Peak
5,710 ft. ▲

Kessler Peak
▲ 6,152 ft.

Ivanpah
Cima Road

▲
Cima Dome
5,745 ft.

Cinder Cone
Lava Beds

○ **Cima**

MOJAVE
NATIONAL
PRESERVE

Mid Hills

Kelbaker Road

Cedar
Canyon Road

Kelso Mountains

Kelso-Cima Road

▲ Kelso Peak
4,747 ft.

▲
Columbia
Mountain
5,673 ft.

○ **Kelso**

PROVIDENCE
MOUNTAINS STATE
RECREATION
AREA

Fountain
Peak ▲

□ ⛺

Providence
Mountains

**Mitchell
Caverns**

Kelso
Sand Dunes

6,611 ft. ▲

Horse
Hills

Granite
Mountains

Granite
Pass

N

Granite
Mountain ▲
6,739 ft.

40

To
Needles

To Barstow

40

0   Kilometers   10

0   Miles   10

To Amboy

eastward to the Colorado River and northward past Death Valley to the dry basins of southern Nevada. The desert's southern boundary is roughly marked by Interstate 10. The immense national scenic area includes twenty-six named mountain ranges, the nation's third-highest dune field, water-sculpted caverns, lava flows, cinder cones, wide basins, dry lakes, and a human history that dates back 10,000 years to early paleo-hunters who camped along ancient lakeshores.

Weather along the drive is generally pleasant in spring, fall, and winter. Expect warm days and cool nights. Winter highs range between forty and seventy, with occasional light rain showers or a dusting of snow. Summers are hot, with daily highs often climbing to 110 degrees in the lower valleys. Temperatures are more moderate in the mountains, including the Mid Hills and Cima Dome, and fall between eighty and one hundred degrees. Summer nights rapidly cool off. The Mojave Desert averages less than 8 inches of annual precipitation, much of it falling in the form of violent summer thunderstorms in July and August. Be aware of flash flooding and don't drive across any flooded section of road.

OVER GRANITE PASS

The drive begins 79 miles east of Barstow on Interstate 40 at the highway interchange with Kelbaker Road. Kelbaker Road heads north, swinging around the east flank of the tall, rounded Granite Mountains. This rough range, studded with gleaming white granite crags, reaches its high point atop 6,753-foot-high Granite Mountain. Van Winkle Mountain, a broad mesa rimmed by an ancient lava flow, towers east of the road.

After almost 6 miles the road turns to graded gravel for 4 miles. This dirt section allows desert bighorn sheep to travel from the Providence Mountains to the east into the Granite Mountains. The finicky sheep won't cross a hard-surfaced highway, only dirt. The diminutive desert bighorn, one of the rarest big game animals in North America, roams these high desert mountains. The sheep find "tinajas" or natural tanks filled with water from summer cloudbursts hidden in steep canyons.

The drive tops out on Granite Pass at 8 miles from the interstate at a wide saddle separating the Granite and Providence Mountains. Kelbaker Road drops arrow-straight north into a broad basin rimmed with mountains. Seven miles north of Granite Pass, a dirt track bumps west 3 miles across a creosote-covered plain to Kelso Dunes. Creosote, *hediondilla,* is called little stinker in Mexico. Creosote is a successful, drought-resistant plant that thrives in conditions that few other plants can endure. The widely spaced bushes suck up all moisture, allowing little competition from other plants. Creosotes are also some of the world's oldest known plants. A creosote stand, called "King Clone," lies 40 miles south of Barstow (see Joshua Tree National Park Scenic Drive). This plant is the clone of a parent bush that lived some 12,000 years ago after the last ice age. Some botanists say that makes it the world's oldest living thing.

KELSO DUNES

The Kelso Dunes form the third-highest dune field in the United States, after Colorado's Great Sand Dunes and California's Eureka Dunes. The Kelso Dunes, one of the Mojave Desert's outstanding features, are protected in a 154,175-acre wilderness area. Windswept and 600 feet high in places, the gleaming white dunes were formed by persistent westerly winds that scoured the dry Mojave River floodplain to the west, transporting loose sand to this natural trap. Other restless winds from the north and east balance the strong westerlies and keep the dune field from advancing eastward.

The dunes are a great place to explore. Park at the road's end and set off on foot. The dunes are closed to all off-road vehicles to protect their fragile plant and animal communities. Springtime brings a tapestry of flowers. Delicate white desert primroses creep among hollows in the dunes, sunflowers display shades of brilliant yellow, and pink sand verbena grows among the fore-dunes. Slender ricegrass stalks, laden with seeds, nod in the wind. Myriad animal tracks meander across the dunes in the morning—a lace work of beetle, lizard, mice, and kangaroo rat tracks and the S-shaped track of the sidewinder rattlesnake. Allow a couple of hours to make a round-trip hike to the dune's high point. When you come down the steep faces of the dunes, listen for a low rumbling vibration caused by the sand grains rubbing against each other. These resonant chords gave the dunes the nickname "the singing dunes."

KELSO

Past the dunes, the drive continues dropping into the Kelso Valley and reaches the old railroad town of Kelso, which is along Kelso Wash 8 miles north of the dunes turnoff. Kelso lies along the Union Pacific Railroad tracks and owes its very existence to the golden age of railroading in the early twentieth century. The town is dominated by the Kelso Depot, a Spanish-style railroad stop built in 1923. The only other remaining Union Pacific Railroad depot is now the city hall of Caliente, Nevada. Kelso's huge station served as a passenger stop and freight office, supplying overnight accommodations for both passengers and crews. The Beanery, the depot's restaurant, reportedly served the finest meals in the California desert. Deep water wells at Kelso supplied water for the steam locomotives. Kelso also housed the "helper engines" that pushed trains up the long grade to Cima. The depot closed in 1985 and has been renovated as a park visitor center.

The drive turns northeast in Kelso on the Kelso-Cima Road. The Kelbaker Road continues northeast past the Devil's Playground and the Cinder Cone Lava Beds to Baker on Interstate 15. The Kelso-Cima Road parallels the railroad tracks for 20 miles to Cima. Creosote scrub dominates the roadside.

PROVIDENCE MOUNTAINS AND JOSHUA TREES

The Providence Mountains, combined with the Mid Hills and the New York Mountains to the north, form a ragged range almost 50 miles long east of the drive.

The highest point in the Providence Mountains is 7,171-foot Providence Peak, a sawtooth ridge of rough limestone. Bold cliffs, steep canyons, and sharp arêtes characterize the entire mountain range. These desert mountains are half-buried in alluvial debris washed by quick flash floods from the peaks, leaving long, low-angle slopes or "bajadas" that drop away from the rocky mountainsides.

The seemingly sun-baked mountains teem with life. Cooler temperatures on the 6,000-foot peaks coupled with 20 to 30 inches of rainfall allow forests of pine and white fir to cloak the upper slopes. The Cedar Canyon Road, 14 miles from Kelso, gives access to the pinyon pine and juniper forest atop the Mid Hills. The twenty-six-site Mid Hills Campground here can be a cool place to stop in summer. Farther south lies **Mitchell Caverns** with two small limestone caves. The state-run park offers cave tours, camping, and hiking.

Joshua trees begin lining the road just before it reaches Cima. Cima is a Spanish word meaning summit. The railroad station was established here in 1907. It is another old railroad stop that is almost deserted. At Cima, the drive turns north on the Cima Road. The paved highway steadily climbs through one of California's thickest and most extensive Joshua tree forests. The Joshua tree is the most spectacular and characteristic plant of the Mojave Desert. It generally grows along the higher, moister margins of the desert. Conditions here, with plenty of water and sunshine, are ideal for the Joshua tree. These Joshua trees are a slightly different species than the ones seen in Joshua Tree National Park to the south. This subspecies, named *Yucca brevifolia Jaegeriana* for the famed California desert naturalist Edmund C. Jaeger, grow larger than their southern cousins.

Joshua trees were named by early Mormon travelers for their resemblance to the prophet Joshua with upraised arms. The trees provide a rich habitat for animals, birds, and insects. This tree-size yucca, reaching heights of 40 feet, depends on the pronuba moth for fertilization of its flowers in a unique symbiotic association. The desert night lizard lives under Joshua tree debris, and more than twenty-five species nest in the yucca trees, including the beautiful Scott's oriole. Flickers and ladder-backed woodpeckers both dig nesting holes in Joshua trees. Look for owls and hawks perched on the branches. Fossilized dung of the extinct giant sloth indicates that as much as 80 percent of their diet was Joshua tree leaves.

CIMA DOME TO SHADOW VALLEY

After a few more miles, Cima Road passes between the long jagged ridge of 6,512-foot Kessler Peak to the east and rounded Cima Dome. This huge, symmetrical dome is composed of quartz monzonite, a granitic rock formed when a large mass of underground magma cooled. The rounded dome is coated with Joshua trees, covers 75 square miles, and is 10 miles in diameter. Craggy, white rock outcrops stud the dome. Teutonia Peak, at 5,755 feet, is the highest crag in the area. A 2-mile-long trail leaves the drive 7 miles north of Cima at a wide parking area and climbs to the peak's rocky summit. Marvelous views of the surrounding ranges and basins

Cima Dome rises above Joshua tree forests.

unfold from here. Cooler temperatures are found along this section of the drive with its 5,000-foot elevation. Good primitive campsites are also found along this road section.

The main road descends northwest from Cima Dome into the broad Shadow Valley. The lofty and roughly upturned layers of the Ivanpah Mountains dominate the eastern horizon. As the road drops, it begins to flatten. The bordering Joshua tree forest slowly thins and gives way to the creosote plant community. The drive ends on I–15, just west of Mountain Pass and the Nevada border and 87 miles northeast of Barstow.

For More Information

GENERAL INFORMATION

Bureau of Land Management
    California State Office
2800 Cottage Way, Suite W-1834
Sacramento, CA 95825-1886
    (916) 978–4400, (916) 978–4416

California State Parks
P.O. Box 942896
Sacramento, CA 94296-0001
www.parks.ca.gov

California Travel & Tourism
    Commission
www.gocalif.ca.gov/state/tourism
www.visitcalifornia.com/state/tourism

National Park Service
1849 C Street NW
Washington DC 20240
(202) 208–6843
www.nps.gov

National Park Service
    Pacific West Region
One Jackson Center
1111 Jackson Street, Suite 700
Oakland, CA 94607
(510) 817–1300

DRIVE 1

Azalea State Reserve
15336 Highway 101
Trinidad, CA 95570
(707) 488–2041
www.parks.ca.gov/?page_id=420

Crescent City-Del Norte County
    Chamber of Commerce
1001 Front Street
Crescent City, CA 95531
(800) 343–8300
www.northerncalifornia.net

Del Norte Coast Redwoods
    State Park
1375 Elk Valley Road
Crescent City, CA 95531
(707) 464–6101, ext. 5120
www.parks.ca.gov/?page id=414

Greater Eureka Chamber of
    Commerce
2112 Broadway
Eureka, CA 95501
(707) 442–3738, (800) 356–6381
www.eurekachamber.com

Humboldt Lagoons State Park
15336 Highway 101
Trinidad, CA 95570
(707) 488–2041

Patrick's Point State Park
4150 Patrick's Point Drive
Trinidad, CA 95570
(707) 677–3570

Prairie Creek Redwoods
    State Park
(707) 464–6101, ext. 5301
www.parks.ca.gov/default.asp?
    page_id=415

Redwood National and State Parks
(Del Norte Coast Redwoods, Prairie
   Creek Redwoods, Redwood
   National Park)
1111 Second Street
Crescent City, CA 95531
(707) 464–6101

DRIVE 2
Crescent City-Del Norte County
   Chamber of Commerce
1001 Front Street
Crescent City, CA 95531
(800) 343–8300
www.northerncalifornia.net

Klamath Chamber of Commerce
P.O. Box 476
Klamath, CA 95548
(800) 200–2335, (707) 482–7165
www.klamathcc.org

Six Rivers National Forest
1330 Bayshore Way
Eureka, CA 95501
(707) 442–1721

DRIVE 3
Golden Gate National Recreation
   Area
Fort Mason, Building 201
San Francisco, CA 94123-0022
(415) 561–4700
www.nps.gov/goga

Kruse Rhododendron State Reserve
(707) 847–3221
www.parks.ca.gov/default.asp?
   page_id=448

MacKerricher State Park
(707) 964–9112
www.parks.ca.gov/default.asp?
   page_id=436

Marin County Convention
   & Visitor Bureau
1013 Larkspur Landing Circle
Larkspur, CA 94934
(415) 449–5000

Muir Woods National Monument
Mill Valley, CA 94941–2696
(415) 388–2595, (415) 388–2596
www.nps.gov/muwo

Point Reyes National Seashore
Point Reyes, CA 94956
(415) 464–5100

Van Damme State Park
(707) 937–5804
www.parks.ca.gov/default.asp?
   page_id=433

DRIVE 4
Annadel State Park
6201 Channel Drive
Santa Rosa, CA 95409
(707) 539–3911

Clear Lake State Park
(707) 279–4293
www.parks.ca.gov/default.asp?
   page_id=473

Golden Gate National Recreation
   Area
Fort Mason, Building 201
San Francisco, CA 94123-0022
(415) 561–4700

Jack London State Historic Park
2400 London Ranch Road
Glen Ellen, CA 95442
(707) 938–5216

Robert Louis Stevenson State
　Historic Park
(707) 942–4575
www.parks.ca.gov/default.asp?
　page_id=472

Sonoma County Tourism Program
520 Mendocino Avenue, Suite 210
Santa Rosa, CA 95401
(800) 5–SONOMA, (707) 565–5383
www.sonomacounty.com

DRIVE 5
Andrew Molera State Park
Big Sur Station #1
Big Sur, CA 93920
(831) 667–2315

BLM Hollister Field Office
20 Hamilton Court
Hollister, CA 95023
(831) 630–5000

Garrapata State Park
(831) 624–4909
www.parks.ca.gov/default.asp?
　page_id=579

Julia Pfeiffer Burns State Park
Big Sur Station #1
Big Sur, CA 93920
(831) 667–2315

Los Padres National Forest
6755 Hollister Avenue, Suite 150
Goleta, CA 93117
(805) 968–6640

Pfeiffer Big Sur State Park
Big Sur Station #1
Big Sur, CA 93920
(831) 667–2315

Point Lobos State Reserve
Route 1, Box 62
Carmel, CA 93923
(831) 624–4909

San Luis Obispo Chamber of
　Commerce & Visitor Center
1039 Chorro Street
San Luis Obispo, CA 93401
(805) 781–2777

DRIVE 6
BLM Hollister Field Office
20 Hamilton Court
Hollister, CA 95023
(831) 630–5000

Pinnacles National Monument
5000 Highway 146
Paicines, CA 95043
(831) 389–4485

DRIVE 7
Klamath National Forest
1312 Fairlane Road
Yreka, CA 96097-9549
(530) 842–6131

Six Rivers National Forest
1330 Bayshore Way
Eureka, CA 95501
(707) 442–1721

Willow Creek Chamber of
  Commerce
P.O. Box 704
Willow Creek, CA 95573
(530) 629–2693

Yreka Chamber of Commerce
117 West Miner Street
Yreka, CA 96097
(530) 842–1649

DRIVE 8

Lava Beds National Monument
Indian Well Headquarters
Tulelake, CA 96134
(530) 667–2282, ext. 232

Tulelake Chamber of Commerce
c/o Tulelake-Butte Valley Fairgrounds
800 South Main Street
Tulelake, Ca 96134
(530) 667–5312
www.tulelakechamber.com

DRIVE 9

Alturas Chamber of Commerce
522 South Main Street
Alturas, CA 96101
(530) 233–4434
www.alturaschamber.org

BLM Alturas Field Office
708 West 12th Street
Alturas, CA 96101
(530) 233–4666

BLM Surprise Field Office
602 Cressler Street
Cedarville, CA 96104
(530) 279–6101

Modoc National Forest
800 West 12th Street
Alturas, CA 96101
(530) 233–5811

Modoc National Wildlife Refuge
P.O. Box 1610
Alturas, CA 96101-1610
(530) 233–3572

DRIVE 10

Lassen National Forest
2550 Riverside Drive
Susanville, CA 96130
(530) 257–2151

Lassen Volcanic National Park
P.O. Box 100
Mineral, CA 96063
(530) 595–4444

Siskiyou County Visitors Bureau
P.O. Box 1138
Mount Shasta, CA 96067
(530) 926–3850
www.visitsiskiyou.org

DRIVE 11

Nevada City Chamber of Commerce
132 Main Street
Nevada City, CA 95959
(530) 265–2692

Sierra County Chamber of
Commerce
P.O. Box 436
Sierra City, CA 96125
(530) 862–0308, (800) 200–4949
www.sierracounty.org

Tahoe National Forest
631 Coyote Street
Nevada City, CA 95959
(530) 265–4531

DRIVE 12

D. L. Bliss State Park
(530) 525–7277
www.parks.ca.gov/default.asp?page_id
=505

South Lake Tahoe Chamber of
Commerce
3066 Lake Tahoe Boulevard
South Lake Tahoe, CA 96150
(530) 541–5255

Truckee Donner Chamber of
Commerce & Visitor Center
10065 Donner Pass Road
Truckee, CA 96161
(530) 587–2757

USDA Forest Service
Lake Tahoe Basin Management Unit
35 College Drive
South Lake Tahoe, CA 96150
(530) 543–2600

DRIVE 13

Amador County Chamber of
Commerce
125 Peek Street, Suite 2
Amador City, CA 95642
(209) 223–0350

Eldorado National Forest
100 Forni Road
Placerville, CA 95667
(916) 644–6084

Humboldt-Toiyabe National Forest
1200 Franklin Way
Sparks, NV 89431
(702) 738–5171

Indian Grinding Rock State
Historic Park
14881 Pine Grove-Volcano Road
Pine Grove, CA 95665
(209) 296–7488
www.parks.ca.gov/?page_id=553

Stanislaus National Forest
19777 Greenley Road
Sonora, CA 95370
(209) 532–3671

DRIVE 14

Humboldt-Toiyabe National
Forest
1200 Franklin Way
Sparks, NV 89431
(702) 738–5171

Stanislaus National Forest
19777 Greenley Road
Sonora, CA 95370
(209) 532–3671

Tuolumne County Visitors Bureau
542 Stockton Road
Sonora, CA 95370
(209) 533–4420, (800) 446–1333
www.thegreatunfenced.com

DRIVE 15

Lee Vining Chamber of
   Commerce
P.O. Box 130
Lee Vining, CA 93541
(760) 647–6629
www.leevining.com

Yosemite National Park
P.O. Box 577
Yosemite National Park, CA 95389
(209) 372–0200

DRIVE 16

Mariposa Chamber of Commerce
Main Street
Mariposa, CA 95311
(209) 878–3074
www.mariposa.org

Mariposa County Visitors Bureau
P.O. Box 967
Mariposa, CA 95338
(209) 966–7081, (866) HALF–DOME
www.homeofyosemite.com

Yosemite National Park
P.O. Box 577
Yosemite National Park, CA 95389
(209) 372–0200

DRIVE 17

Kings Canyon and Sequoia National
   Parks
47050 Generals Highway
Three Rivers, CA 93271-9700
(559) 565–3341

Sequoia National Forest
900 West Grand Avenue
Porterville, CA 93257
(559) 784-1500

DRIVE 18

Angeles National Forest
701 North Santa Anita Avenue
Arcadia, CA 91006
(626) 574–1613

Chilao Visitor Center
Angeles Crest Highway (CA 2)
La Canada, CA 91011
(626) 796–5541

Clear Creek Information Center
Angeles Crest Highway (CA 2)
La Canada, CA 91011
(626) 821–6764

DRIVE 19

Big Bear Chamber of Commerce &
   Visitors Bureau
P.O. Box 2860
Big Bear Lake, CA 92315
(909) 866–4607

San Bernardino National Forest
1824 South Commercenter Circle
San Bernardino, CA 92408
(909) 382–2600

San Bernardino Convention &
Visitors Bureau
201 North E Street, Suite 103
San Bernardino, CA 92401
(909) 889–3980, (800) 867–8366
www.san-bernardino.org

DRIVE 20

BLM Palm Springs South Coast Field
Office
690 West Garnet Avenue, P.O. Box
581260
North Palm Springs, CA 92258-1260
(760) 251–4800
www.ca.blm.gov/caso/wf-palmpine.
html

Mount San Jacinto State Park
25905 Highway 243, P.O. Box 308
Idyllwild, CA 92549
(909) 659–2607
Wilderness permits: (909) 659-2607

Palm Desert Chamber of
Commerce
73-710 Fred Waring Drive, Suite 114
Palm Desert, CA 92260
(760) 251–4800, (800) 873–2428
www.palm-desert.org

DRIVE 21

BLM El Centro Field Office
1661 South Fourth Street
El Centro, CA 92243
(760) 337–4400

Cleveland National Forest
10845 Rancho Bernardo Drive,
Suite 200
San Diego, CA 92127
(858) 673–6180

El Cajon Chamber of Commerce
200 East Main Street
El Cajon, CA 92020
(619) 441–1776

DRIVE 22

Joshua Tree Chamber of
Commerce
61325 Twentynine Palms Highway,
Suite F
Joshua Tree, CA 92252
(760) 366–3723

Joshua Tree National Park
74485 National Park Drive
Twentynine Palms, CA 92277-3597
(760) 367–5500

Twentynine Palms Chamber of
Commerce & Visitors Bureau
6455-A Mesquite Avenue
Twentynine Palms, CA 92277
(760) 367–3445
www.29palms.com

DRIVE 23

Anza-Borrego Desert State Park
200 Palm Canyon Drive
Borrego Springs, CA 92004
(760) 767–5311
www.anzaborrego.statepark.org

Borrego Springs Chamber of
Commerce
622 Palm Canyon Drive
Borrego Springs, CA 92004
(800) 559–5524
www.borregosprings.org

DRIVE 24
BLM Needles Field Office
101 West Spikes Road
Needles, CA 92363
(760) 326–7000

Mojave National Preserve
222 East Main Street, Suite 202
Barstow, CA 92311
(760) 255–8800

Mojave National Preserve Desert
Information Center
72157 Baker Boulevard, P.O. Box 241
Baker, CA 92309
(760) 733–4040
707 West Broadway
Needles, CA 92363
(760) 326–6322
www.nps.gov/moja

Providence Mountains State
Recreation Area
Mitchell Caverns Natural Preserve
P.O. Box 1
Essex, CA 92332
(760) 928–2586

Index

A

Agua Caliente Regional Park, 182
Alturas, 71
Amphitheater Point, 142
Ancient Indian Village Vista Point, 59
Andrew Molera State Park, 41, 43
Angeles Crest Scenic Byway, 143–49
Angeles National Forest, 145
Annadel State Park, 29
Anza-Borrego Desert Scenic Drive,
    177–84
Applegate-Lassen Trail, 72, 74–75
Arcata, 4
Argonaut Mine, 102
aspen, 155–56
Audubon Canyon Ranch, 19
Azalea State Reserve, 4

B

Badger Pass Ski Area, 126
bald eagle, 155
Bale Grist Mill State Historic Park, 33
Banning, 159
Barton Flats Visitor
    Center, 155–56
Bear Gulch Visitor Center, 52

Beringer Vineyards, 33
Big Baldy Saddle, 139
Big Bear Lake, 154–55
Bigelow cholla, 172
Bigfoot, 59
bighorn sheep, 148, 183, 187
Bigler, William, 104, 106
Big Oak Flat Road, 116
Big Pines, 149
Big Sand Butte, 62
Big Stump Basin Trail, 136
Big Sur, 43
Big Sur Coast Scenic Drive, 37–46
Big Valley, 36
Bixby Creek Bridge, 41
Bodega Bay, 22
Borrego Springs, 184
Bothe-Napa Valley State Park, 33
Box Canyon Monument, 182
Brannan, Samuel, 33–34
Bridalveil Fall, 128
Buena Vista Winery, 31
Bumpass Hell, 81–82
Burbank, Luther, 29
Butterfield Overland Mail Company,
    162, 182–83
Butterfield Stage Line, 181

C

Cabrillo, Juan Rodriguez, 39, 44

Cahuilla Tewanet Vista Point, 162

California Desert Conservation
  Area, 162

California fan palm, 181

California Sea Otter Game
  Refuge, 40

California Western Railroad, 25

Calistoga, 33–34

Cambria, 45

Campo, 166–67

Captain Jack's Stronghold, 66, 67

Carmel, 39–40

Carmel River State Beach, 40

Carrizo Badlands
  Overlook, 179

Carson, Kit, 105

Carson Pass Scenic Byway, 100–106

Cascade Fall, 130

Cave Loop Road, 64

Cedar Grove, 138

Cedar Pass–Fandango Pass Scenic
  Drive, 69–76

Cedarville, 72

Chaos Crags, 84–85

chaparral, 159, 165

Chaw'se Regional Indian
  Museum, 103

Chilao Visitor Center, 146

Children's Forest, 153

cholla, 172

Chumash, 46

Cima Dome, 189

Cinder Cone, 83

Clear Creek Vista, 145

Clear Lake, 35

Clear Lake State Park, 35

Clemens, Samuel, 97

Cloudburst Summit, 148

Coalinga, 49

coast redwood, 12

Colorado Desert, 171

Columbia, 109

Columbia Plateau, 61–62

Columns of the Giants, 112

Cottonwood Spring, 170

Cottonwood Visitor Center, 170

Crane Flat, 116

creosote, 171, 187

Crescent City, 8, 11

D

dawn redwood, 12

Deadman Canyon, 112

de Anza, Juan Bautista, 181–82

Del Norte Coast Redwoods State
  Park, 5, 8

desert bighorn sheep, 187

Desolation Wilderness Area, 97

Devastated Area, 84

Devils Canyon, 146

Devil's Garden, 76

Devil's Homestead Lava Flow, 66

Devil's Ladder, 106

Devil's Punchbowl County
  Park, 149

Diablo Range, 49

Diamond Peak, 81

D.L. Bliss State Park, 98

Donnell Vista, 110

Donner Memorial State Park, 99

Downieville, 91

Drake, Francis, 20

E

Earthquake Valley, 183

East Sand Butte, 62

El Capitan, 129

El Capitan Meadow, 130

Eldorado National
  Forest, 103–4

Elk, 24

El Portal, 130

El Portal View, 126

Emerald Bay Overlook, 97

Emerald Bay State Park, 97

Eureka, 3

F

Fairview Dome, 119

Fairview Point, 160

Fandango Pass–Cedar Pass Scenic
  Drive, 69–76

Fandango Pass Massacre, 75

Farallon Islands, 19

Fern Canyon, 6

Fleener Chimneys, 65

Foothills Visitor Center, 142

Fort Bidwell, 74

Fort Bragg, 25

Fort Humboldt State Historic Park, 3

Fort Ross State Historic Park,
  22–23

Fossil Canyon, 179

fossils, 179

Fremont, John C., 97, 105

Fresno Flats Historical Park, 124

G

Garner Valley, 161–62

Garrapata State Park, 41

Gasquet, 14

General Grant Tree, 135

Generals Highway, 138–39

Giant Forest, 141

giant sequoia, 116, 125, 139–40

Gillem's Camp, 67

Glacier Point, 127–28

Glacier Point Road, 126

Glass Mountain
  Geologic Area, 62

Goat Rock State Beach, 22

Golden Gate National Recreation
  Area, 19

Gold Fever Trail, 155

Goose Lake, 75

Granite Pass, 187

Grant, Ulysses S., 3

Grant Grove, 135

Grassy Hollow Visitor Center, 149

gray pine, 49

Grizzly Giant, 125

Gualala, 24

Gualala Point Regional Park, 24

H

Half Dome, 118, 129

Happy Camp, 57

Hat Lake, 83

Heaps Park Arboretum, 153

Hearst, William
  Randolph, 45

Hearst San Simeon State Historical
  Monument, 45

Henry Miller Memorial Library, 43

Hidden Valley, 175–76

Hollister, 52

Hope Valley, 106

Hopland, 36

Horse Creek, 56

Humboldt Bay, 4

Humboldt Bay National Wildlife
  Refuge, 4

Humboldt Lagoons State Park, 5

I

Idyllwild, 161

Indian Cave, 175

Indian Grinding Rocks State Historic
  Park, 102–3

Indian Vista Point, 159–60

Inspiration Point, 148–49, 152

J

Jack London State
  Historical Park, 30

Jackson, 102

jade hunting, 44

Jarvi Memorial Vista, 148

Jedediah Smith Redwoods State Park,
  5, 8, 11–12

Jeffers, Robinson, 40

Jenner, 22

Joshua tree, 173, 189

Joshua Tree National Park Scenic
  Drive, 168–76

Jug Handle State Reserve, 25

Julia Pfeiffer Burns State Park, 44

Junction View, 136–37

K

Karuks, 58–59

Kaspian Recreation Area, 99

Kaweah River, 142

Kelseyville, 35

Kelso, 188

Kelso Depot, 188

Kelso Dunes, 188

Kennedy Meadows, 112

Kennedy Mine, 102

Kenwood, 30

Kenyon Overlook, 184

Keys View, 175

King Clone, 171, 187

Kings Canyon and Sequoia Scenic
    Drive, 132–42

Kings Canyon Highway, 135

Kings Canyon National Park, 135–36

Kings Canyon Overlook, 139

Kings Creek Meadows, 83

Klamath, 8

Klamath National Forest, 55

Klamath Ranges, 57

Klamath River, 7–8

Klamath River Scenic Drive, 53–59

Kruse Rhododendron State
    Reserve, 23

L

La Canada, 145

Lake City, 74

Lake Fulmor, 159

Lake Helen, 82

Lake Hemet, 161

Lake Morena County Park, 167

Lake Tahoe Scenic Drive, 93–99

Lake View Point, 153

Lassen Cutoff, 75

Lassen Peak, 81, 84

Lassen Peak Trail, 82

Lassen Volcanic National Park Scenic
    Drive, 77–85

Lassen Winter Sports Area, 80

Lava Beds National Monument Scenic
    Drive, 60–68

lava tube caves, 63–64

Lee Vining Canyon, 121

Lodgepole, 140–41

London, Jack, 30

Lost Coast, 26

Lost Grove, 140

Lost Horse Mine, 175

Lost Horse Valley, 173, 175

Luther Burbank Home and
    Gardens, 29

M

MacKerricher State Park, 25

Malakoff Diggins State Park, 88–89

Manchester State Beach, 24

Manzanita Lake, 85

Marin City, 18

Mariposa, 131

Mariposa Grove, 125

McKinleyville, 4

Medicine Lake, 62

Meeks Bay, 98

Mendocino, 25

Mendocino Coast–Sonoma Scenic
Drive, 16–26

Mendocino Headlands State Park, 25

Merced River, 130–31

Merrill Cave, 65

Mexican Border Scenic
Drive, 163–67

Middletown, 35

Mill Creek Canyon, 155–56

Miller, Henry, 43

Minkler, 134

Mission San Juan Bautista, 52

Mitchell Caverns, 189

Miwoks, 20, 102–3, 109, 110

Modoc Plateau, 61

Modoc War, 66–67

Mojave Desert, 171

Mojave Desert Scenic Drive, 185–90

Mono Lake, 121

Monterey, 39

Monterey pine, 45

Mormon Emigrant Trail, 104, 106

Moro Rock, 141

Morro Rock, 46

Mountain Palm Springs, 181

Mountain Top Junction, 149

Mount Hoffman, 118

Mount Konocti, 35

Mount San Jacinto State Wilderness
and Park, 160–61

Mount St. Helena, 34–35

Mount Tehama, 81

Mount Wilson, 146

Mount Wilson Observatory, 146

Muir, John, 18, 81, 118, 119, 123, 125,
128–29, 138

Muir Beach, 19

Muir Beach Overlook, 19

Muir Grove, 140

Muir Woods National Monument, 18

Murrieta, Joaquin, 49–50

N

Napa, 31, 32

Napa–Sonoma Valleys Scenic
Drive, 27–36

Nelson's bighorn sheep, 148

Nevada City, 88

Nobles Emigrant Trail, 84

North Fork, Yuba River, 90

North San Juan, 89

O

Oakhurst, 124

ocotillo (plant), 172

Ocotillo (town), 179

Olmsted Point, 118

Onyx Summit, 155

Oregon Creek Day Use Area, 90

Orick, 5

Orleans, 58

P

Pacific Crest National Scenic Trail, 105

Pacific Valley, 44

Palm Desert, 162

Palm Spring, 181

Palm Springs Aerial Tramway, 161

Palms to Pines Scenic Drive, 157–62

Panorama Point, 152

Panoramic Point, 135

Park Boulevard, 172

Patrick's Point State Park, 4

Peninsular bighorn sheep, 183

petroglyphs, 68

Pfeiffer Big Sur State Park, 43

Piedras Blancas, 44

Pinnacles National
    Monument, 51–52

Pinto Basin, 170–71

Pioneer Yosemite
    History Center, 126

Point Arena, 24

Point Lobos State Reserve, 40

Point Reyes National Seashore, 20

Point Sur, 41

Potrero, 166

Prairie Creek Redwoods State Park,
    5, 6–7

Priest Valley, 49–50

Providence Mountains, 188–89

Q

quaking aspen, 155–56

Queen Valley, 172–73

R

Rabbit Valley, 50

Raker Peak, 84

raptors, 65

Red Lake Vista Point, 106

Redwood Highway Scenic Drive, 1–8

Redwood National Park, 5–6

Reflection Lake, 85

Requa, 8

Rim of the World Scenic Byway,
    150–56

river rafting, 57

Robert Louis Stevenson Museum,
    32–33

Robert Louis Stevenson State Park,
    34–35

rock climbing, 118–19, 175–76

Roosevelt elk, 6

Russian-American Fur Trading
    Company, 23

Russian Gulch State Park, 25

S

Salt Point State Park, 23

San Andreas Fault Scenic Drive, 47–52

San Andreas Rift Zone, 19–20, 50,
    149, 152

San Benito River, 52

San Bernardino, 152

San Diego, 165

San Diego Railroad Museum, 167

San Gabriel Mountains, 148

San Jacinto Mountains, 157, 160–61

San Luis Obispo, 46

San Simeon State Beach, 45

Santa Rosa, 29

Sasquatch, 59

Schramsberg, 33

Scott Bar, 56

Seiad Valley, 56–57

Sequoia and Kings Canyon Scenic
    Drive, 132–42

Sequoia National Forest, 136–37

Shadow Valley, 190

Sierra City, 91

Sierra Valley, 92

Silver Lake Recreation Area, 105

Skull Cave, 65

Smith, Jedediah, 11–12

Smith River Scenic Byway, 9–15

Somes Bar, 58

Sonoma, 30–31

Sonoma Coast State Beaches, 22

Sonoma-Mendocino Coast Scenic
    Drive, 16–26

Sonoma–Napa Valleys Scenic Drive,
    27–36

Sonoma State Historic Park, 31

Sonora, 109

Sonora-Mono Toll Road, 112–13

Sonora Pass Scenic Drive, 107–13

Southern Emigrant Trail, 181, 182–83

South Kelsey Historical Trail, 14

South Lake Tahoe, 95

Southwest Information Station, 80

South Yuba River, 88

Spring Valley, 165

Steinbeck, John, 7, 39

Stevenson, Robert Louis, 32–33, 34, 40

St. Helena, 32–33

Stillwater Cove Regional Park, 23

Stinson Beach, 19

Strawberry, 110

Stream Profile Chamber, 96

Sugarloaf Ridge State Park, 29

Sugar Pine Point State Park, 98–99

Sulphur Works, 80–81

Summit Lake, 83

Surprise Valley, 72, 74

T

Tahoe City, 99

Tahquitz Peak, 161

Tallac Historic Site, 95

Tall Trees Trail, 5–6

Tecate, 166

Tecate cypress, 165

Tenaya Lake, 118

Three Points, 148

Tioga Pass Scenic Drive, 114–21

Tragedy Spring, 104

Trail of the Ancient Dwarfs, 110

Transverse Ranges, 146

Trinidad, 4

Truckee, 99

Truckee Canyon, 99

Tule Lake, 67–68

Tuolumne Grove, 116

Tuolumne Meadows, 119

Tuolumne Meadows Visitors
  Center, 120

Twain Harte, 109

V

Vallecito Regional Park, 182

Vallejo, Alferez Mariano, 30–31

Van Damme State Park, 24–25

vineyards, 31–33

Volcano, 102

volcanoes, 79

W

Warner Range, 71–72

Wassama Round House State Historic
  Park, 124

Waterman Canyon, 152

Wawona, 126

Weitchpec, 59

western juniper, 76, 118

Westport, 26

Westport-Union Landing State
  Beach, 26

West Walker River, 113

whale watching, 4–5, 41

White Wolf, 117

William Randolph Hearst Memorial
  State Beach, 45

wineries, 31–33

Woodfords, 106

Y

Yaqui Well, 183

Yosemite Falls, 130

Yosemite Mountain Sugar Pine
  Railroad, 125

Yosemite National Park Scenic Drive,
  122–31

Yosemite Valley, 128–30

Yountville, 32–33

Yreka, 55

Yuba Pass Scenic Drive, 86–92

Yuba Pass Summit, 92

Yuroks, 4, 5

Z

Zumwalt Meadows, 138

About the Author

Stewart M. Green is a photographer and writer based in Colorado Springs, Colorado. He travels the United States and the world working on projects for The Globe Pequot Press and other publications. Stewart has written and photographed many books for Falcon Publishing and The Globe Pequot Press, including *Rock Climbing Europe, Rock Climbing Colorado, Rock Climbing Utah, Scenic Driving California, Scenic Driving Arizona, Scenic Driving New England,* and *Rock Climbing New England.* He is currently working on a world climbing guide and a book about outdoor Colorado. He has over thirty years experience as a photographer and is one of the world's leading rock climbing photographers. His work appears in many catalogs, advertisements, and national publications. View online photo galleries and learn more about Stewart's work at www.stewartgreen.com.

Stewart M. Green